Cynthia Johnston Hallas
Lent, 2013

Toward Our Mutual Flourishing

Toward Our
Mutual Flourishing

STUDIES IN EPISCOPAL AND ANGLICAN THEOLOGY

C. K. Robertson
General Editor

Vol. 3

PETER LANG
New York • Washington, D.C./Baltimore • Bern
Frankfurt • Berlin • Brussels • Vienna • Oxford

LUCINDA ALLEN MOSHER

Toward Our
Mutual Flourishing

*The Episcopal Church,
Interreligious Relations, and
Theologies of Religious Manyness*

PETER LANG
New York • Washington, D.C./Baltimore • Bern
Frankfurt • Berlin • Brussels • Vienna • Oxford

Library of Congress Cataloging-in-Publication Data

Mosher, Lucinda.
Toward our mutual flourishing: the Episcopal Church, interreligious relations,
and theologies of religious manyness / Lucinda Allen Mosher.
p. cm. — (Studies in Episcopal and Anglican theology; v. 3)
Includes bibliographical references and index.
1. Christianity and other religions. 2. Episcopal Church. I. Title.
BR127.M674   261.2—dc23   2012035779
ISBN 978-1-4331-1937-8 (hardcover)
ISBN 978-1-4539-0992-8 (e-book)
ISSN 2168-3891

Bibliographic information published by **Die Deutsche Nationalbibliothek**.
Die Deutsche Nationalbibliothek lists this publication in the "Deutsche
Nationalbibliografie"; detailed bibliographic data is available
on the Internet at http://dnb.d-nb.de/.

Cover art by Barrie Mosher

The paper in this book meets the guidelines for permanence and durability
of the Committee on Production Guidelines for Book Longevity
of the Council of Library Resources.

© 2012 Peter Lang Publishing, Inc., New York
29 Broadway, 18th floor, New York, NY 10006
www.peterlang.com

Printed in Germany

For Bert F. Breiner
with profound gratitude

CONTENTS

PREFACE

"I think you would do us a great service if you presented to us the distinctive attitudes of your church as these are reflected in this document," the message said. *This document* meant the *Theological Statement on Interreligious Relations* adopted by the General Convention of The Episcopal Church in 2009.

This book is for anyone who would like to know what this document—The Episcopal Church's canonical rationale for interreligious work—says and how it came to be. It is for anyone wonders: In addition to this 2009 statement, what other interfaith relations documents has The Episcopal Church issued?

Into what category does this book fall? Historical theology, theology of religions, practical theology—it is about all of these. This book is for those who, like its author, are convinced that interreligious relations is a category of moral theology, a topic to be addressed by ecclesial social teaching.

This book is for Episcopalians—it almost goes without saying. Most especially, Episcopal diocesan interfaith officers will benefit from this book. It is for people in the rest of the Anglican Communion who wonder about the "distinctive attitudes" of The Episcopal Church on interreligious concerns. It is for members of other Christian denominations who are curious about how The Episcopal Church's thinking about interreligious matters compares to theirs. Interfaith activists, ethicists, seminary students, and congregational leaders will find it helpful. But, as well, this book is for Bahá'í, Buddhist, Hindu, Jain, Jewish, Muslim, Sikh, or Zoroastrian neighbors who want to understand what The Episcopal Church has been saying on these matters—and why.

Acknowledgments

I am grateful to the schools, colleges, universities, seminaries, churches, and continuing education programs that have, for the past two decades, given me opportunities to teach about the world's religions, interfaith relations, and Christian theologies of religions. The questions and comments of my students and colleagues enrich this book in many ways. I am grateful to the authors whose works I have digested, and whose ideas and ways of explaining things are embedded in of the way I teach and write. Where I have made good use of them, I do so with great respect and a deep sense of indebtedness. The responsibility for any factual or conceptual errors rests with me.

Some of the ideas developed in this book are drawn from addresses I have given to annual meetings of the North American Academy of Ecumenists, Episcopal Diocesan Ecumenical and Interfaith Officers, and the National Workshop on Christian Unity. This book benefits from many years of research (as consultant to Auburn Seminary and the National Council of the Churches of Christ in the USA) into the role of multifaith education in the preparation of religious leaders, many years of service on a diocesan ecumenical commission, intermittent service as a consultant to various offices at The Episcopal Church Center and the Anglican Communion Network of Inter Faith Concerns [NIFCON]. Thanks are due many people for these opportunities.

This book began with an invitation to participate in an international conference, sponsored by NIFCON, on *Anglicans and Other Faiths: a Century of Engagement*, held at Lambeth Palace in November 2011. I am thankful to Clare Amos (then Director of Theological Studies for the Anglican Communion Office) and to NIFCON colleague David Thomas (University of Birmingham, UK) for the invitation and for guiding me to a topic which would be truly interesting and useful. Much gratitude goes as well to Charles K. Robertson for the invitation to undertake a book-length expansion of my NIFCON paper. Thanks to everyone at Peter Lang for their patience as I did so.

The layout editor of this book is Barrie Mosher, who also built the index. He has been my partner in everything for more than four decades. I accomplish little without his help. In many ways, creating this book has been a team effort. Without his editorial prowess and his ongoing love for exchanging ideas, this book would have taken many more months to complete.

Latent in my writing are numerous conversations with Kusumita Pedersen, since the late 1990s a colleague in the teaching of the world's religions and interpreting interreligious activism. Research conversations with Daniel Appleyard, Bert Breiner, Bill Doubleday, Douglas Dupree, Christopher Epting, Titus Presler, and Pierre Whalon were particularly helpful. All of them also read draft chapters and provided comments. Daniel Joslyn-Siemiatkoski, Marilyn Salmon, and Louis Weil provided expert help with the chapter on Episcopal-Jewish relations. Kurt Dunkle contributed significantly to Chapter Five. They all have my deepest appreciation.

Also helpful were exchanges with Tim Anderson, Ian Douglas, David Green, Tiffany Israel, Drew Kadel, Nancee Martin-Coffey, Helena Mbele-Mbong, Judith Newman, Shanta Premawardhana, Alan Race, Jane Redmont, Jay Rock, and Owen Thomas. Each has my sincere thanks. Gratitude goes as well to Owene Courtney and Douglas Dupree for help with proofreading.

Special gratitude is extended to The Archives of The Episcopal Church—particularly the *Digital Archives*, without which this project could not have been accomplished. Quotations from *Acts of Convention*; *Reports to the...General Convention otherwise known as The Blue Book*; *The Resolves of Executive Council*; and Episcopal Press and News are used with permission from The Archives of The Episcopal Church. Full texts of *Guidelines for Christian-Jewish Relations* (1988), *Principles for Interfaith Dialogue* (1994), Presiding Bishop Frank Griswold's sermon of 21 September 2001, *On Waging Reconciliation* (2001), and the *Theological Statement on Interreligious Relations* (2009) are included in the Appendix with permission of The Archives of The Episcopal Church

Grateful acknowledgment is also given to the National Council of the Churches of Christ in the USA for permission to include the text of the *Interfaith Relations and the Churches* in the Appendix, and to use quotations from it, from Bert Breiner's commentary on it, and from other NCCCUSA interfaith materials in Chapter Two. As well, gratitude is due to Church Publishing Inc. for permission to include a major portion of *Companions in Transformation* in the Appendix, and to quote extensively from it in Chapter Five; and to the Anglican Communion Office for permission to include the text of Lambeth Conference (1978) Resolution 37, *Other Faiths: Gospel and Dialogue*, and to quote from the NIFCON report *Generous Love* (2008).

In actuality, research for this book began while I was a doctoral student at General Seminary—with my preparation of an historical-critical analysis and annotation of the Lambeth Conference (1988) interfaith statements. I wrote on those documents because Bert Breiner suggested that I do so. As will be explained in Chapter One, he played a major role in crafting those statements, so was able to provide me with copious materials related to that process. In fact, Bert was my external advisor throughout my six years of doctoral study at General Seminary. He was a member of the panel for my dissertation defense. This book is a direct outcome of his prodigious gifts of time and expertise during those six years and since. It is for him.

Lucinda Allen Mosher,
Doctors Inlet, Florida
Transfiguration 2012

INTRODUCTION

"By the year 2001 interfaith relations will be far more important to The Episcopal Church than they appear to be today." How ironic this 1997 pronouncement now sounds! Its authors could not have foreseen how iconic the year 2001 would be. In the pages to follow, we will learn how The Episcopal Church has attended to and spoken publicly on interfaith matters during the 20th century and since. We will examine major documents with relevance to The Episcopal Church's teaching on interreligious matters: *Guidelines for Christian-Jewish Relations For Use in The Episcopal Church* (1988); *Principles for Interfaith Dialogue* (1994); *Interfaith Relations and the Churches* (1999); Presiding Bishop Frank Griswold's sermon of September 21, 2001; *On Waging Reconciliation* (2001); *Companions in Transformation* (2003); *Renewing Our Pledge* (2008); and *Theological Statement on Interreligious Relations* (2009). The text for each is provided in the Appendix for easy reference. Through close reading of these and other significant items, we will learn about the theological and practical teaching on interfaith matters by one denomination of Christianity and how it now articulates its theological rationale for this work. We will expect to find the standard elements of Christian theology (doctrines of God, Creation, Salvation—to name but three) at play throughout. We will attempt to discern what is distinctive in The Episcopal Church's handling of them. Before we proceed, however, we would do well to take account of several matters.

Context

"The Episcopal Church" is the preferred—indeed, the canonical—name for the ecclesial entity which is the focus of this book. This is how it will be named throughout (with "the" capitalized, unless quoting material in which this was not the author's practice.) In this book, the folk-reference shorthand ECUSA will not be used, unless it appears in a direct quotation; neither will the now common abbreviation TEC. The entity about which I write (and of which I am a communicant) is multicultural, multilingual, and multilingual. (In the Diocese of New York alone, the main language of worship and discourse in a given congregation may be one of a dozen different languages.) The Episcopal Church is not "*of* the USA;" it is "*in* the USA," which means it may also be elsewhere. In fact it operates in at least sixteen countries.

That said, The Episcopal Church *in* the USA is our primary focus. In 1997, when the Presiding Bishop's Advisory Committee on Interfaith Relations made the pronouncement with which this essay began, it would not have taken an anthropologist of religion to observe and appreciate that The Episcopal Church was now sharing the religious landscape of the United States with expressions and adherents of numerous religions other than Christianity. The same could have been said for most of the fifteen or more other nations in which The Episcopal Church has an institutional presence, but it is reasonable to suspect that, in practicality, the committee was thinking of the US context as it spoke; and likewise in practicality, so shall we.

Defining Religion

This book is about *religion*—a word which has no agreed-upon academic working definition. Whatever this thing *religion* is, it tends to provoke disdain—even in some whose profession is to teach about it. I try to rehabilitate the term by stipulating Byron Earhart's definition of *religion* as "a distinctive set of beliefs, rituals, doctrines, institutions, and practices that enables the members of that tradition to establish, maintain, and celebrate a meaningful world." For me, *religion* is synonymous with *worldview*. Following Ninian Smart, I teach that worldviews have six dimensions: doctrinal and philosophical; mythic and narrative; ethical or legal; ritual or practical; experiential or emotional; social or institutional—in varying degrees of importance. Anglicanism's possession of each of these six dimensions has much in common with the ways they are found in other forms of Christianity, but it has its particularities as well. In this book, attention will be called to this distinctiveness as needed.[1]

Linguistically, *religion*'s roots may lie in Latin words meaning *to bind together* (with regard to a gathering of people), or *to bind back* (to those who have gone before), or *reverence* (for what fascinates and awes). It has a social dimension, as Ninian Smart indicates. So, in coming chapters, I will use the term *religion-communities*—of which The Episcopal Church is one example.

Association with, or adherence to, a religion-community often requires or results in *conviction*. I follow James Wm. McClendon and James M. Smith, who define *conviction* as a belief which cannot be relinquished easily; in fact, relinquishing it will transform the holder (be that a person or a community) into someone or something else.[2] In this book, when I speak of religious *commitments*, I mean this same sense; I mean to signal that we are talking about a belief or practice that cannot be relinquished without disrupting identity.

Related to defining *religion* is the matter of what to call concerns or activities involving two or more religions. This matter of nomenclature is a fluid one. Consider that the tagline for my consulting service announces that I am in the business of "enabling interreligious relations;" my position at Hartford Seminary is "Faculty Associate in Interfaith Studies;" and I am the director of that institution's "Graduate Certificate Program in Chaplaincy in Multifaith Contexts." My media-savvy millennial friends tell me that *interfaith* yields higher search-engine returns than *interreligious* or *multifaith*. I often argue that, frequently, the context is *multifaith*, whereas the work may be *multi-* or *inter-*. Some of my friends and colleagues in this field use *interreligious* when referring to formal interactions between official representatives, reserving *interfaith* for more informal interactions. With all of this in mind, in this book I have chosen to be quite random in using *interfaith* and *interreligious*; unless otherwise noted, they are interchangeable. In this book, *multifaith* and *multireligious* name situations in which the concern or the activity involves three or more religions.

The Fact of Manyness

This book is about how a particular branch of Christianity has made sense of and related to other religion-communities. Since 1981 at the least, historian Catherine Albanese has been speaking of "the manyness of religions." She uses this turn of phrase in her acclaimed textbook, *America: Religions & Religion*, when teaching about the diversity of traditions coexisting, even flourishing together, in the United States. Borrowing from her, I use the term *religious manyness* to name a situation provoking a theological response.[3]

Speaking of *religious diversity* might serve equally well. *Diversity*, after all, connotes variety or multiplicity, difference or unlikeness. Does this term have a downside? Perhaps, in the realm of theology, it is this. In the 21st century, particularly in educational institutions, *diversity* connotes more than merely the state of variety; it often connotes the deliberate inclusion of different people because of their differences (and those differences themselves are many). *Diversity* thus names a stance of promotion of respect for difference, of provision of a safe and nurturing environment for the exploration of differences. To say *religious diversity* would thus imply a degree of activism toward acceptance, rather than a mere naming of a state of affairs. To the contrary, *religious manyness* names a state of affairs, a *construction site for theology*, to borrow an idiom from Terrence Tilley's *Religious Diversity and the American Experience*.[4]

In the arena of multireligious concerns, *pluralism* is indeed used by some to name a phenomenon: the fact of the presence of many religions. Many anthropologists and sociologists of religion use it in a way that is synonymous with my use of *religious manyness*. Might it have sufficed to speak of *religious pluralism*? I think not; the term is also problematic. How so? Since the 1980s at the least, others have used *pluralism* to denote an attitude toward this fact. But what is that attitude? I have heard it used pejoratively to name perceived willingness to water down Christian beliefs when embracing religious diversity. Diana Eck, on the other hand, defines *pluralism* as "response to diversity via engagement."[5] As she uses the term, *pluralism* is not a synonym for diversity, nor is it mere acknowledgment of *diversity*. Rather, it is "a dynamic process through which we engage with one another in and through our deepest differences."[6] I concur with her wholeheartedly, and have often cited her frequently in this regard.

Sociologist Robert Wuthnow also uses the term *pluralism* to label "our response to diversity—how we think about it, how we respond to it in our attitudes and lifestyles, and whether we choose to embrace it, ignore it, or merely cope with it."[7] Following Professors Eck and Wuthnow, I use *pluralism* when referring to response to the multireligious context. I use the term *religious manyness* to refer to that context.

Furthermore, in a great many discussions of multireligious concerns, *pluralism* does not denotes a situation calling for a theological response, nor an attitude toward diversity. Rather, *pluralism* names a theological stance itself. This stance might be defined as "a move away from insistence on the superiority or finality of Christ and Christianity toward a recognition of the independent validity of other ways," as Paul Knitter puts it rather straightforwardly in the preface to *The Myth of Christian Uniqueness*.[8] Or, defining this stance might require a long and detailed list of attributes, such as Raimundo Panikkar provides later in the same book.[9] This, in turn, has generated its own industry: books and articles arguing for or against various definitions and models of a "pluralistic theology of religions," and meaning by that something somewhat different from a "theology of religious pluralism." Discussions of (for example) the difference between "universalistic religious pluralism" and "particularistic religious pluralism" are a case in point.

Even when I stipulate the working definition of pluralism, I find it very difficult to hold its meaning stable in a conversation of any length. I prefer, therefore, the term *theology of religious manyness* because it unambiguously names the context and the concern.

The Theological Construction Zone

"Episcopal Churches across the country are finding themselves increasingly aware of religious diversity in their own communities," asserted the Church's

Principles for Interfaith Dialogue in 1994. "We now live side by side with organized groups representing many of the great religious traditions of the world who share our concern for peace, justice and the common good," it continues. Harvard University's Pluralism Project has been documenting, analyzing, and teaching about this changing religious landscape since 1991. In her widely read study, *A New Religious America: How a "Christian Country" Has Become the World's Most Religiously Diverse Nation*, Pluralism Project founder and director Diana Eck points to changes in U. S. immigration policy in 1965 as a major reason behind that reality. Even more significantly, she also notes, not only do many US cities (and not just a few towns) include the adherents of a range of the world's religions, a second interesting dynamic is at play: the US religious landscape now includes *multiple expressions* of each of the world's religions, often as next-door neighbors. In short, the US is now home to intra-religious diversity as well as interreligious diversity in interestingly complex ways.

In her *Interfaith Encounters in America*, Kate McCarthy notes that it is not that US multireligious vastness is so unique, but that it seems to hold more meaning than it does in other contexts. Talk among Americans about religious diversity, she has observed, is very often a discussion about Americanness itself. The United States, argues Catholic theologian Terrence Tilley, is a "distinctive cultural site" in which to construct a theology of religious difference. That is, he explains, the US combines social (thus religious) diversity with a political tradition of nonestablishment of religion. The result is an environment in which it is rather easy to choose to practice a religion other than the religion into which one was born. Tilley calls this "a cultural 'live option'" not available in many other parts of the world.[10] Such is the cultural site in which The Episcopal Church has endeavored to construct its own theology of religious difference. The pages to follow take us inside the construction process.

Sources of Episcopal Church Teaching

To discern or distill the teaching of The Episcopal Church on any particular topic or in any particular domain, where must one look? The Episcopal Church embraces Anglicanism's self-understanding as a *via media*—a middle road both catholic and reformed, for which authority is found in a triumvirate of scripture, tradition, and reason. By scripture, Episcopalians mean the Bible (which, in the Anglican tradition, includes the Apocrypha—books which are used in worship, but not for the establishment of doctrine). Anglicanism's moral vision as corporate, liturgical, sacramental, and ordered is embodied in its hallmark worship resource, the Book of Common Prayer. The Episcopal Church uses an edition authorized in 1979. When it comes to a theological warrant for positive interreligious relations, I am not alone among Episcopalians in pointing to the Baptismal Covenant, as found therein.[11] That the Baptismal Covenant is The Episcopal Church's starting-point can be sensed in the late-20th- and early-21st-century documents which receive major attention in this book.

In order of priority, the other sources of Episcopal Church teaching are: General Convention; the Executive Council; Pastoral Letters from the House of Bishops; interim pastoral letters from the Presiding Bishop; actions of Standing Commissions; and Lambeth Conference resolutions, teachings, and encyclicals. The process of discerning The Episcopal Church's theology of religious manyness draws upon all of these sources.

General Convention

The primary governing and legislative body of The Episcopal Church (and ultimate authority—with the exception of the Bible, the Book of Common Prayer, and the Constitutions and Canons) is the General Convention, which meets every three years. General Convention is bicameral: to take effect, resolutions must be passed by both the House of Deputies and the House of Bishops. Resolutions so passed become the voice and policy of The Episcopal Church. Such actions bear canonical weight. *Reports to the [#] General Convention otherwise known as The Blue Book* is the official publication of the combined reports of Committees, Commissions, Agencies and Boards of The Episcopal Church presented to the Church every three years. *The Journal of General Convention... of The Episcopal Church* is the official record of The Acts of Convention.

The very nature of General Convention means that The Episcopal Church "relies on predilection rather than recollection," Robert Hood notes. At each General Convention, more than 30% of delegates will be new; many bishops will be new. The result, he says, is that General Convention outcomes have "an episodic, transient character even in social policies, with a noticeable absence of sustained theological debate and discussion."[12] This can make outcomes flexible and relevant; it also risks that they will be trendy and insubstantial. With regard to General Convention actions on interreligious matters, relevance rather than trendiness is undoubtedly to be hoped.

Particularly since the mid-twentieth century, a number of resolutions with interreligious implications have been passed by General Convention. Some have been oriented toward some peace-and-justice concern; some address a liturgical matter. Others have fallen under the rubric of calls for (or endorsements of) dialogue. In coming chapters, we will examine interreligious-relations documents endorsed by General Convention in recent decades.

Executive Council

Next in authority is the Executive Council, comprising twenty members elected by General Convention (four bishops, four priests or deacons, and twelve laypersons) and eighteen persons elected by the Church's nine provinces. Between General Conventions, the Executive Council may speak for The Episcopal Church. Occasionally, it has had something to say about interreligious matters, which has, in turn borne on The Episcopal Church's theology of religious manyness.

Pastoral Letters

For Episcopalians, *Pastoral Letter* is a technical term, referring to a genre of document issued occasionally by the House of Bishops or the Presiding Bishop. According to the canons of The Episcopal Church, Pastoral Letters are to be shared with every congregation within a month of its publishing—either by reading it aloud during a Sunday liturgy or disseminated in print form (by including in the parish newsletter, for example). Typically, such epistles convey information or make a particular point, often accompanied by a theological rationale.

Occasionally, the Presiding Bishop of The Episcopal Church is a signatory to a pastoral letter issued by the Anglican Communion's Primates and Moderators as a body, or to a letter issued ecumenically—and sometimes, these too have interreligious-relations implications. For example, on 11 May 2004, the National Council of Churches USA, by means of a letter signed by representatives of its 36 member communions, called for a change of course in the Iraq War. As is typical of pastoral letters, this one included reiteration or clarifying of theological teachings. Similarly, on 14 September 2006, a joint pastoral letter was co-signed and issued by the Presiding Bishops of The Episcopal Church and the Evangelical Lutheran Church in America, underscoring their communions' commitment to pursuit of the Millennium Development Goals [MDGs] regarding eradication of global poverty which had just been adopted by the United Nations, laying out a theological basis for doing so, and proposing a strategy.

Presiding Bishops' Sermons and Public Addresses

Closely related to official pastoral letters, Presiding Bishops' sermons and public addresses are excellent means by which to appreciate the Church's theological stance on an issue. In Chapter Four we will engage one such sermon.

Standing Commission Actions

Standing Commissions are task forces comprising clergy and laity. Often, the work of a Standing Commission is integral to the development of a major teaching document. In addition to the Standing Commission on Ecumenical and Interreligious Relations, several other Standing Commissions figure prominently in the discussion to come.

Lambeth Conference

The Lambeth Conference is a gathering of the bishops of the Anglican Communion which has been convened by the Archbishop of Canterbury once in almost every decade since 1867. Recent assemblies have included ecumenical participants, and typically have involved worship, study, informal conversation, and formal discussion. Most of these gatherings have issued a variety of resolutions and documents from which "the mind of the communion" on various issues and teachings on various topics can be discerned. However, because the member churches of the Anglican Communion are autonomous, Lambeth Conferences are collaborative and consultative rather than legislative in function. Since the last quarter of the twentieth century, Lambeth Conferences have taken on the task of deep engagement with issues occasioned by religious manyness. Several theologically helpful documents have been issued as a result, and have had particular impact on official teachings of The Episcopal Church.

Citation of Sources

In the process of contextualizing and analyzing the interfaith documents around which this book is organized, each of the authoritative sources just described will come into play. I have chosen to use a light hand with regard to citing sources. Unless otherwise stipulated, the source for references to or quotations from official documents of The Episcopal Church, and references to or quotations from Episcopal News Service stories, is the Digital Archives of The Episcopal Church: www.episcopalarchives.org. Where endnotes are not provided for references to or quotations from these sources, it is assumed that the reader has been given enough information to call up the item in the Digital Archives database.

Episcopalians customarily refer to General Conventions by number. (It would be said, for example, that the 77th General Convention of The Episcopal Church took place in July 2012.) However, in this book, meetings will be identified by year rather than number. Thus, for example, rather than speaking of the adoption of the *Theological Statement on Interreligious Relations* as an act of the 76th General Convention, this text will describe it as an act of the 2009 General Convention. It is the custom of The Episcopal Church to assign an identifying number and name to each resolution brought to General Convention. In this book, I have used a light hand in providing these identifiers, in order not to overburden the reader (especially the non-Episcopalian) with technical data. Enough information has been supplied to enable the interested reader to find full texts of resolutions in the Digital Archives. In endnotes, "*The Blue Book, year*" is shorthand for *Report to the...General Convention* for the year given. *Journal of General Convention* is shorthand for *General Convention Journal of...The Episcopal Church, City, year* (New York: General Convention, year).

Throughout this book, the reader will find remarks by or reports from unnamed observers. These are composites, for the most part: collective insights, objections, and comments of students and others with whom I have discussed this material.

Themes

Since the 1970s, as The Episcopal Church's teaching on religious manyness has developed and become manifest, a number of significant, somewhat overlapping, themes have emerged. Chapter I, *Interfaith Movement*, considers The Episcopal Church's affirmation of interfaith dialogue *per se*. Chapter II, *Embracing Ecumenism*, explains The Episcopal Church's preference for collaborative interreligious work and the importance for Episcopalians of the interfaith work of the National Council of the Churches of Christ in the USA. Chapter III, *Eschewing Contempt*, examines the Church's concern for Jews and Judaism. In Chapter IV, *Common Words*, the focus is on the Church's engagement with Islam and Muslims. Chapter V, *Relating Multireligiously*, discusses the establishment of a location and a rationale for the interreligious work of The Episcopal Church—thus a consideration of its relation to missiology. Chapter VI, *Interreligious Ecclesiology*, considers the theological grammar of interreligious understanding, reviews the theological understanding latent in The Episcopal Church's major interreligious-relations documents of the past several decades, and considers these documents' present implications. My hope is that, as a study in Anglican and Episcopal theology, this book will clarify the arena of enabling positive interreligious relations, inspire further effort therein, and allow all to see this work as an act of Christian faithfulness.

Notes

1. See H. Byron Earhart, *Religious Traditions of the World* (New York: HarperCollins, 1992), 7; and, Ninian Smart, *Worldviews: Crosscultural Explorations of Human Beliefs* (Upper Saddle River, New Jersey: Prentice Hall, 1999).

2. James Wm. McClendon, Jr. and James M. Smith, *Convictions: Diffusing Religious Relativism* (Harrisburg, Pennsylvania: Trinity Press International, 1994), xii.

3. Catherine Albanese, *America: Religions & Religion*, 4th ed. (Belmont, California: Thomson Wadsworth, 2007) 15 and throughout.

4. Terrence Tilley, et al., *Religious Diversity and the American Experience: A Theological Approach* (New York: Continuum, 2007).

5. Diana Eck, "American Religious Pluralism: Civic and Theological Discourse," in *Democracy and the New Religious Pluralism*, ed. Thomas Banchoff (New York: Oxford University Press, 2007), 245.

6. Eck, "American Religious Pluralism," 266.

7. Robert Wuthnow, *America and the Challenges of Religious Diversity* (Princeton University Press, 2005, 2007), 286.

8. Paul Knitter, Preface to *The Myth of Christian Uniqueness: Toward a Pluralistic Theology of Religions*, eds. John Hick and Paul F. Knitter (Maryknoll, New York: Orbis Books, 1995), viii.

9. Raimundo Panikkar, "The Jordan, the Tiber, and the Ganges," in *The Myth of Christian Uniqueness: Toward a Pluralistic Theology of Religions*, eds., John Hick and Paul F. Knitter (Maryknoll, New York: Orbis, 2005), 110–11.

10. Tilley, *Religious Diversity and the American Experience*, 12, 14, 19, 24.

11. 1979 Book of Common Prayer, 304–305.

12. Robert E. Hood. *Social Teachings in the Episcopal Church: A Source Book* (Harrisburg, Pennsylvania: Morehouse, 1990).

I

INTERFAITH MOVEMENT

THE EPISCOPAL CHURCH'S
PRINCIPLES FOR DIALOGUE

"Episcopal Churches across the country are finding themselves increasingly aware of religious diversity in their own communities." Thus opens *Principles for Interfaith Dialogue*, the earliest comprehensive statement in The Episcopal Church on interreligious relations. While more practical than theological, this document, adopted in 1994, is nevertheless a significant step in the Church's development of a formal rationale for such engagement—a necessary step toward its articulation of its own theology of religious manyness. By publishing *Principles for Interfaith Dialogue*, the Church acknowledged that it was indeed a player in what was coming to be called the interfaith movement. The goal of this chapter is threefold: to define the interfaith movement and the concerns it raises; to place The Episcopal Church within this phenomenon; and to lay out the content and significance of the document *Principles for Interfaith Dialogue*.

A Global Phenomenon

The biggest, most colorful beach umbrella you can find—that is an excellent icon for the modern interfaith movement. As an umbrella term, the *interfaith movement* encompasses the full range of positive interaction among and outreach by representatives of religion-communities or by individuals with differing religious commitments for the purpose of deeper understanding, cooperation, or collaboration. Scholar-activist Kusumita Pedersen defines *movement* as "an activity that can spread horizontally by using particular, known methods, without necessarily depending either on charismatic leaders or on material support or authority from one or a few centers." Throughout the world are thousands of interfaith (sometimes called *interreligious* or *multifaith*) groups and activities which are "loosely related by a cluster of shared methods, aims, and values." A great many are local, grassroots in nature. This given, says Pedersen, "the word 'movement' seems accurate and evocative."[1]

It is also practical. As Pedersen explains, use of the term *movement* to name "the totality of interfaith work presently going on in the world" gained currency near the turn of the 20th century. The driving factor was "the need to avoid referring to interfaith work by any term that could inaccurately imply a high degree of centralized and/or hierarchical structure with top-down direction." It would be an exaggeration, she notes,

> …to imply that interfaith activity is exhaustively contained in the programs of self-described 'interfaith organizations,' [but] it is just as misleading to allow any misconception that interfaith work somehow consists mainly of formal cooperation between religious institutions.[2]

So, the umbrella term *interfaith movement* casts its shade over myriad groups and activities, but it is unlikely that what Pedersen calls "umbrella-fication"—in the sense of central governance—will ever be possible or even desirable.

Indeed, *the interfaith movement* has gained traction as an umbrella for this work, yet *faith* is not the best rubric under which to put each and every one of the traditions which somehow participate. *Religion* may be the more accurate term, yet it is at least as problematic as *faith*. As we saw in this book's Introduction, *religion* has no universally accepted definition in the academic arena. Too often it has been used to dismiss groups of people who believe and practice differently from us—as in, *they* have "a religion," where as *we* have a "way of life." With some frequency, I encounter individuals—among them, occasionally, religious leaders-in-training and professors of religious studies—who sneer at the word *religion* itself and disdain whatever they think it names. Such an attitude can demean interfaith activism and dialogue because it dismisses the underlying *commitment*. Other scholars wonder whether *religion* is merely a Western fiction, thus rendering talk of "interreligious" dialogue nonsensical. Nevertheless, the movement is vibrant, as is well illustrated by the Harvard University Pluralism Project's *America's Interaith Infrastructure* study. Indeed the study's website, pluralism.org/interfaith/, is laden with evidence in a broad variety of forms.

Landmarks

It has become commonplace to assert that the modern interfaith movement was launched by the World's Parliament of Religions (Chicago 1893). Certainly, scholars can call our attention to several inspiring examples of prolonged and fruitful periods of interreligious interaction at earlier points in history.

However, the 1893 gathering in Chicago was indeed significant because of its methodology. Not only did it bring together representatives of a number of religions—Buddhism (both Theravada and Mahayana), Confucianism, Hinduism, Islam, Jainism, Shinto, Taoism, Zoroastrianism—it positioned Christianity as one among the many. We might note, however, that Christian voices were most dominant in the proceedings, and that Christian concerns and concepts set the agenda. This would remain the case for the next many decades of the interfaith movement's emergence.

Among the two-dozen presenters at that first parliament was Thomas Richey, Professor of Ecclesiastical History in the General Theological Seminary of The Episcopal Church (New York City), who gave a paper on "The Relations Between the Anglican Church and the Church of the First Ages."[3] Thus it can be said that The Episcopal Church played a role in the interfaith movement's launch event. However, the Parliament seems to have gone unnoticed by The Episcopal Church's 1895 General Convention. The proceedings contain no report, message, or resolution pertaining to it. Only well after World War II would The Episcopal Church (or most other US ecclesial bodies, for that matter) take official note of the need to engage in, or provide guidance for, interreligious relations as a category of its own. Indeed, an entire century would elapse before another Parliament of the World's Religions would be mounted. While the 1893 event failed to establish an ongoing program, it did succeed in establishing a normative model: formal encounters between clergy and scholars of diverse religions, meeting in a spirit of openheartedness for the purpose of promotion of mutual understanding and enrichment.

Some analysts see the World Missionary Conference of 1910 (Edinburgh, Scotland) as an event of at least equal significance to the World's Parliament of Religions—as a second landmark in the formation of the modern interfaith movement. Episcopalians were present in this gathering of some 1200 persons. Each day of the conference had a theme. "Carrying the Gospel to All the Non-Christian World" and "The Missionary Message in Relation to Non-Christian Religions" are two examples. As discussions ensued, new questions about the Christian's relation to people with other religious commitments were provoked by missionaries' reflections on their own lived experience of the religions of the people among whom they had worked, by evaluations of evangelization methodologies provided by recent converts from several of the world's religions who numbered among the attendees, and by insights from the rather new academic field of comparative religion. These new pastoral, missiological, and theological questions—especially those pertaining to soteriology—would persist, as we will see in subsequent chapters.

A third landmark in the emergence of the modern interfaith movement is *Nostra Aetate* (Declaration Concerning the Relationship of the Church to Non-Christian Religions). This decree, issued by Vatican II in 1965, opened the door for heightened Roman Catholic theological generosity toward and appreciation of the truth and beauty in other religions. A consequence of the promulgation of *Nostra Aetate* has been the articulation and promulgation of a much broader range of Christian theologies of religious difference, thus a much livelier interest by Christians in deeper interreligious understanding than previously had been the case. Anglicans, some Evangelicals, and most mainline Protestants took note of *Nostra Aetate,* and allowed their own theological reflection to follow in the direction it had set. In some cases, this resulted in formal statements which went much farther than it had. An example is *Christ and People of Other Faiths*, an elegant and lengthy theological rationale for positive interfaith relations produced by the Anglican Communion's 1988 Lambeth Conference, which we will examine carefully later in this chapter. In the early 21st century, Episcopal Church interfaith documents would acknowledge a debt to *Nostra Aetate,* as we shall see in Chapter Five.

A fourth landmark of the emergence of the interfaith movement has been the development of various sorts of structures which facilitate positive interreligious engagement for a broad range of purposes. Some of these agencies and programs exist primarily for the purpose of helping us to see religious manyness; others exist primarily for the purpose of helping to make sense of that manyness. The Episcopal Church has been a member of several. (The NCCC Interfaith Commission and Religions for Peace–USA are two examples.) Certain Episcopalians as individuals have founded or directed such organizations. Several Episcopal dioceses have had their own. Out of (or parallel to) this work has developed a vast interreligious-relations publications industry: books, journals (print and online; for both scholarly and popular readerships), and teaching materials on multifaith matters. The range of ways to go about this work is as fascinating as religious diversity itself.

Early Records

In The Episcopal Church's early records, concerns with religious difference are far from overt. The reports of 1892 and 1895 note countries and geographical regions in which missionary activity was being supported, but make no mention of the religions embraced by the peoples being evangelized. The *Journal of General Convention* 1952 notes that, since 1949, The Episcopal Church had been fully involved in the World Council of Churches—whose efforts would include the addressing of interfaith concerns of missionaries. The report of the Ecumenical Commission to General Convention 1961 mentions India, Pakistan, Burma, Ceylon, and Lanka—but with no reference to the multireligious context of the Church in these places. In the 1967 *Journal of General Convention*, various references to the Viet Nam War do not mention its interreligious implications, nor does the Ecumenical Relations report for that year mention Vatican II (let alone the promulgation of *Nostra Aetate*).

The Episcopal Church took explicit action on Christian-Jewish concerns at least as early as 1964. As we will see in Chapter Three, work on the theological and ethical implications of Episcopal-Jewish relations has been ongoing. Broader attention to multifaith matters would come later. In a 1987 report to the House of Bishops, Presiding Bishop Edmund Browning included interfaith concerns in the list of his eight mission imperatives. According to an Episcopal News Service story dated 8 October 1987, he had asserted that the time had now come for inclusion of "a realistic world view of interfaith dialogue with Islam, Judaism, Hinduism and other world religions," in the agenda of The Episcopal Church.

It would be several more decades before The Episcopal Church's actions regarding broader interfaith concerns were as clear. Meanwhile, the Church was then, and remains, a participant in the interfaith movement by virtue of its membership in the worldwide Anglican Communion, and this in turn has informed its theology of interfaith involvement.

Lambeth Conference and Interfaith Concerns

As a record of the mind of the Anglican Communion, Lambeth Conference reports often contain interesting discourse and insights. Through their resolutions, Lambeth Conferences declare and advise. So, while not binding on member churches or individuals of the Anglican Communion, Lambeth Conference actions are often taken quite seriously. A glance through Lambeth Conference records reveals theological reflection on religious diversity which in turn influences reflection and action of The Episcopal Church.

The proceedings of Lambeth 1920 and 1930 indicate enthusiasm for the embryonic ecumenical movement. Attention to other religions (slight though it was in these decades) arose in the context of Anglican commitment to the notion that Christian unity is key to Christian flourishing in the 20th century. Interfaith concerns begin to be addressed more overtly with Lambeth Conference 1948's assertion that human rights are universal, regardless of religion. At Lambeth 1958, interfaith concerns are addressed indirectly, embedded primarily in resolutions on religious freedom and the right to proclaim the Gospel. The theology underpinning these moves is more implied than spelled out.

Lambeth 1968 is the first of these decennial conferences to commend the attitudes and activities characteristic of the emerging interfaith movement. Its Resolution 11 frames cultivation of positive interreligious relations in terms of "obedience to Christ's mission," calling upon Christians to study other religions seriously, and endorsing interfaith collaboration in the economic, social, and moral arenas. Resolution 13 urges vigorous support for interreligious dialogue already being conducted by the World Council of Churches and others. Both resolutions commend Christian study of, and dialogue with those who profess, atheism. Given the era, both resolutions more likely have Communism rather than Buddhism or Jainism in mind.

With Lambeth 1978, consideration of interfaith matters increases in prominence somewhat, by virtue of the fact that its working-group on *The People of God and Ministry* had a committee for *Other Faiths and Religions*. Actions of Lambeth 1978 include the passing of Resolution 37: *Other Faiths: Gospel and Dialogue:*

1.   Within the Church's trust of the Gospel, we recognize and welcome the obligation to open exchange of thought and experience with people of other faiths. Sensitivity to the work of the Holy Spirit among them means a positive response to their meaning as inwardly lived and understood. It means also a quality of life on our part which expresses the truth and love of God as we have known them in Christ, Lord and Saviour.

2.   We realize the lively vocation to theological interpretation, community involvement, social responsibility, and evangelization which is carried by the Churches in areas where Hinduism, Buddhism, Taoism, Confucianism or Islam are dominant, and asks that the whole Anglican Communion support them by understanding, by prayer, and, where appropriate, by partnership with them.

3.   We continue to seek opportunities for dialogue with Judaism.[4]

The work of Lambeth 1978, limited though it was, ensured that interfaith issues would be a major part of the work of Lambeth 1988. Indeed, Lambeth 1988 was the first of these conferences to articulate in depth an Anglican theology of the Other-than-Christian, to lay out principles behind and guidelines for dialogue. Especially, this was the first Lambeth Conference to speak of a positive place for Islam in an Anglican-Christian worldview and to give specific attention to warm-hearted dialogue with Muslims on theological grounds.

Lambeth 1988's Dogmatic & Pastoral Concerns Section included an Interfaith Committee which produced a lengthy document articulating theology and practice of interfaith relations. Entitled *Christ and People of Other Faiths: The Statement on Interfaith Relations of the Dogmatic & Pastoral Concerns Section Report*, it comprises the middle portion (paragraphs 41–69) of the Section's much larger report.[5] Its principal author was Episcopalian Bert Breiner, secretary to this working group—a career missionary of The Episcopal Church, serving at the time at Selly Oak Colleges, University of Birmingham (UK).

The theology of *Christ and People of Other Faiths'* interfaith argument is profoundly Trinitarian and Incarnational. "The very life of God is a 'being with,'" it asserts from the start, picking up on language which permeates the preceding portion of the larger report. Thus Christian encounter with people of other faiths is (as Paragraph 48 puts it) an opportunity "to overhear what dialogue there may be between God and these people—between the God who calls all into being by a process of sharing and communication, and other peoples in their religious cultures." As well, it draws heavily on early church thought, particularly Cappadocian theology. In that regard, its eschatological leaning is toward a universalism grounded in the notion of *anakephalaiosis*—that is, the notion that ultimately, all things will be summed up through Christ (which was the Father's will from before the foundation of the world).

Paragraph 66 takes up the question of whether persons of differing religions may worship together—a question raised by the expansion of the interfaith movement, and particularly by the decision of Pope John Paul II to hold a Day of Prayer for Peace (Assisi, 27 October 1986). The sense of *Christ and People of Other Faiths* is that we may "pray alongside each other" but "cannot share anything like a common liturgy." Attention is also given (in Paragraph 65) to the question of Christian hospitality to persons of different faiths, (in Paragraph 66) to concern for freedom to worship as a fundamental human right.

Appendix Six of the Dogmatic & Pastoral Concerns Section Report, entitled *Jews, Christians and Muslims: The Way of Dialogue*, was designed to stand alone, and was commended (via Lambeth 1988 Resolution 21, *Inter-faith Dialogue: Jewish/Christian/Muslim*) for study Communion-wide. Its preamble acknowledges that, while any interfaith dialogue has value, Christian dialogue with Jews and Muslims is founded on a unique interrelationship (that is, "a common relationship to Abraham") and unique potential for furthering the well-being of humanity. The body of the document has three parts. Part One, *The Way of Understanding*, lays out points about Judaism and Islam about which Christians ought to lay aside stereotypes and become better informed.

Part Two, *The Way of Affirmation*, is a brief presentation of aspects of Judaism and Islam which, because they "resonate with the Gospel," Christians should be willing to affirm. Part Three, *The Way of Sharing*, suggests forms this sharing might take while acknowledging its real challenges.

Resolution 21 also recommended that Abrahamic dialogues be initiated wherever possible at the provincial level, and that the Anglican Consultative Council create a structure through which (working cooperatively with the World Council of Churches Inter-Faith Dialogue Committee) "a common approach to people of other faiths on a Communion-wide basis" could be honed, and "more detailed guidelines for relationships with Judaism and Islam and other faiths as appropriate" might be crafted. This recommendation gave rise to the establishment, in 1993, of the Network of Inter Faith Concerns of the Anglican Communion (NIFCON).

In spite of the degree of parallelism between *Nostra Aetate* and Lambeth 1988's *The Way of Dialogue*, the latter has received miniscule attention in comparison. The critical difference between the two documents is that *Nostra Aetate* was promulgated as an official teaching of the Roman Catholic Church, and has, as a consequence, received global scrutiny and acknowledgement; the Lambeth interfaith report was merely "commended for study" in the Anglican Communion.

Of what value have the Lambeth 1988 documents been to The Episcopal Church? In April 1997, I had a conversation about this with William Norgren, who had served as The Episcopal Church's ecumenical officer during the years 1979–1994. He noted that the interfaith material from the 1988 Lambeth Report was included in a handbook produced by the Ecumenical and Interfaith Office for use by diocesan ecumenical officers who function in the interfaith field. Presumably, Norgren said, it had also been used by The Presiding Bishop's Advisory Committee on Interfaith Relations, which (at the time) dealt with relations between The Episcopal Church and other religious groups and was the main contact point for the promotion of such.

One aspect of Lambeth 1988's legacy which has remained influential to the present is found in the conference's Resolution 20, *Inter-faith Dialogue*, which commends and encourages interfaith dialogue as compatible with discipleship and mission. Embedded in the resolution's text is the formulaic principles-of-dialogue articulated in 1981 by the British Council of Churches: that dialogue begins in meeting; depends on mutual understanding, respect, and trust; makes collaborative community service possible; and can be a vehicle for "authentic witness." The resolution then clarifies that, while dialogue does not replace evangelism, it can facilitate interreligious work for the common good in arenas of peacemaking or social-justice religious-liberty advocacy. The principles-of-dialogue formula—its origin and incorporation into The Episcopal Church's theological rationale for interfaith work—will be discussed in Chapter Five below. For now, we take note of it because Lambeth 1988's encouragement of interreligious dialogue is a factor in The Episcopal Church's decision to clarify principles of engagement.[6]

Principles for Interfaith Dialogue (1994)

For much of the second half of the 20th century, the most robust interfaith work of The Episcopal Church was conducted by the Presiding Bishop's Committee on Christian-Jewish Relations. In 1992, this committee was disbanded in favor of a new entity: the Presiding Bishop's Advisory Committee on Interfaith Relations. Lambeth 1988's call for dialogue with Jews and Muslims by member churches of the Anglican Communion was cited as one of the factors in this restructuring. Other factors were the obvious expansion of religious diversity in the US, particularly the growth of the Islamic community, and the sense that a Committee on Christian-Jewish Relations was now insufficient to the needs of The Episcopal Church, given its changing context. In fact, the committee itself had been steering the Church in this direction. In its 1991 report to General Convention, it had asserted: "The increasingly pluralistic expression of religion in the United States fosters a particularly conducive environment for those in each religious tradition to meet each other as equals." In that same report, it pledged to work with the Executive Council's Committee on Partnerships "to find an improved way of working with non-Christian religions while affirming the special relationship which…links Christian faith with Judaism." In 1991, it had helped to craft a successful General Convention resolution (about which we will hear more in Chapters Three and Five) articulating a theological attitude for interfaith relations broadly construed.[7]

The decision to appoint an Advisory Committee on Interfaith Relations was an acknowledgment on the part of the Office of the Presiding Bishop that interfaith concerns simply could not be added to the already too full agenda of the Standing Commission on Ecumenical Relations. The new Advisory Committee was independent of, but its membership included a liaison from, the ecumenical commission. For the triennium 1992–1994, it kept its focus primarily on Jewish and Muslim relations. Its tasks included the brokering of meetings between the Presiding Bishop and significant Jewish and Muslim leaders, address of "sensitive interfaith issues with and for the Presiding Bishop" (as its 1997 report to General Convention), working closely with the National Council of Churches Interfaith Commission, and participation in various dialogues.

The Advisory Committee on Interfaith Relations also took on the task of drawing together resources useful for interfaith work by parishes. To this end, one of its early achievements was the development of *Principles for Interfaith Dialogue*. With General Convention's endorsement of this document in 1994, The Episcopal Church took a significant step toward teaching of interfaith dialogue as valuable in and of itself.

In fact, essential for participation in the interfaith movement is an attitude that in difference there is value; essential also is comfort and skill with dialogue as a methodology. Dialogue is a term which is much used, often disparaged, yet necessary to any consideration of interreligious relations. Therefore, a moment spent in definition may prove helpful. While the term's linguistic origins cannot be traced neatly, it is often asserted that the term dialogue comes from the Greek *dia* (through) + *logos* (word), thus talking something through. We are reminded, then, that *dia* does not mean two. A *dialogue* can be multilateral.

As Plato used the word, *dialogue* names a reciprocal discourse, the purpose of which (different from debate) is gaining clarity rather than winning an argument; there is parity (at least roughly) among its participants, who practice courtesy and forbearance throughout the discussion.

Social scientist Daniel Yankelovich would add that dialogue is reciprocal discourse featuring empathetic listening, the airing of participants' prior assumptions, and the absence of coercive influences. His popular handbook, *The Magic of Dialogue*,[8] defines dialogue as a transformative activity—a constellation of strategies employed for the purpose of strengthening relationships or solving problems. Thus dialogue is something quite specific. It entails a certain degree of formality, but not every formal exchange qualifies as dialogue. Casual encounter may have value, but it is not dialogue. A single meeting is not likely to qualify as dialogue. Rather, dialogue is a dialectical mode of relationship requiring time and patience.

The conduct of dialogue comes with its own obstacles, such as: Who should be at the table? Which religions? Which sub-groups of those religions? If it is to be a dialogue among religious leaders, by what standard is it determined who is a leader and who is not? Will there be some attempt to achieve gender balance in the dialogue circle? Ethnic balance? Is there room at the table for the secular humanist? What can be done to get the very conservative to participate? How do we make sure minority voices are heard? How do we conduct a bilateral religious dialogue without causing harm to religion-communities not at the table?

The need for overt movement into multireligious concerns was occasioned, as the brief prologue to *Principles* (1994) explains, by US Episcopal congregations' increasing awareness that they were now living "side by side with organized groups representing many of the great religious traditions of the world who share our concern for peace, justice and the common good." Episcopalians were coming to realize "the need to affirm spiritual values in a materialistic society," as well as to embrace "the duty to remove any supposed religious justification for discrimination based on prejudice and ignorance."

The body of the document comprises two roughly equal sections. The first, *Dialogue as Mutual Understanding*, asserts and explains five principles:

- Make the effort to get to know adherents of other religions (and through them, their traditions), taking full advantage of whatever structures are in place to facilitate interfaith understanding;

- Engage in dialogue ecumenically whenever possible;

- Allow adherents of other faiths to speak for themselves regarding their religion (thus minimizing the tendency to stereotype);

- Be aware of the "cluster of theological commitments and cultural loyalties" which each dialogue participant (ourselves included) cannot help but bring to the table; and,

- Prepare for dialogue carefully—which includes careful preparation for presenting one's Christian perspective.

This last principle implies that Christians should take time to rehearse their responses to questions the dialogue partner might raise about core Christian doctrines and practices. As well, under this rubric is found calls for respectful listening and for willingness to take up painful issues charitably. Here also is noted the need for fairness in making comparisons—a warning against the highly problematic tendency to talk about our own religion in its ideal form and best practices, while assessing another religion only in terms of its worst manifestations in everyday life.

The second section, *Dialogue as Common Action*, offers and explains three directives:

- "Deal with issues related to living together as part of the human condition"—such as "joint approaches to government on matters of economic, social, political, and cultural concern," human rights, religious freedom, world peace, the environment, an hunger relief;

- "Foster efforts at education and communication among people of different faiths"—both to enrich community understanding and to mitigate stereotyping and "inaccurate media coverage of minority religious groups;" and,

- "Share spiritual insights and approaches to worship that respect the integrity of each tradition."

Under this third directive are included cautions against participating in worship in ways "which blur very real differences of theology or world view," or which appropriate other people's "religious symbols or sacred texts." Here also is modest encouragement for attending "another community's acts of worship," but only with careful preparation, a respectful attitude, and an opportunity to debrief.

Finally, in the last paragraph of the 1994 *Principles,* a note of humility emerges. In mentioning the value of "prayer for people of other religious traditions" and commenting on the appropriateness of Christian prayers for the conversion of others, *Principles* asserts: "In any event, it is God who converts people. Christians themselves are far from fully understanding or obeying God's will. It is inappropriate to single out any one religious group as being in particular need of conversion in a way that fosters prejudice."

Principles (1994) draws heavily upon the Anglican Church of Canada document *Guidelines for Interfaith Dialogue* (1988), using its same two-part format (albeit with new names for the two sections) and even quoting it directly in places. Interestingly, however, the Canadian document concludes with a caveat: no single set of guidelines can cover all situations. *Principles* (1994) omits this paragraph.

Continuing Involvement

Ironically, the Advisory Committee which produced *Principles* (1994) replaced the Presiding Bishop's Committee on Christian-Jewish Relations, which had been in service for at least two decades. Yet, within a year, the need for two "Relational Committees" had been recognized: one each for Episcopal-Jewish and Episcopal-Muslim Relations. The membership of each included persons from the Advisory Committee on Interfaith Relations, but also other persons selected for their particular expertise, and met occasionally for some years.

From its beginning in 1992, the Presiding Bishop's Advisory Committee on Interfaith Relations articulated repeatedly the need to expand the scope of its efforts (thus those of The Episcopal Church) beyond the Abrahamic concerns. As early as 1993, it recommended the addition of someone with expertise on Christian-Buddhist concerns to its roster; this step was indeed taken. By 1997, the Advisory Committee could report its own involvement in learning about

Buddhism and attendance by at least some members at national Jewish-Buddhist relations events. Again, the Advisory Committee called for establishment of more interfaith relationships—perhaps with Buddhists and Hindus as the logical next step. However, it acknowledged that such a move would require additional members to be appointed to its roster, and additional relational committees (i.e. Episcopal-Buddhist, Episcopal-Hindu) to be formed. As well, it recognized that the necessary funds were unlikely to be budgeted. Such advisory committees await their moment still.

Even with these challenges in mind, the Advisory Committee, through the Standing Commission on Ecumenical Relations, brought two resolutions to General Convention 1997, both of which passed. One of these, Resolution A023, encouraged Episcopal seminaries "to prepare their graduates on what it means theologically to live in a permanently interfaith and religiously pluralistic world." In 2009, Auburn Seminary (New York City) conducted a major study of the state of multifaith education in the formation of religious leaders for the religiously diverse North American context. Seven Episcopal seminaries were included in the research sample for that study. Multifaith education was evident at each at that time; at some seminaries, it has expanded dramatically since. For example,

- The General Theological Seminary's Center for Jewish-Christian Studies and Relations [CJCSR], established in 1986 by James Carpenter, sponsors an annual lecture on Jewish-Christian relations, maintains an ongoing formal dialogue between General Seminary and Hebrew Union College-Jewish Institute of Religion students, and holds an annual interfaith Service of Remembrance for victims of the Holocaust. In recent years, the CJCSR's efforts have expanded in multifaith directions to an extent. Courses on the world's religions, theology of religions, Christian-Muslim relations, and related topics have been available most semesters since the early 1990s at least.

- Virginia Theological Seminary has, for many years, offered courses and other opportunities for learning about world religions, Judaism and Jewish-Christian relations, and Islam and Christian-Muslim relations. More recently, "Interfaith Conversations" have been located within the Center for Anglican Communion Studies. These have taken a number of forms, including a series of major conferences on interreligious topics. In light of actions by the 2012 General Convention, it has reiterated a strong, public commitment to interreligious education and conversation.

- Whereas, at the time of the Auburn study, Episcopal Divinity School had been offering occasional courses with multifaith implications, its commitment to multifaith education is now far more robust. Since Spring 2011, a grant from the Henry Luce Foundation has enabled EDS to expand interfaith learning opportunities in varied and creative ways. This has included a conference on *Abrahamic Religions on the Silk Road: Remapping our understanding of the geography of the Christian world,* lectures and panel discussions on the current state of Christian-Muslim relations, a travel-seminar to China, and student participation in the Cambridge Interfaith Environmental Group.

The other of these two General Convention actions, Resolution A022, encouraged every diocese of The Episcopal Church "to identify existing faith groups within its boundaries and to open channels for dialogue." Such dialogues were to make use of the *Principles for Interfaith Dialogue* (1994) and were to be conducted ecumenically wherever possible. The same resolution requested each diocese to designate a liaison to the Presiding Bishop's Advisory Committee on Interfaith Relations. These designees were to be skilled in communicating online. Action of General Convention does not, however, guarantee action at the diocesan level. Research in early 2002 by the Interfaith Education Initiative—a program created in the aftermath of the attacks of 9/11/2001—indicated that the number of dioceses with an interfaith officer or liaison was far from 100%.

The Interfaith Education Initiative [IEI], which ran from January 2002 through December 2004, was funded by and housed in the offices of Episcopal Relief and Development [ERD]. Oversight was shared by ERD and The Episcopal Church's Ecumenical and Interfaith Relations Office, with help from a steering committee of individuals with educational, theological, or interfaith expertise. The initiative's mission, according to its promotional literature, was "to promote better understanding within the Church of the world's religious diversity, complexity and interconnectedness by developing a curriculum and providing educational resources." To this end, the IEI website offered downloadable resources on some dozen religions and published a handbook on Jewish-Christian-Muslim understanding.

During the summer of 2002, the IEI offered three week-long seminars. Two of these offerings (held in Dearborn, Michigan, and in New York City) helped participants understand the changing US religious landscape.[9] The third focused on the Anglican encounter with Islam (historically and presently). The IEI concluded with a conference at the Washington National Cathedral in early fall 2004. Entitled *Charged to Do What is Right and Just*, its focus was on forma-tion for local-level dialogue and activism.

In part, at least, the Interfaith Education Initiative was an effort to act on concerns such as those voiced in the past by the Advisory Committee on In-terfaith Relations about the need to improve Christian understanding of and response to America's religious diversity writ large. In a March 2002 news brief about the IEI, Christopher Epting (then Presiding Bishop's Deputy for Ecu-menical and Interfaith Relations) underscored this need for improvement, say-ing: "the global situation and changing demographics in this country make understanding the world's major religions no longer a matter of mere curiosity but a real necessity."[10] The Interfaith Education Initiative stands as an example of The Episcopal Church participating in the interfaith movement independent of its ecumenical partners.

The Ecumenical Preference

In her assessment of the interfaith movement in 2004, Kusumita Pedersen commented that "the pace of interfaith activity seems to be accelerating."[11] The Episcopal Church's actions during the decade preceding her study can be seen as contributions to that acceleration.

In his 1998 publication, *Faith and Interfaith in a Global Age,* Marcus Bray-brooke complained that, in spite of rapid expansion and significant progress, the interfaith movement was "still very weak."[12] Some of the obstacles men-tioned then are still with us:

- The reluctance to fund interfaith work vigorously, thus the expectation that much of the work be done by volunteers;

- The need for better collaboration between interfaith organizations—which is impeded by the reality that they may be in competition for the same funding sources;

- The perception within our respective religion-communities that inter-faith matters are "fringe" rather than "core" concerns;

- The attitude within our own religion-community that interfaith work such as most of us conduct it is antithetical to the tenets of that religion itself;

- The difficulty of involving very conservative adherents of the various religious in interfaith activities and conversations–which in turn points to the need for more vigorous intra-religious conversation.

As a player in the interfaith movement, The Episcopal Church has encountered each of these stumbling blocks in some way.

Theologically, The Episcopal Church may have been helped into the interfaith movement by changes in missiology which gained strength in the mid-1980s. For example, Buddhist, Muslim, and Jewish guests were among the speakers to the Sixth Assembly of the World Council of Churches (Vancouver 1983). Canadian missiologist Katharine Hockin saw this as indicative of a shift toward inclusivism, an example of "new patterns of relationship and faithfulness on a companion way."[13] The Episcopal Church's approval of a major revision of the Book of Common Prayer—particularly, the 1979 prayer book's Baptismal Covenant, which emphasizes neighbor-love and service, calling upon the baptized to "strive for justice and peace among all people, and respect the dignity of every human being"—may also have been helpful to Episcopalians in coming to see interfaith dialogue as compatible with Christian faithfulness and witness.

Methodologically, throughout the 20th century at least, The Episcopal Church's normative mode of engagement in interreligious relations had been ecumenical. This preference was quite clear to the Presiding Bishop's Advisory Committee on Interfaith Relations, as was noted in its 1997 report to General Convention:

> The Committee understands that dialogue with members of other religions should be carried on at the national level through that body where Christians cooperate to work together—The National Council of the Churches of Christ in the USA....The major work of our Interfaith Relations Committee is understood to be that of supporting the NCCC process and facilitating appropriate relations at the local level between The Episcopal Church and other faith communities.

The fruit of working on interreligious matters ecumenically is the topic to which we turn next.

Notes

1. Kusumita P. Pedersen, "The Interfaith Movement: An Incomplete Assessment," *Journal of Ecumenical Studies* 41, no. 1 (Winter 2004): 74.

2. Pedersen, 76.

3. For Richey's text, see: http://www.parliamentofreligions.org/_includes/FCKcontent/file/ Richey.pdf. Last accessed: 22 November 2011.

4. For the full text of this resolution, see http://www.lambethconference.org/resolutions/ 1978/1978-37.cfm. Last accessed: 9 July 2012.

5. For the text of *Christ and People of Other Faiths,* see http://nifcon.anglicancommunion. org/resources/documents/lam88_section_report.pdf; for Appendix 6, see http://nifcon. anglicancommunion.org/resources/documents/lam88_ap6.pdf. Last accessed: 24 July 2012.

6. For the full text of this resolution, see http://www.lambethconference.org/resolutions/ 1988/1988-20.cfm

7. *The Blue Book, 1991,* 536, 537. See also Resolution Number: 1991-A060 "Reaffirm Commitment to Evangelism and Recognize Religious Pluralism." *Journal of General Convention,* 397.

8. Daniel Yankelovich, *The Magic of Dialogue: Transforming Conflict into Cooperation* (New York: Simon & Schuster, 1999).

9. The Dearborn offering has persisted as the annual *Worldviews Seminar* at the University of Michigan-Dearborn. For a discussion of its founding, sponsorship, and methodology see Lucinda A. Mosher and Claude Jacobs, "The University of Michigan-Dearborn Worldviews Seminar," in *Teaching Religion and Healing,* ed. Linda Barnes (New York: Oxford University Press, 2006), 261–70.

10. Pedersen, 74.

11. *News Briefs,* Episcopal News Service 2002-058-1 (March 6, 2002).

12. Marcus Braybrooke, *Faith and Interfaith in a Global Age* (Grand Rapids, Michigan: CoNexus, 1998), 97–100.

13. Katharine B. Hockin, "My Pilgrimage in Mission," *International Bulletin of Missionary Research* (January, 1988): 30.

II

EMBRACING ECUMENISM

INTERFAITH RELATIONS AND THE CHURCHES

"We are living in a religiously diverse and highly globalized world, a world of shared vulnerabilities and hopes," opens *Interfaith Relations and the Church: The Theological Challenge*, a resource produced by the National Council of the Churches of Christ in the USA [NCCC] in 2010. This 12-page booklet endeavors to be both educational and pastoral. It is not *from* The Episcopal Church, but it is intended for Episcopalians nonetheless. It represents ecumenical theologizing about religious manyness, which is the focus of this chapter.

As we learned in Chapter One, in *Principles for Interfaith Dialogue* (1994), its earliest comprehensive statement on the matter, The Episcopal Church is explicit in its preference for conducting interreligious work ecumenically. During the 20th century, it was the policy of The Episcopal Church *not* to engage in serious formal theological dialogue with agencies representing other religions, a point made by one ecumenical officer I interviewed in the late 1990s. Time and again, moves toward taking up interreligious relations work were resisted by the Executive Council and General Convention with the argument that The Episcopal Church was a member of the NCCC, which was already conducting interreligious relations on its behalf.[1] One church officer described this to me as a positive way for the various Christian bodies to be of one voice in interfaith matters. This preference for conducting interreligious relations ecumenically is a second theme in The Episcopal Church's engagement and theological understanding of religious manyness.

By the late 1950s, interfaith matters had become a concern of the NCCC—thus a concern of The Episcopal Church as a founding member. As early as 1961, we find General Convention directing The Episcopal Church's Joint Commission on Ecumenical Relations to study the content of NCCC literature (as a step toward adopting such material for use by Episcopalians). It seems that questions had been raised about the Council's claim that its "educational materials are designed to further the search for truth".[2] The Joint Commission determined that adequate safeguards had indeed been put in place as the Council developed materials on, for example, "Christianity and Buddhism". Authoritative statements on Buddhism (from Buddhists, one might hope) would have to be considered, even if Christian members of NCCC did not like what was said.[3]

The Episcopal Church always has been represented on the NCCC Interfaith Relations Commission. Late in the 20th century, it provided even more vigorous support. At its meeting in November 1993, the Executive Council expressed official appreciation for four missionary appointments made in recent months by Presiding Bishop Edmund Browning. Among these was the seconding of career missionary Bert Breiner to the NCCC. Collaborating with The Episcopal Church to underwrite Breiner's position were the United Methodist Church and the American Baptist Church. At NCCC Headquarters in NYC, he would join Jay Rock, a Presbyterian, as Co-Director for Interfaith Relations. The Episcopal Church would thus play a particularly vital role in ecumenical interreligious-relations efforts for nearly eight years.

Interfaith Relations and the Churches (1999)

An important outcome of the era of robust Episcopal Church support of the interfaith office of the NCCC was the formulation and promulgation of *Interfaith Relations and the Churches: A Policy Statement of the National Council of the Churches of Christ in the U.S.A.* Terry Muck (then on the faculty of Austin Presbyterian Seminary) wrote the first draft. It was then critiqued by the council's Interfaith Relations Commission—a disparate group in terms of denominational membership and theological perspective. As part of the revision process, the council's Faith and Order Commission, the Black Church caucus, and interfaith officers of various Protestant denominations and Orthodox churches were also consulted. By unanimous vote of the NCCC General Assembly on 10 November 1999, the document was accepted as the council's official policy. Because Episcopalian Bert Breiner was a member of the *Policy Statement* writing team (and in fact wrote the final draft), and because it was embraced by General Convention in due course, this important document was shaped in part by, and would help to shape further, The Episcopal Church's own theology of religious manyness.

Breiner later wrote a companion resource, *Interfaith Relations and the Churches: A Brief Theological Introduction to the Policy Statement* (2001), which (with the original document) remains available on the NCCC website.[4] Breiner's published commentary, amplified by notes from numerous conversations with him about the Policy Statement, will guide us here.

Interfaith Relations and the Churches has two major components: the Policy Statement *per se* and Recommendations. The Policy Statement itself comprises three main sections: *Preamble*; *Reflections on Theology and Practice*; and *Marks of Faithfulness*. Throughout, it keeps the reader aware of the diversity of theologies extant within the council's membership. For points on which the members cannot speak with a common voice, a reference to the range of positions is built into the text. It encourages further deep ecumenical dialogue on such points. "In doing so," Breiner writes, the NCCC Policy Statement "stands squarely in the mainstream of ecumenical experience." As a theological argument, it "seeks to make a positive contribution to the understanding of interfaith relations" by taking up particular themes in light of a question fundamental to all of its member communions (and, for that matter to non-member Christian bodies as well): What does it mean to live as a faithful disciple of Christ side by side with persons whose religious commitments are other than Christian?

Preamble

The *Preamble*, which itself has three parts, establishes the context for which a policy statement is needed. By opening with John 17:18: "As you have sent me into the world, so I have sent them into the world," it underscores that establishing an ecumenical policy for interfaith relations will be construed as a matter of discipleship, a "common effort to understand ever more fully how to live as the body of Christ in this religiously plural and culturally diverse time and place." It will be informed by new experiences of religious diversity in the US, thus new awareness "of the significance of the world's religions and their influence on politics, economics, and cultures." It does this while deliberately avoiding the need to define *religion* or to set the boundaries of *Christianity*.

"The Americas have always been religiously plural," begins the sub-section entitled *Historical, Political and Social Context*. Its six paragraphs provide an oft-requested brief history of US religious diversity, acknowledging its ugly aspects as well as the positive developments, the present challenges as well as the opportunities. It recognizes that interfaith relations actually *matters* to the inner dynamics of families in American society. This section notes some of the arenas in which interfaith cooperation is particularly important: local problems such as housing and job opportunities; stereotyping based on religious difference; and international concerns such as the rise of "fundamentalism"—a term it uses without offering a definition. The term remains controversial: sociologists and scholars of religious studies do not agree on a working definition of this term; the Policy Statement simply ignores that. In fact, the Policy Statement says only little about the international dimension of US interfaith relations—primarily because other NCCC policy statements had addressed international concerns already.

The sub-section headed *A Continuing Dimension of the Church's Life* suggests that life in a religiously complex situation has always been part of the Christian story, with antecedents in biblical times. Currently, the intersection between interfaith concerns and ministry raise questions of theology and practice which call for extended ecumenical consideration. That is, there is need for clarification of understandings of relationship between Christian groups, between Christians and people of other religions, and between such people and God. Likewise, there is need for consideration of how Christians can "best live a life of faithful witness and service in a multi-faith context." In short, the *Preamble* lays out the overarching theme of faithful Christian life in the midst of religious diversity, furthered by interreligious understanding and cooperation.

Reflections on Theology and Practice

Reflections on Theology and Practice, the second main section of the Policy Statement, devotes two paragraphs to expressions of gratitude for and indebtedness to prior work on these matters which inform the NCCC Policy Statement: the Roman Catholic document *Nostra Aetate* (1965); post-1965 statements from the Lambeth Conference of the Anglican Communion, the Lutheran World Federation, and the World Alliance of Reformed Churches; the World Council of Churches' *Guidelines on Dialogue* (1979); and "policies or study documents on interfaith relations or on specific bilateral interreligious relationship" developed by NCCC member communions—plus insights gleaned from member communions' participation in local or regional interreligious councils, social ministries, and advocacy efforts.

All of the foregoing serves as prelude to some two-dozen paragraphs of theological argument spun out under three sub-headings: *God and Human Community; Jesus Christ and Reconciliation;* and *The Spirit of God and Human Hope.* As this organizational structure implies, the content is enthusiastically Trinitarian and Incarnational.

God and Human Community

The sub-section *God and Human Community* asserts that relationship itself is a divine gift; in fact, in Christian understanding, God's very essence is "dynamic interrelationship." Taking "the life of the Trinity as a model for relationship," explains Breiner, the Policy Statement "reflects a respect for the integrity of the distinction of persons in the Trinity"—an approach "particularly developed in Eastern Orthodox theology and in some strands of Anglican theology."

Human diversity is a divine gift, the statement asserts, as is community. It emphasizes that the will of God in creation is that human beings should be in relationship "for their mutual support and fulfillment," Breiner points out, making "the search for true community, respect, and justice a theological imperative." In this portion of the argument, he says, the document's emphasis is on God's will in creation, not the act of creation itself. The document attempts to focus attention on the will of God by carefully avoiding any hint of modalism that some have attached to these doctrines. He explains:

> The statement studiously avoids such a theology which would contradict its respect for the Trinitarian life of God as a model of human relationship and community. Human beings are not reducible to their functions or roles in human society and the document affirms a theological foundation for the integrity and theological worth of every human person. It is the will of God which makes the search for true community, respect, and justice a theological imperative and not a matter of sociological, historical, cultural, or political importance only.

The Creation account of Genesis 2–3 as evidence of God's will for all of humanity to be in common relationship makes possible some talk of "a universal family of humankind." Such use of "family language" in a way that included non-Christians, Breiner notes, caused some controversy during early discussions. In response, biblical examples of "family language" referring to non-Christians were added to the discussion of reconciliation which comes later in the document.

Noting that human beings "have a propensity for taking the gift of diversity and turning it into a cause of disunity, antagonism and hatred," the argument includes biblical evidence of separation and alienation, plus a number of historical examples of Christians acting "unfaithfully" toward Jews, Muslims, and others. It acknowledges that the Christian record on building loving community and stewarding creation is mixed. Balancing this is biblical teaching on hospitality. "The discussion of hospitality is central to this section of the Policy Statement," Breiner notes. It provides "a biblical basis for its concentration on the theme of Christian discipleship." As was true also of the previous category, much more biblical material could have been included here, he observes—and provides further suggestions as part of his commentary.

Missing in the Policy Statement's account of hospitality shortcomings and successes, Breiner notes, is some "mention of the continued hospitality which has been provided to the Church" by non-Christians. This is a serious lack, in his opinion; in his commentary, he provides some examples for those who might be willing to expand upon paragraph 26 in this regard. The next paragraph (#27), which urges rejection or reform of "human actions and systems that destroy or deny the image of God in human beings or that tear down the structures of human community," is a link in the document's chain of efforts to provide a foundation for authentically Christian participation in interfaith struggles toward the common good.

"Because God is at work in all creation," we read in paragraph 28, "we can expect to find new understandings of our faith through dialogue with people of other religions." Breiner calls special attention to the nuances of this paragraph, which was crafted with care and is open to a range of interpretations. In fact, he says, this paragraph draws on "a doctrine of creation…fully developed in the Policy Statement, although it is clearly a central theological affirmation of the document as a whole."

Jesus Christ and Reconciliation

With an affirmation of the necessity of repentance and reconciliation, transition is made to the next sub-section (*Jesus Christ and Reconciliation*), the theme of which is Incarnation. "It is our Christian conviction that reconciliation among people and with the world cannot be separated from the reconciliation offered in Jesus Christ," it proclaims. That given, the Policy Statement concedes that many perspectives on reconciliation in Christ are brought to the ecumenical conversation by the NCCC's member communions. It issues a reminder that scripture is multivocal about Christian relationship with people of other religious convictions. It also asserts the inseparability of the "love of God and love of neighbors."

The Policy Statement's summary of the gamut of Christian views on the relationship between non-Christians and God is particularly interesting. Without using the labels common in academic analyses of these attitudes, about which more will be said in Chapter Six, paragraphs 33 and 34 of the document make reference to two, which (following Breiner) can be described as follows:

- *Christian exclusivism*, which sees "no possibility of salvation apart from confession of faith in Jesus Christ as Lord and Savior," thus, "Jesus' work can have effect only if certain conditions are met on the part of human beings."

- *Christian inclusivism*, which "is somewhat more ambivalent about the role that human faith plays in appropriating the saving work of Jesus."

Two scriptural warrants are included for each of these viewpoints. This move, says Breiner, illustrates "the theological and exegetical approach of the document as a whole." By being evenhanded, the Statement affirms that ecumenical theological deliberations "need to be informed by the whole breadth of the Scriptures and of the theological traditions of the Church."

Again, without labeling it, a third viewpoint is also described, in which "the saving power of God is understood as a mystery...." This attitude is sometimes termed *holy agnosticism* with regard to the question of God's relationship to people who are not Christian.

A fourth position, pluralism, is often included in discussions of theologies of religious manyness, as we saw in the Introduction. The pluralist position may be defined as understanding "the truth about God to transcend any and every religious tradition," says Breiner, and the Policy Statement has nothing to say about that viewpoint, because pluralism so defined "does not reflect a consensus of the official positions of the member communions." (It may, however, be a view held by individuals within some member churches.)

In wrapping up the reconciliation sub-section, attention is refocused on the overarching theme of Christian discipleship. The Policy Statement suggests the need for further ecumenical consideration of "issues of interpreting scriptural teaching," then asserts that Christian discipleship involves living "by the clear obligation of the Gospel." In this latter regard, it quotes the Summary of the Law. The first draft of the Policy Statement had used the Gospel of Matthew to convey this; upon further consideration, the authorial committee had opted for the summary as found in Luke 10:25–28. In Luke, the Summary of the Law is followed by the Parable of the Good Samaritan—and by this story, as Breiner explains, makes two points with serious implications for interfaith relations:

- "Love of neighbor crosses boundaries of community adherence. It applies to loving even those of another faith and even those of faith communities with whom we are not on the best of terms."

- Such conduct "is not limited to those of our own community of faith." Non-Christians "can and do love their neighbor as themselves."

With regard to Christian discipleship, Breiner stresses: "Any understanding of Jesus' teaching on how we are to relate to men and women of other faiths and how we are to value the lives and deeds of such people needs to take both implications into account."

The Spirit of God and Human Hope

As we take up the sub-section *The Spirit of God and Human Hope* (the third and final category of the Policy Statement's *Reflections on Theology and Practice*), it is helpful to recall the theological anthropology at play in the document as a whole. In his *The Christian Moral Vision*, Earl Brill notes that traditional Anglican theological anthropology "recognizes the fact of sinfulness, but denies that this is the last word to be said."[5] Similarly, the anthropology of the

Policy Statement begins with a pair of assertions (developed under the rubric God and Humanity and implied as the present stage of discussion commences) that human beings are created for a life of community with God and with each other; yet human beings tend to behave in ways destructive to both relationships. Thus, Breiner points out, the Policy Statement describes the human condition in a manner "traditionally associated with the doctrine of original sin." It then balances this with a robust pneumatology—that is, an account of the nature and action of the Holy Spirit. To begin, it declares: "The presence and power of the Holy Spirit fill us with hope." Christians have hope, it explains, because the same Holy Spirit who (as Christians read Genesis 1:2) brought order out of chaos in Creation "can reshape our warped societies."

As this argument unfolds, we are reminded that (as the Gospel of John puts it) the Holy Spirit "blows where it chooses." Perhaps audaciously, the document declares: "We believe that our relationships with people of other religious traditions are being shaped by the Spirit." Christians "need never be without hope, for neither we nor the rest of creation are ever without the Spirit of God." The point is made several times that Christians may not always understand what God is up to. Thus there is need for discernment—which Breiner defines as "the ability to become aware of the presence and activity of the Holy Spirit wherever it is to be found;" and discernment is a crucial element of Christian discipleship. Breiner reminds us of the Christian tradition's association of the Holy Spirit with discernment: lists of gifts of the Spirit always include "wisdom and counsel," he notes.

As the Policy Statement asserted earlier, a "loving community" is God's intention. The statement now explains that it is the Spirit which helps Christians work toward this, and to "witness in word and deed to this hope." Implying that Christian behavior outside the Christian community is to be consistent with behavior within, the Policy Statement explains that Christians are to "be a sign of the restored community" and to "be open to the presence of God's Spirit" in the varied circumstances of encounter (family, workplace, community-action coalitions, while on daily errands, yet elsewhere) with persons of other religions. As Breiner puts it, the point here is that, "since the Spirit blows where it wills, one cannot preclude the possibility that the Spirit may use any and all of those present in such an encounter to challenge us and to give us inspiration and hope."

In paragraph 43, the Policy Statement allows that Christians "do not always agree…on how best to love our neighbors." Questions of evangelism, witness, and dialogue are, in fact, a major area of disagreement among the NCCC's member churches, as Breiner's commentary confirms. The Policy Statement describes three differences of emphasis:

- Those who see "practice of Christian love" as "the most powerful witness to the truth of the Gospel";

- Those who "believe that love demands the verbal proclamation of the Gospel and the open invitation to all people to be reconciled to God in Christ;"

- Those who "understand evangelization as our participation in God's transformation of human society."

In any case, the Policy Statement comes down emphatically against "coercive proselytism," described as interactions which "do violence to the integrity of human persons and communities." Returning to the theme of discipleship, it prays that all may be "instruments of God" in working toward an era of faithfulness, righteousness, and peace. Drawing upon biblical warrants, the argument concludes that Christian relationship to people of other religions must be founded in willingness "to engage in the struggle for justice," genuine respect for all, and love.

Marks of Faithfulness

Marks of Faithfulness, the Policy Statement's third main section, outlines characteristics of open-minded, open-hearted approach to "the challenges of our multi-religious society" which remains in tune with notions of Christian discipleship:

- All relationship begins with meeting (which may be encumbered by the baggage of "bitter memories," but to which Christians are to bring recollection of having been "created for loving community").

- True relationship involves risk.

- True relationship respects the other's identity.

- True relationship is based on integrity. (That is, neither side will be asked "to betray their religious commitments.")

- True relationship is rooted in accountability and respect.

- True relationship offers an opportunity to serve.

Thus, as Breiner puts it, the Policy Statement has sought "to translate its theological stance into a series of guidelines for interfaith encounter."

Some Observations

Having now laid out what the NCCC Policy Statement is, it is important, says Breiner, to note what it is not. It is not an attempt to resolve matters of intra-Christian controversy—such as the salvation of non-Christians, mission-as-evangelism versus mission-as-service, the nature and role of dialogue; nor is it a handbook for dealing with practical interfaith-relations matters—such as interfaith marriage, interfaith worship, and more. While it contains many biblical quotations, it is not an example of scholarly biblical exegesis.

Much of the theology of the Policy Statement is latent, rather than spelled out overtly. For example, as Breiner points out in his commentary, the Policy Statement provides two theological bases for ongoing divine relationship with the whole of humanity. In the sub-section on *God and Human Community*, it does so by means of the doctrine of creation. In the sub-section on *Jesus Christ and Reconciliation*, it turns to the doctrine of incarnation.

With regard to the doctrine of creation, the Policy Statement asserts (in paragraph 28) that "because God is at work in all creation, we can expect to find new understandings of our faith through dialogue with people of other religions." It makes a similar point (in paragraph 34) by quoting Romans 1:20, "Ever since the creation of the world, (God's) eternal power and divine nature, invisible though they are, have been understood and seen through the things [God] has made;" and again (in paragraph 42) by insisting that "since God is the Lord of history, we can be open to the presence of God's Spirit in these encounters [with men and women of other faiths]." Thus we find in the NCCC Policy Statement, as Breiner puts it, "a theological rationale for an interfaith encounter which assumes that all human meeting takes place in the context of God's abiding presence, power, and purpose." As a whole, *Interfaith Relations and the Churches* does not, Breiner insists, try to offer "a common theological principle for a Christian understanding of interfaith relations." Rather, as a Policy Statement for a fellowship of communions, it focuses a spotlight on "some theological resources widely available throughout the varied traditions of [Christianity] which might help to inform an ongoing ecumenical dialogue." The Episcopal Church has always been, and remains, a participant in this conversation.

With regard to the doctrine of Incarnation, arguments based on it with particularly usefulness in furthering positive interfaith understanding were worked out from diverse perspectives during the latter third of the 20th century. Breiner makes note of post-Vatican II Roman Catholic theologians on the one hand, the neo-Barthian perspective of David Lochhead on the other. Whichever the approach, he asserts, the case is well made that, through the doctrine of the Incarnation, Christians can learn much "about the things of God from the whole of the human family."

Consider the Chalcedonian Definition of the two natures of Christ, Breiner urges. If it is correct, an important implication for interfaith understanding follows from the Christology of the Early Church Fathers. "Jesus assumed 'human nature' in its entirety, sin only excepted. This means that we can learn about the true breadth of our Lord's humanity only to the extent that we are willing to explore the breadth, depth, and variety of human nature. The questions and experiences of men and women can help us to deepen our understanding of the human condition and so of human nature." People whose convictions differ from ours may ask questions we would never ask, in terms we would not think to use. But, Breiner concludes, if the thinking enshrined at Chalcedon is correct, we cannot fully understand the reality of Christ's human nature if "we close ourselves to the insights, perceptions, and experiences of our common humanity which have been articulated throughout the millennia by all men and women."

Further Resources

Recall that, near the beginning of this chapter, the document *Interfaith Relations and the Churches* was described as having two major components: the Policy Statement *per se* and *Recommendations*. Where the paragraphs of the Preamble and the argument which followed had been numbered, this practice was not continued after the conclusion of the *Marks of Faithfulness* section. This is an indicator that the remainder of the document should be considered an appendix to the Policy Statement *per se*.

The component labeled *Recommendations* is just that: some three pages of practical mandates for the NCCC as a whole, for its Interfaith Commission, and for its member churches themselves "in service to each other as a community of communions." The final recommendations: that this policy statement be commended "to member communions, congregations and local ecumenical and interreligious gatherings for study, and as a catalyst to reflection and action;" and, "to other religious communities in the United States for their study, and invite their reactions to it in the hope and expectation of deepening friendship." This begs the question: did this happen?

Margaret Orr Thomas, of the Office of Ecumenical and Interfaith Relations of the Presbyterian Church (U.S.A.) wrote and published "A Liturgy Based on *Interfaith Relations and the Churches*," for use by the NCCC General Assembly on Sunday, November 14, 1999, just four days after it had adopted the Policy Statement. The liturgy follows a typical Protestant Order of Service, and includes a ritual of commitment to the Policy Statement's *Marks of Faithfulness*, constructed in responsorial fashion. This liturgy is still available on the NCCC website.[6]

In 2000, the NCCC released *Interfaith Relations and Christian Living: Study and Action Suggestions for use with* Interfaith Relations and the Churches: *A Policy Statement of the National Council of the Churches of Christ in the USA*. This 28-page resource, planned by the NCCC Commission on Interfaith Relations, was prepared by interfaith officer Jay Rock, with editorial assistance from Margaret Thomas. It provides detailed plans for a course with six sessions:

- What Shall We Ask About Living With People of Other Faiths?;

- Living Among Women and Men of Other Faiths;

- God and Human Community;

- Jesus Christ and Reconciliation;

- Hope and the Holy Spirit;

- Our Vocation as Christians Among People of Other Religious Traditions.

Suggestions are included for adapting the course for situations, such as a day-long workshop. The booklet also includes guidelines for planning a visit to a different religion's house of worship, and an annotated resource list. This last item, while admittedly now more than a decade out of date, is still worth consulting.

More importantly for the present, however, is to note that the Policy Statement continues to provide the foundation for new teaching materials on interfaith understanding for Christians, Episcopalians included. In 2010, the NCCC Interfaith Relations Office put forth a booklet series called *Interfaith Relations and the Church*. The five individual booklet titles, all available as free downloads from the NCCC website, are: *The Ecumenical Challenge, The Identity Challenge, The Missional Challenge,* and *The Theological Challenge*. All incorporate new writing, but the language, tone, and message is consistent with the 1999 document. All encourage Christians to be clear about their own convictions while teaching openness to people who do not share them. Altogether the material developed to teach the *Policy Statement* (1999) provide an excellent model for how The Episcopal Church's recent interfaith statements might be taught—a point to which we will return in Chapter Five.

Certainly, the NCCC Policy Statement itself was read by Episcopal Diocesan Ecumenical Officers and their counterparts in other communions affiliated with the Council. It was assigned to seminarians by various course-syllabi then and since. Assuredly, the items developed to make the NCCC Policy Statement accessible at the congregational level were indeed put to use. It is reasonable to assume that Episcopalians were among those who did so. In its report to the

2000 General Convention, the Standing Commission on Ecumenical Relations applauded the NCCC Policy Statement, noting that copies could be obtained from The Episcopal Church's Office of Ecumenical and Interfaith Relations. Furthermore, it said:

> ...the NCCC's Interfaith Commission maintains that, theologically, it is crucial to connect interreligious work to Christian Unity. For that reason, and because for many years any connection between ecumenical and interfaith relations was resisted in our church, one of the first tasks of the Episcopal Interfaith Relations Committee will be to explicate clearly the theological reasons for linking interfaith relations with the search for Christian unity.

On the basis of this comment, three points are worth highlighting. First, by 2000, seeing interfaith concerns as something to be addressed by the same structures handling ecumenical relations is no longer being resisted. Second, the Presiding Bishop's Advisory Committee on Interfaith Relations had given way to a new structure: the Episcopal Interfaith Relations Committee of the Standing Commission on Ecumenical Relations. Third, while a theological explication of the link between interfaith relations and ecumenism was on this new structure's agenda from its inception, nearly a decade would elapse before The Episcopal Church would have such an explication officially. Meanwhile, it would continue to support and celebrate the interfaith work of the NCCC. For example, in its report to the 2006 General Convention, the Standing Commission on Ecumenical and Interreligious Relations celebrated the ongoing interfaith work of the NCCC, noting that the council "seeks to promote harmonious relations among Christians, Jews, Muslims, and many other faith groups in a society that is increasingly multireligious."

These three points will be examined further in Chapter Five. Before we take that step, we will take a close look at The Episcopal Church's bilateral interfaith relationships. The theme of Episcopal-Jewish concerns will occupy us in Chapter Three. In Chapter Four, we will turn to Episcopal-Muslim relations.

Notes

1. The National Council of the Churches of Christ in the USA is an association of some thirty-five churches: Eastern Orthodox, Oriental Orthodox, Anglican, Lutheran, and Reformed; historic Black Churches and historic Peace Churches are also members. The major Evangelical denominations and the Roman Catholic Church do not participate.

2. *Journal of General Convention,* 1961, 507; quoting a memorandum from NCCC.

3. *Journal of General Convention,* 1961, 508.

4. http://www.ncccusa.org/interfaith/brieftheocom.html. Last accessed: 10 April 2012. Dr. Breiner's commentary is excerpted in this chapter with permission of the National Council of the Churches of Christ in the USA.

5. Earl H. Brill, et al., *The Christian Moral Vision* (New York: Seabury Press, 1979), 11.

6. See http://www.ncccusa.org/interfaith/ifrliturgy.html. Last accessed: 13 July 2012.

III

Eschewing Contempt

Episcopal Guidelines for Christian-Jewish Relations

When The Episcopal Church adopted *Guidelines for Christian-Jewish Relations*, the *New York Times* applauded. In a story dated 24 July 1988, the Gray Lady commented that the recent action by General Convention in Detroit provoked "neither fanfare nor controversy;" but it may indeed have signaled the opening of "a whole new era" in interfaith relations. At least some prominent Jewish leaders had said as much. This chapter focuses on Episcopal-Jewish relations as one of several themes in the development of The Episcopal Church's theology of religious manyness.

Christian Anti-Judaism and Supersessionism

Different from the themes explored in other chapters, this interfaith concern takes us beyond the realm of commissions and offices of ecumenism and inter-religious relations per se. Although these certainly remain centers of reflection and action, Episcopal-Jewish relations is on the agenda of the Church's Standing Commission for Liturgy and Music and its peace-and-justice office as well. Throughout, of prime theological concern is anti-Judaism, defined as prejudice against the Jewish religion. Christian anti-Judaism, explains the Standing Commission on Liturgy and Music, in its report to The Episcopal Church's 2009 General Convention, "is not, in the first place, about Judaism. It is about authentic Christianity and the church's truth-telling." It is an attitude created and perpetuated by the Church "in its story of [Christian] origins, its biblical interpretations and its theology."[1] The term *anti-Semitism* is less precise for purposes of this discussion. Technically, it names prejudice against Jews as a race or ethnic group, but—as we shall see—it is used in some Episcopal resolutions and writings as a synonym for anti-Judaism.

Any current discussion of Christian anti-Judaism will take us almost at once to the term *supersessionism*. Derived from the Latin to *sit on or above*, the term names the fact of having taken over someone else's chair, of now having the right to sit in a place which once properly belonged to someone else. While this term dates back many centuries, it may be surprising that there is no entry for it in *The Oxford Dictionary of the Christian Church* or the *Evangelical Dictionary of Theology*. Be this as it may, the term is now used routinely in discussions of Christian-Jewish relations. As it is defined in many books and articles, *Christian supersessionism* labels the notion that the Church has replaced Israel as God's chosen people. Sometimes called *displacement* (or *replacement) theology*, it names a theological position encompassing a number of claims:

- God has rejected the Jewish people because they have rejected Jesus as the Messiah.

- God has, therefore, abrogated the divine covenant with the People Israel; that covenant relationship is now between God and the Body of Christ (the Church).

- The Law of Moses is annulled, replaced by faith in Jesus as Messiah.

- Those who accept Jesus as Messiah have replaced Jews (who reject him) in God's plan of salvation.

- Since the Church is now the True Israel, the Jews comprise a false Israel.

- Christians now are the heirs of all biblical promises to Israel; all prophetic criticism and condemnation, however, still applies to the Jews.

When addressing a meeting of the Standing Commission on Liturgy and Music in October 2010, Daniel Joslyn-Siemiatkoski, Assistant Professor of Church History at Church Divinity School of the Pacific, explained that such notions have in turn generated four highly problematic notions about Judaism:[2]

- That Judaism is merely preparatory for Christianity; therefore it is spiritually bereft—obsolete, in fact.

- That the relationship between Judaism and Christianity is unequal: where Judaism is "temporary in nature, legalistic in its teachings, and carnal in its understanding of Scripture," Christianity is eternal, permanent, "compassionate in its teachings, and possessing spiritual insights in Scripture."

- That the Gospels' Pharisees epitomize the ills of Judaism, responsible for having "distorted Judaism into a legalistic religion;" thus "Pharisee"

becomes a pejorative used in a host of contexts—too often "as a synonym for 'hypocrite' or 'sanctimonious jerk,'" as blogger Sarah Dylan
Breuer points out.[3]

- All Jews (from the time of Jesus henceforth) carry guilt for the trial and execution of Jesus.

One hardly needs now point out the consequent slippery slope of this line
of thinking: the formerly-chosen/no-longer-chosen people have forfeited their
right to existence; since they've been replaced, they can/should be eliminated
(by means of forced conversion, expulsion, pogroms, genocide). The worst instance of this to date was the Shoah, the Holocaust. "Christians are not responsible for the Holocaust," asserts Marilyn J. Salmon, Episcopal priest, esteemed
scholar of Judaism, and professor of New Testament. "Christianity itself is
not responsible for the Holocaust," she continues. "Christianity is culpable,
however, for creating the environment that made the Holocaust possible."[4]
Episcopal-Jewish relations becomes a clear concern of the Church only in a
post-Holocaust world, with full awareness of the need to repent for Christian
complicity in the Shoah, but not always so aware of continuing (often inadvertent) Christian anti-Judaism.

Toward a Dialogical Relationship

Not surprisingly, given the Shoah and its immediate aftermath in the mid-
20th century, Christian-Jewish matters received The Episcopal Church's attention earlier than did those of relationship to any other religion particularly, or
concern for interreligious relations broadly. As early as the 1960s, the Church
had a Committee on Jewish-Christian Dialogue. Action by the 1964 General
Convention ruled out the validity of the charge of deicide and any other "unchristian accusations against the Jews"—in fact, condemned anti-Semitism
entirely—although, in light of the vocabulary lesson above, "condemnation
of anti-Judaism" better names what was intended. The 1964 General Convention's action, as the text of the resolution indicates, was based theologically on
two points: that centuries of Christian implication that all Jews everywhere
are responsible for Jesus' death was an "un-Christ-like witness;" and that lack
of communication with (thus ignorance and suspicion of) Jews has impeded
"Christian obedience of the Law of Love."[5]

The 1964 resolution committed the Church to initiate "dialogue with appropriate representative bodies of the Jewish Faith." This led to official dialogue
between The Episcopal Church and the Synagogue Council of America, out of

which came the decision to mount a mutually sponsored conference. The 1967 report to General Convention indicates that, because of diversity of viewpoint among the Synagogue Council's constituents, a non-theological theme for the conference had to be found. The result: on 5–6 March 1967, Temple Emanu-El (NYC) hosted a highly successful Episcopal-Jewish conference on "The Family: Tradition and Transition."

The 1973 Joint Commission on Ecumenical Relations report to General Convention is interesting. It discusses the situation of Christians in North India, Pakistan, and Bangladesh. Obviously, this would have interfaith implications, but no mention of that is made. It speaks of Anglicanism in the Middle East, but without referencing Islam or Judaism. It discusses the efforts of the National Council of the Churches of Christ in the USA, but nothing is said about any interfaith dimension to this. In the section on the World Council of Churches, the situation is a bit different: the sixth paragraph mentions civil war in Sudan, but says nothing of Islam; then, interestingly, in the seventh paragraph, we read: "Dialogue between Christians and people of other living faiths and ideologies is beginning to prosper."[6] As well, this report includes an entry on Jewish-Episcopal Relations in particular.

In that same 1973 report, the Joint Commission acknowledged that Jewish-Episcopal relations reach beyond the situation in the Middle East. It explained that it had "[taken] counsel with the Presiding Bishop and the President of the House of Deputies concerning the best way in which this Church can best listen to the concerns of the Jewish community and work together for increased mutual co-operation, for the purpose of an expansion of these relationships." Its solution was to establish a small committee to advise the Presiding Bishop on Jewish-Episcopal matters, "with staff service by the ecumenical officer and the public-affairs officer." The task of the committee would be to coordinate Episcopal-Jewish relations and to bring concerns in this area to the attention of the appropriate operating units—for example, the Commissions on the Church in Human Affairs and on Ecumenical Relations; units of the Executive Council such as education, social work, and overseas relations; and the theological seminaries.

Thus, 1973 saw the establishment of the Presiding Bishop's Advisory Committee on Christian-Jewish Relations (later, the Presiding Bishop's Committee on Christian-Jewish Relations). This development was, as I see it, the first major move by The Episcopal Church into the arena of interreligious relations, and grew directly out of 1964 General Convention action. The purpose of this Committee on Christian-Jewish Relations was never to develop programs. Rather, it was to observe, report, advise, and to serve as a bridge between The Episcopal Church and five major national Jewish organizations—and, as well, between the Church and offices of the National Council of Churches (USA) and the World Council of Churches charged with Jewish-Christian relations. Throughout its history, it encouraged dialogue—defined as "a mutual witness, for witness is a sharing of one's faith conviction without the intention of proselytizing." It also sought "to raise the consciousness of the whole Church to the theological issues inherent in a religiously pluralistic world with particular reference to Christian-Jewish relationships," thus to encourage sensitivity when producing church materials and programs for education or evangelism.

Observing that "interfaith relationships interlock with ecumenical relationships in many American communities, especially those with a significant Jewish population," the Standing Commission on Ecumenical Relations [SCER] included proceedings of the Presiding Bishop's Advisory Committee on Christian-Jewish Relations in its own report to the 1979 General Convention—even though, it noted, "the arena of Christian-Jewish relationships is not on the assigned agenda of SCER." The brief report commented that "the memory of virulent anti-semitism [sic] let loose again and again during the long history of the church should always warn us against taking good Christian-Jewish relations for granted."

General Convention 1979 responded by adopting a lengthy resolution calling upon Episcopal Church leadership—lay and ordained—to deepen its dedication to Episcopal-Jewish dialogue and local-level collaboration. It urges Episcopal leaders to familiarize themselves with Jewish scholarship (ancient and modern), toward the goal of better understanding of Scripture. It argues that Christians will benefit from learning how Jews read and interpret the texts which nurtured Jesus. The preamble to this resolution is interesting, in that it mounts an argument, with biblical citations backing each step, for the deep and continuing spiritual link between Christians and Jews, with a strong reminder that God's covenant with the Jews still obtains: "the Jews remain precious to God," who "does not withdraw the gifts he has bestowed or revoke the choices he has made." Further, it reminds Episcopalians of the Jewishness of Jesus and "the first apostles and witnesses," noting that Jesus led an observant-Jewish life. It is Christian denial or ignorance of these common roots which has most often lain at the base of anti-Semitism. Since improved "mutual understanding between Episcopalians and Jews by way of biblical and theological enquiry and through friendly discussion" is much to be desired, the Presiding Bishop's Advisory Committee on Episcopal-Jewish Relations is to look into methods and issues for such dialogue, and is to report its findings to General Convention 1982. This report seems not to have been forthcoming; but work no doubt was undertaken. We have the fruit, in the form of a document adopted by General Convention in 1988—a major step in building Episcopal-Jewish dialogical relationships.

Guidelines (1988)

In 1988, *Guidelines for Christian-Jewish Relations for Use in The Episcopal Church*, prepared by the Presiding Bishop's Committee on Christian-Jewish Relations, was adopted by General Convention "as a policy intended to assist the members of this Church in facilitating understanding and cooperation between Christians and Jews."[7] This move was not exactly ground-breaking; the story about it in the *New York Times* (mentioned at this chapter's opening) said as much. The World Council of Churches had condemned anti-Semitism in 1948 on theological and moral grounds. The Second Vatican Council had issued its Declaration on the Relationship of the Church to Non-Christian Religions (*Nostra Aetate*) on October 28, 1965. This document was applauded then, and still receives praise, as a landmark in Christian reevaluation of the relationship between Christian ecclesial bodies and Judaism. As we saw earlier in this chapter, The Episcopal Church had itself adopted a resolution eschewing the validity of the charge of deicide against the Jews a full year earlier. However, it can hardly be expected that documents issued by The Episcopal Church's General Convention would command the attention accorded Vatican II statements. Thus *Nostra Aetate* has had far more impact.

Specifically, four teachings in its fourth section make it significant in the history of Christian-Jewish relations:

- Its affirmation of a spiritual link between Jews and Christians.

- Its affirmation, based on Romans 9:4–5, that the covenant between God and the Jews continues.

- Its affirmation of the Jewishness of Jesus, the apostles, and the earliest disciples.

- Its denunciation of the charges of blood guilt, deicide, and blanket assertion of guilt against the Jews; it also repudiated persecution of Jews.[8]

Thus in *Nostra Aetate* the Roman Catholic Church expresses its desire to encourage and promote better interreligious relations, and "deplores all hatreds, persecutions, displays of anti-Semitism directed against the Jews at any time or from any source." However, this document does not (as critics have noted) acknowledge that the Church has been such a source.

By way of follow-up, in December 1974, the Vatican Commission for Religious Relations With The Jews had issued *Guidelines and Suggestions for Implementing the Conciliar Declaration Nostra Aetate*. In November 1975, a *Statement on Catholic-Jewish Relations* had come forth from the US Conference of Catholic Bishops. In 1987, the United Church of Christ General Synod had authorized the resolution *The Relationship Between the United Church of Christ and the Jewish Community*; and, the Presbyterian Church (USA) had issued *A Theological Understanding of the Relationship between Christians and Jews*. The committee tasked with composing *Guidelines* (1988) acknowledged that it built on teachings gleaned from these earlier official statements. Nonetheless, the issuance of *Guidelines* (1988) was an important step in Episcopal interreligious relations.

Turning now to the structure and content of *Guidelines* (1988), this document has a Preface. "Self-serving descriptions of other people's faiths are among the roots of prejudice, stereotyping and condescension," it asserts. Dialogue mitigates this by enabling people to talk about their own religion in their own terms. While almost every religion, as an element of its self-understanding, will have something to say about the other religions around it, interreligious dialogue provides for the "mutual questioning" of these prior understandings that participants cannot help but bring with them into the process. *Guidelines* (1988) calls for careful listening and reciprocity out of obedience to the commandment not to bear false witness against one's neighbor.

The remainder of the document is divided into five sections. Section One, *Principles of Dialogue* offers six aids for more substantive exchange. Beginning with a warning that the vocabulary of religious discussions is "not innocent or neutral," its second point is a reminder that "a 'theological' understanding of Christianity is not of the same significance" for Jews as is a theological understanding of Judaism for Christians. "A profound sense of penitence is the necessary response" to the fact that Christian self-definition in relation to Judaism—and the resultant reinterpretation of vocabulary, divine agency, and scripture—has led too often to "overt acts of condescension, prejudice and even violent acts of persecution." Christians ought not to be surprised "that Jews resent [Christian] scriptural and theological interpretations in which they are assigned negative roles."

Section One continues by noting that too many Christians think, mistakenly, that all they need to know about Judaism is to be found in the Bible. Christians are, therefore, urged to learn *from Jews* about how "Jews understand their own history, their Scriptures, their traditions, their faith and their practice," all the while keeping in mind that Judaism (as does Christianity) "contains a wide spectrum of opinions, theologies, and styles of life and service"—which dialogue will benefit from including. Christians who wish to take up this challenge will do well to get to know Jews from more than one denomination. They may also wish to do some reading about Judaism from various denominational perspectives.

Most of what is included in Section One seems helpful enough. Some objections to it, however, have been raised. Paragraph 5, for example, asserts that Christians ought to know something about how Jews understand Jewish history, scripture, traditions, faith, and practice. This is very much in line with its Preface's insistence that dialogue-participants ought to be allowed to discuss their own religion in their own terms. But now, the document goes one bold step further by suggesting that "mutual listening to *the way each is perceived by the other* can be a step toward understanding the hurts, overcoming the fears, and correcting the misunderstandings that have separated [Jews and Christians] throughout the centuries."

This is risky. How exactly would this happen? Much "in-house" work would be necessary in advance of sharing. *Which* Christian perceptions of Jews are worth bringing to dialogue with Jews? *Which* Jewish perceptions of Christians? *Guidelines* (1988) seems to thinking of the negative ones. Nor does the document offer a method. Would the Christians at the table sit silently while the Jews brainstormed a list of Jewish (mis)perceptions of Christians (after which the roles would reverse)? Various diversity-awareness training methodologies do provide techniques for taking such a step, but *Guidelines* (1988) makes no mention of this. As veterans of some of these trainings (such as the *Consultation on Racism* model used with church congregations in the 1970s) can testify, unless sessions are moderated skillfully and unless adequate follow-up is in place, "mutual listening" can cause considerably more harm than good. Fortunately, much has been published since 1988 on the theory and practice of dialogue—some of it arising from the corporate world's need for efficient problem-solving. Paragraph 5 of *Guidelines* (1988) must be appreciated with this in mind.

The section concludes with a recommendation that, because Judaism and Christianity each "contain a wide spectrum of opinions, theologies, and styles of life and service," therefore, "Jewish-Christian dialogue must try to be as inclusive of the variety of views within the two communities as possible." This guideline begs clarification, especially since it is part of a document does not address all Christians everywhere; rather it was prepared "for Use in The Episcopal Church." Does it mean to suggest that the preferred dialogue's circle of participants would have Christians from several denominations (an Episcopalian, a Baptist, a Quaker, and a Roman Catholic at the least), while the Jewish delegation ought to include at least one person each from the Orthodox, Conservative, Reform, and Reconstructionist wings? Does this guideline mean to say that a dialogue between an Episcopal parish and a neighboring Reform Jewish congregation would be insufficiently inclusive of variety?

Section Two, *The Necessity for Christians to Understand Jews and Judaism* is the document's longest portion. Rather than offering pointers for Christians who wish to organize and conduct a dialogue with Jews, as the overarching title of the document would lead the reader to expect throughout, the real purpose of Section II is to provide a rationale for doing so. Having begun with the premise that an appreciation of the vitality of Judaism can enrich Christian "understandings of Jesus and the divine will for all creatures," the remaining sixteen paragraphs of this section detail topics and concepts in need of improvement or revision in Christian understanding. Among these are the Jewishness of Jesus; the diversity of Judaism in Jesus' time; the need for continued inter-Christian conversation about how to interpret anti-Jewish New Testament passages; the emergence and development of Rabbinic Judaism; the dangers of certain theological moves; traditions of scripture interpretation in Judaism as well as Christianity; notions of election and stewardship. Exploration of common ground (not just differences) is encouraged.

Paragraphs 14 through 17 put forth Jewish understandings of "the land of Israel and the city of Jerusalem" as an area needing appreciation by Christians. In doing so, the document notes the importance of this geography to Christians and Muslims as well, if differently so. The section concludes by referencing a 1979 General Convention resolution affirming Israel's right to a secure existence; but also stressing that "the quest for homeland status by Palestinians" cannot be ignored.

The decades since the penning of the "Necessity" section of *Guidelines* (1988) have seen the publication of many excellent resources suitable for use in parishes and seminary classrooms by Episcopalians and other Christians who wish to embrace the recommendations it makes—among them, *Irreconcilable Differences? A Learning Resource for Jews and Christians*, by David F. Sandmel and others, to name but one. Meanwhile, a number of authors (Jewish as well as Christian) have explored the Jewishness of Jesus—some writing for a popular audience, others for an academic readership. Likewise, a steady stream of books examining the fact of the modern State of Israel and Israeli-Palestinian issues from a range of vantage-points is readily available.

In the same vein, many new resources can be found for addressing the issues raised in the comparatively short Section Three, *Hatred and Persecution of Jews—A Continuing Concern*. The three paragraphs of this section reiterate the need for thorough understanding of the history of persecution of Jews. Particular attention is given to the Crusades, the Inquisition, pogroms, the Holocaust, extremist behavior by groups such as the Ku Klux Klan, and less violent yet still pernicious behaviors such as synagogue defacements and economic or political discrimination or scapegoating. Episcopalians wanting to act on this guideline by learning more about this history have many places to turn. James Carroll's *Constantine's Sword: The Church and the Jews* has been a very popular (and controversial) option.[9]

This third section stresses as well the necessity that Christians "learn to proclaim the Gospel without generating contempt for Judaism or the Jewish people." During the first years of the 21st century, this important guideline has been revisited and addressed in depth—as we shall see in the coming portion of this chapter.

Section Four, *Authentic Christian Witness*, a mere two paragraphs, condemns "coercive proselytism" aimed at Jews, while also affirming the need for Christians to "bear witness by word and deed" to God "embodied in the person of Jesus Christ." It asserts, however, that "dialogue can rightly be described as a mutual witness"—with witness defined as "a sharing of one's faith conviction without the intention of proselytizing."

The concluding Section Five, *Practical Recommendations* offers six ways forward. First it suggests an annual liturgical observation of the relationship between Christians and Jews—by means of a Yom ha-Shoah service, for example. Second, it urges "careful explanations be made of the New Testament texts which appear to place all Jews in an unfavorable light," most especially those in John's Gospel, in church preaching and teaching. Third, it urges every diocese to have a Committee on Christian-Jewish Relations. Local dialogues between Episcopal and Jewish congregations are also encouraged—the fourth recommendation. Fifth, Episcopal seminaries are asked to do more to "promote a greater understanding and appreciation of our common heritage with the Jews as well as for living Judaism." Finally, *Guidelines* (1988) calls for the intensification of "cooperation with Jewish and interreligious organizations concerned with service and the common good, interreligious programs, cultural enrichment and social responsibility."

In short, *Guidelines* (1988) is much more than a set of principles. As a primer on Christian-Jewish relations, it signals a major move on the part of The Episcopal Church to teach neighborliness toward Jews. The document emphasizes the Jewishness of Jesus. It affirms that God has called Jews and Christians alike "to be holy and to exercise stewardship over the creation in accountability to God;" that Jews and Christians alike "are taught by their Scriptures and traditions to recognize their responsibility to their neighbors, especially the weak, the poor, and the oppressed;" and, that Jews and Christians, await the coming of God's reign, albeit in "various and distinct ways." It should be seen (and celebrated) as one of a cluster of efforts by church bodies in the second half of the 20th century to repudiate a theological position frequently called *supersessionism*.

At the urging of the Presiding Bishop's Committee on Christian-Jewish Relations, Forward Movement published *Guidelines* (1988), with a foreword by William Weiler (a past committee-member), as a small booklet for easy distribution in parishes and elsewhere. The booklet remained in the Forward Movement catalogue for several years. Forward Movement also published a companion resource, a Forward Day-by-Day devotional booklet for February-April 1990, focusing on insights gained from Christian-Jewish dialogue. Among the authors of these short pieces for day-by-day reflection were three Episcopalians, all of them associates of the Committee on Christian-Jewish Relations.

Under the leadership of John Burt (then Bishop of Ohio), the Presiding Bishop's Committee on Christian-Jewish Relations set an agenda for itself for the triennium following the release of *Guidelines* (1988). In addition to promoting *Guidelines* (1988) itself, it encouraged local and diocesan Episcopal-Jewish dialogue through its work with the Episcopal Diocesan Ecumenical Officers, and by making available news of and materials for such dialogues. In cooperation with General Seminary's Center for Jewish-Christian Studies and Relations, it also encouraged Christian-Jewish dialogue, education, and training in seminaries, and commended efforts in that regard at Nashota House and Sewanee. The committee vowed that, during the triennium leading toward the 1994 General Convention, it would "press for more adequate treatment of Judaism (both in its historic and contemporary expressions) in the curricula of [Episcopal] seminaries"—a matter which still begs for attention.[10]

In fulfillment of its founding mandate, the committee advised Episcopal Church efforts in Christian education and evangelism on the Christian-Jewish relations implications of their materials and programs. It continued to work ecumenically with Jewish relations offices of the National Council of the Churches of Christ in the USA [NCCC], the World Council of Churches, and the National Conference of Catholic Bishops. As a corollary to its mandate to advise the Presiding Bishop on Christian-Jewish relations issues, the committee facilitated relations between Episcopal and Jewish leaders which might lead to "discussion of current, and sometimes stressful, issues in an atmosphere of theological candor and truth," as the committee's 1991 report to General Convention explained. In fact, this committee saw its reports to General Convention as a means by which "to raise the consciousness of the whole Church to the theological issues inherent in a religiously plural world with particular reference to Christian-Jewish relationships."[11]

From the Committee on Christian-Jewish Relations report to General Convention 1991, we learn that The Episcopal Church was a sponsor of the 1989 and 1990 National Workshops on Christian-Jewish Relations.[12] With encouragement from the committee, some 100 Episcopalians participated in the 1989 gathering; more than 80 participated in 1990—with committee chairperson John Burt numbering among the presenters. We also learn of the deepening of Episcopal Church relations with major national Jewish bodies: the American Jewish Committee, the American Jewish Congress, the Anti-Defamation League of B'nai Brith, the Synagogue Council of America (a network with Orthodox, Conservative, and Reform members), and the Union of American Hebrew Congregations (predecessor to the Union for Reform Judaism). One result was committee facilitation of a formal conversation (Fall 1989) between representatives of these organizations and Presiding Bishop Browning, plus select members of his staff, on "Implications for Christian-Jewish Relations in the United States of the Crisis in the Middle East."

The report discusses four of the many factors contributing to improvement in Christian-Jewish relations between the mid-1960s and 1991: "a new spirit of openness and mutual respect…[making it possible] to speak not just words of introduction to one another but also words of deep and abiding meaning;" interreligious work on societal issues; "a virtual revolution…theologically in current Christian biblical studies which some call 'the rejudaization of Jesus'" (i.e. fresh exploration, celebration, and consideration of the meaning of Jesus' Jewishness); and increased Christian acknowledgement of Christians' complicity in centuries of anti-Semitism. With regard to this fourth factor, the Committee on Christian-Jewish Relations strove to convince The Episcopal Church to add *Yom ha-Shoah* and *Kristallnacht* to the calendar of observances of The Episcopal Church.

The report also includes considerable comment on concerns in anticipation of The Episcopal Church's Decade of Evangelism. John Burt is the probable author of the report's outline of the range of viewpoints held by Christians (Episcopalians included) regarding evangelization of Jews, concluding that most Episcopalians "would simply include any individual Jews who so wish in the one Christian invitation that is extended to all non-Christians." The report also makes note of conversations on this topic between the Committee on Christian-Jewish Relations and the Standing Commission on Evangelism, saying, "We found ourselves grateful that our Anglican tradition, in its more enlightened moments, has been particularly respectful of God's truth as it exists outside the Church, yet without compromising our devotion to Jesus Christ as Lord and Savior."[13]

Many of the points made in *Guidelines* (1988) were reaffirmed by a 1991 General Convention resolution, *Reaffirm Commitment to Evangelism and Recognize Religious Pluralism*. Submitted jointly by the Presiding Bishop's Committee on Christian-Jewish Relations and the Standing Commission on Evangelism, it obligated The Episcopal Church to reaffirm "its commitment to the fullness and uniqueness of God's self-revelation to humankind in Jesus Christ, while recognizing that to proclaim the Gospel in a pluralist society requires us to be aware of the significance of God's self-revelation outside the Church." It further determined that "even as we seek new opportunities to share our Christian faith with those who do not know Christ, we recognize that God's activity in the world is not confined to the Church and we affirm our willingness to listen carefully to and to learn humbly from those whose perception of God's mystery differs from our own." A representative of the Jewish Congress sent a congratulatory message to the Christian-Jewish Relations committee. So did Jay Rock, then director of Christian-Jewish Relations for the National Council of the Churches of Christ in the USA.[14]

It is worth noting that, as had the *New York Times*, many Episcopalians would have applauded *Guidelines* (1988). Their practice was in harmony with these teachings already. But where the *Guidelines* fall short—where, indeed, almost all documents of this genre fall short, say some critics—is in dealing pastorally with Christians who see nothing wrong with doing what they are being asked not to do. By what method, for example, does one help the parish priest who quite routinely and comfortably speaks of Jewish converts to Christianity as "completed Jews"? Just as the need for strategies for improved understanding between Episcopalians and Jews will always be with us, so too the need for continual intra-Episcopalian work on better understanding of the issues. For the past decade at least, it has fallen to the Standing Commission on Liturgy and Music [SCLM] to take up this challenge most consistently and earnestly. It is the fruit of SCLM's work on anti-Judaism issues to which we turn next.

Episcopal Worship and Jewish Concerns

In its report to General Convention 1991, the Presiding Bishop's Committee on Christian-Jewish Relations pledged that, during the next triennium, it would "work toward removing the doctrine of supersession from the canon, eucharistic [sic] liturgy, reading of the Hebrew Scripture, prayers of the people and the lectionary."[15] Among the actions of General Convention 1991 was a mandate that "whenever liturgical materials are developed for or adopted for use by the Church on the national level, a member of the Presiding Bishop's Committee on Christian-Jewish relations, or a person recommended by that body, be consulted so that the Church may honor its Jewish heritage and Jewish sisters and brothers in utilizing materials appropriately sensitive." This resolution reinforced the recommendation from Section Five of *Guidelines* (1988) that Episcopalians guard against anti-Judaism in worship and in church school teaching. In a similar move, the 2006 General Convention directed the Standing Commission on Liturgy and Music "to collect and develop materials to assist members of the Church to address anti-Jewish prejudice expressed in and stirred by portions of Christian scriptures and liturgical texts, with suggestions for preaching, congregational education, and lectionary use."

Theologically, these mandates rest on the notion *lex orandi lex credendi*: the notion that praying shapes believing. Thus Episcopalians should take care not to pray in ways disrespectful of or harmful to Jews, and this has enormous implications—not only for the development of new liturgical materials, but also for the continued use of traditional ones. For example, on more than one occasion, the great Lutheran bishop Krister Stendahl said that our task as Christians is to answer the question: "How can I sing my love song to Jesus, how can I sing my song to Jesus with abandon, without disrespecting other religions—without telling negative stories about (or, mistreating) others?" It is unlikely that the beloved Advent hymn "O come, O come, Emmanuel" will be set aside by Episcopalians anytime soon. How are Episcopalians being helped to be "appropriately sensitive" while singing hymns so easily interpreted in supersessionist terms?

Toward Changing Old Habits

A response to the 2006 mandate, SCLM determined, would necessarily require clear answers to four key questions:

- Why is it important that the Church address anti-Jewish prejudice?

- Where does anti-Judaism present itself in congregational life?

- What resources are available to deal with the problem of anti-Judaism?

- What additional resources are needed, and how can they be made accessible?

Marilyn Salmon, introduced above, was enlisted to write the 2009 report in which these questions are addressed. In that essay, entitled "Dismantling Christian Anti-Judaism,"[16] she says,

> The imperative to address Christian anti-Judaism is grounded in the following convictions: (1) anti-Judaism is antithetical to the Christian Gospel; (2) Christian supersessionism depends on half-truths and misrepresentations of Judaism; (3) the Christian Gospel of Jesus Christ is compelling on its own terms, without creating a foil, an "other" to display its merits; and (4) Jesus does not need our help to make him look good by demonizing his Jewish brothers and sisters, even those who may have disagreed with him.

Furthermore, Salmon asserts, not only is it unethical to promote "one's own religion by misrepresenting another's, eliminating anti-Judaism is an especially necessary response to the Holocaust." Anti-Judaism should be eradicated from Christian preaching, teaching, and biblical interpretation in order to break the long pattern of "teaching of contempt" toward Judaism and Jews—a behavior which "undermines the Gospel of Jesus we proclaim." She explains:

> The Christian story of origins was constructed by creating a caricature of Judaism, an inferior Judaism designed to display the superiority of Christianity. We continue to perpetuate this caricature in careless readings of our scriptures, Old and New Testament, and in any definition of Jesus over and against his Jewish brothers and sisters.

In this essay for the 2009 SCLM report, Salmon defines supersessionism as "the viewpoint that Christianity displaced Judaism in the story of God's salvation because of Judaism's inferiority." It is an attitude, she says, which Christians reinforce, sometimes unconsciously, "by asserting that Christianity proclaims a universal salvation while Judaism insists on ethnic exclusivity; by contrasting the freedom of the Gospel with the supposed burden of Jewish Law; by Christian acceptance of Jesus over against Jewish rejection of Jesus; by defining Jewish people in terms of obstinacy, disobedience and blindness."

In light of the lessons of the Holocaust, Salmon affirms, "theologians, church historians, and biblical scholars have responded to the ethical imperative to examine Christianity's anti-Judaism." It takes positive note as well that, for the past thirty years (i.e. since 1979), The Episcopal Church and many others "have passed Resolutions and voted statements affirming the continued validity of God's covenant with Jews and denouncing efforts to convert Jews to Christianity." Yet, the commission stresses, "very little has changed in liturgy, preaching and teaching in congregational life. Supersessionism persists in sermons, preaching resources, educational material, bible studies and liturgies."

Persistent supersessionism is a problem, Salmon explains, because the way Christians speak of Jews and Judaism in worship affects their pastoral relationships: "Sermons, hymns, prayers that exclude, diminish or insult any other group potentially cause alienation or harm, and undermine our most sincere expressions of hospitality and acceptance." However, the report is clear: "This is not in the first place about offending Jews. It is about being fully aware of how our public expressions of faith compromise the gospel we proclaim."

As first steps toward changing old habits, the SCLM (2009) makes three recommendations. First, it calls for "consciousness-raising"—that is, learning to hear the Christian story "with Jewish ears" and trying "to imagine how what we preach or teach or read from scripture might sound to a Jewish person." Since not just a few Jews do attend Eucharist regularly with an Episcopal family-member or friend, this is not an abstract suggestion. Second, it suggests that Episcopalians simply "resolve not to repeat misinformation about Jews and Judaism."

Third, Episcopalians can take care "not to presume we know more than we do about Judaism, especially in the time of Jesus, by relying solely on the New Testament as a source of information."

The 2009 SCLM report concludes with an annotated list of resources primarily for church leaders responsible for preaching the lectionary, but also for decision-makers regarding liturgical music, and for anyone willing to reimagine church education for all ages.[17]

In response, the 2009 General Convention did authorize the SCLM to "collect, develop and disseminate" resources to assist Episcopalians in addressing "Christian anti-Judaism expressed in and stirred by portions of scriptures and liturgical texts," and to collaborate with the Standing Commission on Ecumenical and Interreligious Relations in preparing "a statement defining anti-Judaism and why it matters."

In a blog-post in March 2012, SCLM member Louis Weil recalled that, from the first meeting after the 2009 General Convention, he had misgivings "about how this work might be accomplished most effectively." Ideas such as pamphlets and children's-education materials had been posited, but he questioned whether these would command attention in the long term. He proposed an alternative, which the SCLM embraced: the production of a commentary designed to address the problem of anti-Judaism in preaching and teaching the lectionary. Special attention would be given to the "most difficult texts"—many of which occur during Holy Week and Eastertide. This would be an online resource, rolled out gradually, thus readily available to the Church. Given the scale of undertaking, the SCLM asked for, and received, authorization from General Convention 2012 to extend work on this project into the 2013–15 triennium.[18]

As we can see, in its work on this matter, SCLM has looked beyond "liturgical materials" to "elements of liturgy"—which include the lectionary, preaching, hymnody, and the language of the liturgy itself.

Preaching the Lectionary Without Contempt

As is true for Roman Catholics, Orthodox Christians, Lutherans, and several other denominations, the Bible passages read aloud in Anglican worship are determined by a lectionary—a predetermined list of sets of lessons. For Episcopalians, a set includes an Old Testament passage, all or part of a Psalm, a portion of an Epistle, and a portion of a Gospel.

The norm in Episcopal churches is to preach according to the lectionary. Recall that *Guidelines* (1988) called upon Episcopalians to "learn to proclaim the Gospel without generating contempt for Judaism or the Jewish people." As

Daniel Joslyn-Siemiatkoski and others have stressed, supersessionism colors the way many Christians understand the Bible. In a Christian supersessionist worldview, the Old Testament is seen merely as preparation for the New, and is to be read only through a New Testament lens; Jewish exegesis has no value. It ignores any meaning Old Testament prophetic literature may have for its community of origin and preservation. "The law given by God to Moses on Sinai was meant to control wayward Israel and its propensity to sin. The condemnation of Israel by the Hebrew prophets attests to the continued sinfulness of Israel and the fittingness of the divine abrogation of the covenant."[19] Rather Jesus stands in stark contrast to first-century Judaism; his own identity as an observant first-century Jew is ignored. The place of messianism in Judaism is exaggerated. The lectionary's pairings of readings can exacerbate this.

In the years since *Guidelines* (1988) was issued, many resources have been published to help Christians do exactly this. Marilyn Salmon's *Preaching Without Contempt* (mentioned above) has received high praise for its clarity and practicality. Salmon encourages preachers to let go of reliance on anti-Jewish stereotypes and facile dismissiveness of "deficient" Judaism in contrast to "superior" Christian faith. She explains why "a demeaning portrayal of the Pharisees denigrates modern Judaism." Concerning the lectionary's pairing of "Older Testament" texts with passages from the "Newer Testament" in a way which "reinforces an uncritical and traditional Christian view" that the Hebrew prophets "literally foretold" things about Jesus, Salmon explains that such an "understanding of prophecy in effect denies any meaning the prophecy had in its…context or for the communities of faith that recorded and handed down the prophetic literature to succeeding generations." When read in worship without immediate teaching to the contrary, the effect of certain pairings of texts, Salmon explains, "is to reinforce the common themes of Christian anti-Judaism: the sole purpose of the Old Testament is to point to the New Testament, specifically to Jesus; the New Testament supersedes the Old Testament, and Christianity replaces Judaism as the New Israel; Jews did not (and do not) understand their own Scriptures." In order to counter the tendency (albeit often inadvertent) to preach contempt, she advocates gaining deeper knowledge of the diversity of first-century Judaism, that the Gospels might be interpreted within that context.[20]

Amy-Jill Levine, a Jewish scholar of the New Testament at Vanderbilt University, cautions against decontextualizing Jesus—against operating from the assumption that Jesus' insights are somehow independent of the fact that he is an observant Jew. For Episcopalians striving to abide by principles laid out in the 1988 *Guidelines* (even if the actual document be unfamiliar to most at this point), Levine, with co-editor Marc Z. Brettler (Brandeis University), is responsible for another valuable resource: *The Jewish Annotated New Testament*.[21] This is not the first book about the New Testament by Jews. It is, however, the first thorough annotation of and commentary on the New Testament made entirely by Jews. It bears witness to improvements in Jewish and Christian perceptions of each other, while pushing forward the agenda of rectifying persistent misunderstandings.

Bound with the annotated scriptural text is a set of some thirty essays by Jewish scholars. Levine's "Bearing False Witness: Common Errors Made About Early Judaism," is among them. In it, she mentions The Episcopal Church's 1988 document in a list of denominational guidelines for teaching or preaching about Jews and Judaism. Her list of ten areas of persistent anti-Jewish stereotyping in Christian preaching and teaching is quite consistent with the concerns described in the *Guidelines* under "Principles" and "Necessity", and some readers may prefer her approach to outlining them. Levine suggests five reasons why, in spite of these official teachings, problems continue, one of which is obvious: just because a church has guidelines for presentation of Jews and Judaism does not guarantee that its clergy are well versed about them. Indeed, *Guidelines* (1988) is not included among interreligious-understanding resources on the current website of The Episcopal Church.

Pairings of Old and New Testament passages feed supersessionism in one way; feeding it in another is the Eastertide lectionary practice of reading a passage from the Acts of the Apostles in the point of the liturgy usually given to an Old Testament reading. This implies, as Daniel Joslyn-Siemiatkoski explains, that God's revelation to Israel "(and the abiding revelation enshrined by the Jewish people) has no relevance as Christians celebrate the cornerstone of their faith." Even more problematic is that the Eastertide readings from Acts reinforce the notion of Jewish responsibility for the death of Jesus and "perpetuate a sense of Jewish animosity toward Christians."[22]

Mitigating contempt of Jews and Judaism in preaching by Episcopalians has been given pride of place in SCLM's ongoing address of the General Convention of directive "to collect and develop materials to assist members of the Church to address anti-Jewish prejudice." The commission's first priority, as was noted above, is development of commentaries on readings assigned by the Lectionary which have, in the past, been used to fuel anti-Judaism—especially the Lessons for Holy Week and Easter.

Excursus: Passion Play and Pop Culture

Closely related to the issues just explored is the way in which Christ's Passion is portrayed, not only in liturgy, but in popular culture. One such instance of note,

Mel Gibson's controversial movie, *The Passion of the Christ,* offers an example of The Episcopal Church opting to address Christian-Jewish concerns ecumenically. This preference had been true in 1979, when—even though the Church had by then a task force dedicated to Episcopal-Jewish concerns (the Presiding Bishop's Advisory Committee), it remained committed to working on these concerns ecumenically. That year the SCER report to General Convention asserted the Church's moral and financial support of the NCCC Office of Christian-Jewish Relations, for which an Episcopalian (William Weiler) had been the first director in 1974. Even having issued its own *Guidelines for Christian-Jewish Relations,* the preference of The Episcopal Church to work on interfaith matters ecumenically has always been strong—as was discussed in depth in Chapter Two.

Therefore, when Mel Gibson's movie provoked controversy while still in production, response came from the NCCC Interfaith Relations Commission, on which The Episcopal Church was represented by associate ecumenical and interfaith officer Thomas Ferguson. In anticipation of the film's release on Ash Wednesday 2004 (and its re-release in 2005), the NCCC constructed a Reflection Guide and other resources. The purpose of these materials was to help Christians understand the issues involved in the way Jews were depicted and the way in which the story of Jesus' crucifixion was being told in this film, and what consequences all of this could have potentially on Jewish friends, neighbors, and family-members. Thus, rather than telling its constituents not to see the Gibson film, the NCCC provided a frame within which Christians might watch it, reflect on it, and discuss it at home and at church.

Immediately upon its publication, the NCCC study guide for the Gibson film was endorsed by The Episcopal Church's ecumenical and interfaith officer, Christopher Epting, who called it consistent with The Episcopal Church's approach to controversial matters.[23] Taking an approach quite consistent with The Episcopal Church's *Guidelines* (1988) and the NCCC's just-issued suggestions, a "Forum for Inter-Religious Understanding" was held at the Cathedral of St. John (Providence, RI), with Amy-Jill Levine and Krister Stendahl as keynoters. The Forum's purpose was to address concerns raised by anticipation, not only by the Gibson film's portrayal of Jews, but by its extremely graphic cinematography; it was an early offering among many by Episcopal churches which sought to encourage deeper exploration of soteriological questions, persistent anti-Semitism, and unintentional anti-Judaism. Levine's message during the Providence forum included many strategies for biblical interpretation developed further in her best-selling *The Misunderstood Jew.*[24]

Hymnody

We now return to the effort of the Standing Commission on Liturgy and Music to address anti-Judaism in the various elements of Episcopal Church liturgy—specifically, to the texts sung in worship. Supersessionist theology is particularly easy to find in Christian hymnody. When challenged, Christians may protest that they have placed themselves inside the story: rather than condemning "the Jews" or "the people Israel," they are speaking of themselves. As one Holy Week hymn (No. 158 in *The Hymnal 1982*) puts it: "Alas, my treason, Jesus, hath undone thee. 'Twas I, Lord Jesus, I it was denied thee: I crucified thee." This is how Christians often read the Psalter, for that matter: "I" and "we" in a psalm is taken to mean the Christian at prayer in the here and now.

The problem, as Daniel Joslyn-Siemiatkoski sees it, is that some hymns allow the Christian "to disassociate the Jewish people from their covenant from God." Others mischaracterize the first-century historical Jewish context. By way of example, he points to the Advent favorite, "O come, O come, Emmanuel" (No. 56 in *The Hymnal 1982*). The problem with this hymn is its implication that "all Jews were collectively eagerly awaiting the Messiah in the first century," when current scholarship now indicates that messianism was far from the dominant mindset in and around Jerusalem in Jesus' time. "In other words," he explains, "this text is not about the actual, historical people of Israel.

> While claiming to speak in the voice of Israel, the author of this hymn displaced the Jewish people as Israel and replaced it with the Church....[This hymn] claims to speak for the Jewish people when in actuality it is only representative of later Christian aspirations. Thus, it does not equitably represent the Jewish experience of living in a covenanted relationship with God.

In evaluating the appropriateness of the biblical imagery in hymns, Joslyn-Siemiatkoski offers this guideline: "Are Christians understood as exclusively having claim to this story with no room for the experience of the historical people of Israel and their descendants, the Jews? Or is there a sense of a shared narrative in which both Israel and the Church are blessed in having received God's revelation?"[25]

Liturgical Language

For Anglicans, the language of corporate worship is determined primarily by the Book of Common Prayer. Listening to the language of the prayer book with an ear for supersessionist theology is part of the dynamics of any effort to change it. It is, therefore, interesting to look back on the proceedings of General Convention 1976. The Standing Liturgical Commission's report that year was laden with matters pertaining to an all-encompassing prayer book revision. Recounting one episode illustrates something of what is at stake when inter-faith concerns intersect with liturgical reform.

As the SLC report explained, trial versions of the Good Friday Liturgy had been tested by various Episcopal congregations, and most of the proposed changes in the rite had been received well in these parishes. However, the op-tion to incorporate *The Reproaches* met with resistance from some quarters. In creating the very first Book of Common Prayer, Thomas Cranmer had chosen not to include any of the medieval Good Friday liturgy. So, *The Reproaches* had not been an element in the beginning, and had never become an official ele-ment in the time since. However, some Episcopal churches were using it in the mid-20th century; some still do.

The text of *The Reproaches* dates from the seventh or eighth century. In a series of stanzas, God speaks directly to the worshipers: "we" are asked why, in spite of what God has done for us in the past, we have crucified our Savior. The first stanza is representative:

> My people, what have I done to you?
> How have I offended you?
> Answer me!
> Holy God, Holy Mighty, Holy Immortal One: have mercy on us.
> I led you out of Egypt, from slavery to freedom,
> but you led your Savior to the cross.

The question at stake: to whom does the pronoun "you" refer?

In the discussion of whether to add this anthem to the new edition of the prayer book, some scholars complained that this poem broadcast "undesirable anti-Jewish overtones;" it was far too easy to hear "you" and think it meant "the Jews"—at the time of Jesus' crucifixion, and at present. They backed up their assessment by rehearsing evidence of Christian anti-Jewish behavior over the centuries. "I have contested this interpretation of *The Reproaches* ever since the debate began," Louis Weil, professor emeritus of liturgics, told me. "I was a member of a parish during college in which the Good Friday rites were re-stored; and, as a Jew, it never entered my mind that these texts were anything other than a judgment on the members of the Church." It is clear that many Commission members, and many of the parishes which had been using this material on a trial basis, likewise understood "you" in these texts as did Weil: to mean the Church; indeed, all of sinful humanity.

However, those who heard "anti-Jewish overtones" in *The Reproaches* ar-gued further that adding this item to the Book of Common Prayer would fly in the face of the 1964 General Convention resolution on Christian-Jewish rela-tions. This side prevailed. *The Reproaches* were not included in The Episcopal Church's major prayer book revision of 1979.

In this case, the matter under contention was whether to add something to the liturgy. The situation is thornier when the call is to delete something. On what basis should something be taken *out* of the liturgy? For example, The Episcopal Church's Eucharistic Prayer D reads, "Again and again you called us into covenant with you, and through the prophets you taught us to hope for salvation. Father, you loved the world so much that in the fullness of time you sent your only Son to be our Savior." This prayer's theology is blatantly supersessionist, notes Professor Joslyn-Siemiatkoski, by virtue of its use of first-person plural pronouns in conjunction with God's pre-Incarnation acts. As a result:

> ...the Old Testament narratives of Israel are presented as events that happened only to those who count themselves as Christians. The primary meaning of God's covenant with Israel, or the exodus from Egypt, or the activity of the prophets is solely Christological. The actual history of the historical Israel and the Jewish people is erased from these prayers. The Christian claim that things happened for them, with no mention of the original people who experienced these events, is to claim that it is the Church that is the true Israel. This stance of Church as Israel is an essential part of supersessionist theology and a key ingredient for Christian anti-Judaism that makes possible negative representations of Jews and Judaism in worship, preaching and teaching.[26]

A number of Episcopalians have mounted strong arguments that liturgical elements like this should be removed from the Book of Common Prayer. Others take a different approach. Louis Weil's concern, as he explained to me, "related to the larger issue of the imperative for liturgical catechesis, which is gravely lacking in Episcopal adult formation programs. As a liturgical church, it is imperative (especially in American society, where 'symbol' is so radically not understood) that liturgical catechetical work be done to enable people to enter into the liturgical symbols." He has conducted this kind of parish education; and, as a consequence, he reports, "the participation of the people in the Triduum rites was extraordinary." Weil insists that Christian hymnody and ritual language are not the primary sources of anti-Judaism anyway. Historically, he points out, anti-Judaism behavior has been shaped by the anti-Judaism which people heard from the pulpit. He sees more value in attention to preaching education than in liturgical reform as a means toward reducing anti-Jewish behavior.

Reconstructing Theology

The Episcopal Church is right to look seriously at its liturgical language, says Professor Joslyn-Siemiatkoski. However, it is merely "the presenting symptom of the underlying theological problem." Constructing a truly non-supersessionist Christian theology "is a massive challenge," he admits, "because it involves revisiting many doctrinal and theological categories." He himself has offered guidance in rethinking Christian notions of Torah and covenant.[27]

Supersessionism has been the normative Christian theology for centuries; and, as we have seen, it raises a number of concerns. For example, it leaves no room for Jews to remain Jews and still to be appreciated. It leads quite directly to the teaching of contempt for Jews and Judaism, which in turn has led time after time to anti-Jewish (and quite unchristian) behavior. It implies something quite problematic about God's steadfastness: if the coming of Jesus could nullify God's promises to the people Israel, what guarantee do Christians have that God will honor newer promises? How can anyone be certain of God's reliability? It poses a conundrum: if Jews no longer have a place in God's plan of salvation, what theological sense can Christians make for the fact that, not only has the Jewish community continued to exist, it has produced numerous faith-filled people and not just a few outstanding theological minds?

It also has its skeptics (fine biblical scholars and theologians among them). Some question the assumptions driving the argument of, for example, Rosemary Radford Reuther who, in her now classic *Faith and Fratricide*, claims that the Christian practice of interpreting the Old Testament christologically leads inexorably to supersessionism.[28] They caution that the effort by some Christians to rid Christianity of supersessionism has been taken to an unhelpfully self-denying extreme, resulting in evisceration or abandonment of the Christian faith itself. Nothing, then, is left to bring to the table of dialogue.

In a 1999 *Cross Currents* article, Episcopal moral theologian Thomas Breidenthal (now Bishop of Southern Ohio) offers a *via media*.[29] His close reading of the New Testament has determined that "while the New Testament is at no point explicitly supersessionist (although it is certainly not innocent of anti-Judaic polemic), it is also at no point explicitly antisupersessionist. Indeed, the various texts of the New Testament can easily be read either way." He argues in favor of "a more original Christian teaching," which he calls "neighbor-christology." Working with a definition of neighbor as "one who is different from me and yet has a claim on me," this theology make a series of assertions:

- Difference (rather than sameness) draws human beings to one another.

- "Kinship with the stranger" is encountered "in the event of nearness, in which we discover the other as someone who is near to me and has a claim on me."

- "Human sinfulness involves both the denial and the exploitation of nearness."

- Jesus is he who "refuses all false distinctions, assumes his connection with everyone he meets, and embraces nearness even and especially from the cross."

There is more to be said; but Breidenthal's point is that neighbor-christology offers Christians authentic grounds "for saying yes to difference," on which "to seek out fellowship with non-Christian communities of faith [Jews, especially], and to contribute positively to the development of a genuinely pluralistic society."

Competing Commitments

Institutionally-driven interreligious work often suffers from competition with other institutional commitments. Anti-Judaism has been a concern of The Episcopal Church's Standing Commission on Liturgy and Music for many years, but it is but one concern among many which command the attention of this taskforce. Only occasionally has the commission as a whole been fully invested in this topic. Continued work on anti-Judaism sometimes falls victim to the attitude that, since guidelines exist, or since a report has been issued, "we've been there and done that, and don't need to be working on it now." The political context also affects this work. In the 1980s, all major Christian denominations in the US were on board with the call to address anti-Judaism, Marilyn Salmon pointed out in a conversation with me. The current context is different, she remarked: early 21st-century politics concerning the modern state of Israel have an effect on theological and liturgical work on anti-Judaism.

In this last regard, some Jewish observers have told me that they hear dissonance from The Episcopal Church: what they hear from one commission or office clashes with what they hear from another. Preparation for, and resolutions adopted by, General Convention 1991 offer a case in point. In its report to that convention, the Presiding Bishop's Committee on Christian-Jewish Relations had acknowledged that, in spite of overall improvement in Jewish-Christian relations during the previous quarter-century, "serious areas of divergence" continued to strain Christian-Jewish dialogue—chief among them, "developments in the Middle East and criticism of Israel by many American Christians."[30]

Successful 1991 General Convention resolutions included several responding to tensions in the Middle East. We will look briefly at three which originated with the Standing Commission on Peace's Middle East Task Force, whose lengthy report to General Convention had been decidedly pro-Palestinian. One resolution insisted on the appropriateness of "legitimate criticism of Israeli governmental polity and action" and distinguished this from "anti-Jewish prejudice" (which it called upon the Church to deplore in all forms).

A second resolution called upon the Church to support "a Two-state Solution for Israel and the Palestinian People." A third, the longest and most detailed, celebrated successes in Jewish-Christian dialogue. While it too deplored anti-Jewish prejudice, it likewise deplored *anti-Arab* prejudice, and made a number of demands on the Israeli government with regard to the situation of Palestinian Christians. Further, it ordered copies of *all resolutions* adopted by the 1991 General Convention with any relevance to the Palestinian-Israeli situation to be sent to the President of the United States, the Prime Minister of Israel, the Secretary General of the United Nations, and a number of other officials.[31]

In a 1992 lecture for the Center for Jewish-Christian Learning (University of St. Thomas, Minnesota), Marilyn Salmon reported on this action:

> In the opinion of now-retired Bishop John Burt, chair of the Presiding Bishop's Committee on Christian-Jewish Relations, the resolution was one-sided and unfair—asking much more of Israel than of Arab neighbors. Rabbi Robert Kravitz, an official observer, was invited to address [General Convention] on behalf of the America Jewish Committee. He expressed "keen disappointment with the tone, the substance and the timing of the major Middle East resolutions and their lack of fairness." Authors of the resolution were hurt and offended, believing that they had achieved…balance and fairness, and they were dismayed that Rabbi Kravitz spoke so frankly and critically about a resolution already voted.[32]

Not only Jewish observers, but also some members of Committee on Christian-Jewish Relations found the Middle East resolution disturbing. The committee had already pledged to take on "special responsibility to interpret the Jewish point of view" to Episcopal Church officers and task forces working on Middle East concerns. The need was even clearer now, as they saw it. In correspondence with me, Salmon noted the irony that, in the very same General Convention (1991), The Episcopal Church passed two resolutions: one which took a very progressive theological stand in the midst of the decade of evangelism, and which was applauded by American Jews; and another which was critical of Israel and which upset American Jews—to the apparent surprise of its authors.[33]

Indeed, during the second half of the 20th century and beyond, Episcopal Church efforts toward better Christian-Jewish relations have always been waged in tension with concerns for (and often, activism on behalf of) Palestinians. Many Episcopalians consider Palestinian Christian concerns a "family matter:" Anglican Christianity has long had deep roots in the Middle East; St. George's College (Jerusalem) is an Anglican institution, as is a major hospital in Gaza.

In a December 2000 interview, Brian Grieves, then director of the office of Peace and Justice Ministries, insisted that The Episcopal Church had always striven for balance when dealing with the Israeli-Palestinian situation. That is, the Church had always shown emphatic support for solutions which accorded respect to, and expected accountability from, both sides. The Episcopal

Church, he stressed, had "long distinguished between our deep concern about anti-Semitism and our criticism of Israeli policy. The two are not the same."[34]

The involvement of The Episcopal Church in peace-and-justice issues, particularly with regard to the Middle East, is a story fraught with complexity, and to tell it properly would take us beyond the goals of this book. It has been raised here because it is an apt illustration of the Anglican commitment to holding together *difference;* and because the work of the Committee on Christian-Jewish Relations *and* the Middle East Task Force, it can be argued, have the same theological foundation. Theologically, this dual activism on the part of The Episcopal Church—for Palestinians on the one hand, and Jews on the other—is founded upon the baptismal mandate to "seek and serve Christ in all persons," to "strive for justice and peace among all people, and [to] respect the dignity of every human being."[35]

More dialogue is necessary—intra-Episcopal as well as interreligious. Already in Section II 71 of *Guidelines* (1988), an official document on Christian-Jewish relations specifically, we find recognition that interreligious dialogue is never entirely and cleanly bilateral. With regard to Middle East issues, consideration of Islam and its adherents is essential. Thus, as we saw in Chapter One, The Episcopal Church would move in 1994 to establish guidelines for interreligious dialogue which might well be multilateral—and might well include Muslims. It is to that theme to which we turn in Chapter Four.

Notes

1. Marilyn Salmon is the author of this report—an essay she wrote as a consultant to the Standing Commission on Liturgy and Music in preparation for the 2009 General Convention.

2. I am grateful to Daniel Joslyn-Siemiatkoski for his kind invitation to draw generously upon his 2010 unpublished paper entitled "Anti-Judaism and the Liturgy: Theological Reflections on Covenant and Language."

3. See *dylan's lectionary blog*: Fifth Sunday in Lent, Year C. http://www.sarahlaughed.net/lectionary/pharisees. Last accessed 2 August 2012. Sarah Dylan Breuer, currently a member of the Executive Council of The Episcopal Church, is a public theologian who has written extensively on Christian misuse and misinterpretation of the term *Pharisee*.

4. Marilyn J. Salmon, *Preaching Without Contempt: Overcoming Unintended Anti-Judaism* (Minneapolis, Minnesota: Augsburg Fortress, 2006), 9.

5. The full text of the 1964 resolution "Deicide and the Jews" is available online at http://www.ccjr.us/dialogika-resources/documents-and-statements/protestant-churches/na/episcopalian/685-ecusa64oct. Last accessed: 25 July 2012.

6. *Journal of General Convention*, 504–505.

7. The full text of *Guidelines for Christian-Jewish Relations* (1988) is provided in the Appendix.

8. Joslyn-Siemiatkoski, "Anti-Judaism and the Liturgy." For the text of *Nostra Aetate* see http://www.vatican.va/archive/hist_councils/ii_vatican_council/index.htm

9. James Carroll, *Constantine's Sword: The Church and the Jews—A History* (Boston: Houghton Mifflin, 2001).

10. *The Blue Book* 1991, 405–15; particularly, 409–12.

11. Resolution 1991-D122, "Distinguish Between Criticism of Israeli Policy and Expression of Anti-Jewish Prejudice."

12 The National Workshop on Christian-Jewish Relations began in 1973 as a Catholic-Jewish initiative. It met fourteen more times between 1975 and 1996 with broader Christian support and participation.

13. *The Blue Book* 1991, 535.

14. From Marilyn Salmon, "In Our Times: What Has Changed Between Jews and Christians?" *Proceedings of the Center for Jewish-Christian Learning* 1992 Lecture Series, vol. 7 (Spring 1992), 32.

15. *The Blue Book* 1991, 538.

16. For the complete essay see *The Blue Book* 2009, 189–91.

17. All of the items on the SCLM 2009 resource list have been incorporated in this volume's bibliography.

18. Louis Weil, "Some Words about the Anti-Judaism Resolution," SCLM Blog, March 29, 2012 http://liturgyandmusic.wordpress.com/2012/03/29/some-words-about-the-anti-judaism-resolution/#comments. Last accessed: 25 July 2012. Used with the author's permission.

19. Joslyn-Siemiatkoski, "Anti-Judaism and the Liturgy."

20. Salmon, *Preaching Without Contempt*, 3, 4, 14; this is the focus of her Chapter One.

21. Amy-Jill Levine and Marc Z. Brettler, *The Jewish Annotated New Testament* (New York: Oxford University Press, 2011).

22. Joslyn-Siemiatkoski, "Anti-Judaism and the Liturgy."

23. See Episcopal News Service, 17 February 2004.

24. Amy-Jill Levine, *The Misunderstood Jew: The Church and the Scandal of the Jewish Jesus* (New York: HarperCollins, 2007).

25. Joslyn-Siemiatkoski, "Anti-Judaism and the Liturgy."

26. Joslyn-Siemiatkoski, "Anti-Judaism and the Liturgy."

27. Joslyn-Siemiatkoski, "'Moses Received tm he Torah," 447. Rethinking Christian understanding of "Torah" is the focus here; rethinking of "covenant" is the focus of a forthcoming paper based on an essay prepared for SCLM. See Joslyn-Siemiatkoski, "Anti-Judaism and the Liturgy."

28. Rosemary Radford Reuther, *Faith and Fratricide: The Theological Roots of Anti-Semitism* (Eugene, Oregon: Wipf & Stock Publishers, 1996).

29. Thomas E. Breidenthal, "Neighbor-Christology: Reconstructing Christianity before Supersessionism," *Cross Currents* (Fall 1999): 320–48.

30. *The Blue Book* 1991, 536. The Presiding Bishop's Committee on Christian-Jewish Relations' 1991 report is a robust example: lengthy, detailed, interesting. It is signed by John Burt, and almost certainly was penned by him. See *The Blue Book* 1991, 532–38.

31. Resolutions 1991-A147, "Support a Two-state Solution for Israel and the Palestinian People;" 1991-A150, "Support an Anglican Presence in the Middle East;" 1991-A152, "Deploring Anti-Jewish Prejudice."

32. Salmon, "In Our Times," 32.

33. Salmon, "In Our Times," 32.

34. "Episcopalians in Ecumenical Delegation Seek Understanding of Mideast Conflict." ENS 2000–240, 20 December 2000.

35. 1979 Book of Common Prayer, 305.

IV

COMMON WORDS

THE EPISCOPAL CHURCH CONSIDERS ISLAM

Islam had been on The Episcopal Church's mind for a long time, Bishop Epting explained:

> For more than 20 years, our General Convention has passed resolutions with language like this: "Whereas the Church today recognizes the vitality and often impressive resurgence of the communities of the faithful of Islam, both in foreign nations and among peoples of our own nation; and acknowledges the impact of the Islamic community on the religious, cultural and sociological aspects of the lives of many people... [Therefore be it resolved that we] endorse substantive dialogue between Christians and Muslim communities, dialogue that maintains the theological integrity of both faith communities and commitment to genuine human rights and religious freedom."[1]

It was September 2004. Christopher Epting, Presiding Bishop's Deputy for Ecumenical and Interfaith Relations, was addressing the 41st Annual Convention of the Islamic Society of North America [ISNA]—the US's largest (perhaps most influential) Muslim umbrella organization. In fact, by this point, improved understanding of Islam and bettering Christian relations with Muslims had been at least an intermittent concern of The Episcopal Church for a full quarter-century.

Indeed, in 1979, General Convention had instructed the Standing Committee on Ecumenical Relations of The Episcopal Church [SCER] to "identify existing conversations between the Christian community and Islam in our country [i.e. the USA] and in countries where this Church has jurisdiction;" to "devise and formulate, in consultation with the Presiding Bishop, a means of initiating such conversations on a formal level involving The Episcopal Church;" and further, to "commend and encourage the present dialogues of the National and World Council of Churches with the Islamic communities."[2]

The impetus for this move is not immediately evident. No mention of Islam or Muslims appears in any of the reports prepared for the 1979 General Convention. However, the Iran Revolution climaxed in 1979: on 17 January, the Shah of Iran left the country; on 1 February, Ayatollah Ruhollah Khomeini returned to Tehran in triumph; on 1 April, by popular vote, Iran became an Islamic Republic.

The situation in Iran must have influenced the mind of General Convention. Whatever the motivation, the 1979 call for deeper consideration of Episcopal-Muslim concerns was informed by a notion that formal interreligious conversation has value; and, that such conversations should be pursued—not merely ecumenically—but by The Episcopal Church itself.

In its report to the 1982 General Convention, SCER indicated that it had "explored the possibility of fulfilling" the mandate issued by General Convention in 1979—albeit not terribly energetically, it would appear. As the report notes, SCER soon "discovered that The Episcopal Church is already involved in Christian-Muslim relations through an ecumenical agency and realized that to take on the full scope of this assignment without more staff, funding, and membership would interfere with the work entrusted to the Commission by the Canons of the Church." It therefore submitted the resolution *Encourage Islamic Relations Through the NCC:*

> *Whereas,* the energies and resources of the Standing Commission on Ecumenical Relations are totally absorbed in ecumenical relations with other Christian bodies looking toward visible unity in the Body of Christ; and
>
> *Whereas,* The Episcopal Church is already participating in the National Council of Churches' Task Force on Christian-Muslim Relations; therefore be it
>
> *Resolved,* the House of Deputies concurring, That this 67th General Convention encourage continued Episcopal involvement in the National Council of Churches' Task Force on Christian-Muslim Relations; and be it further
>
> *Resolved,* That the Standing Commission on Ecumenical Relations be discharged from further responsibility for the development of additional programs or agencies, other than those through which it currently operates in dealing with Islamic relations.

This resolution passed, effectively asserting that the National Council of the Churches of Christ in the USA [NCCC]—not The Episcopal Church *per se*—would be the source of most Episcopal Church teaching on Christian-Muslim relations for the foreseeable future.

Yet, in 1991, General Convention urged "dioceses of our Church to engage in study and dialogue with respect to Muslim/Christian relations," with the hope of inspiring better understanding at the local level. Some did so in response to this urging. However, the Diocese of New York Ecumenical Commission had already added an Episcopal-Muslim Relations Committee to its structure in March of that year. The newly constituted committee made its first report to the full Commission (ironically, it would turn out) on September 11, 1991.

Also as a direct result of General Convention's action in 1991, a group of distinguished US Muslim leaders met with the Presiding Bishop's Advisory Committee on Interfaith Relations in November 1995. While The Episcopal Church had been (and would continue to be) a participant in Christian-Muslim dialogue via the NCCC, as then Presiding Bishop Edmund Browning made clear at the time, the purpose of this high-level Episcopal-Muslim gathering was to explore "ways to improve the climate between Episcopalians and Muslims at the local level." Theologically, the exchange was grounded in Christian mandate to hospitality and neighbor-love, and themes of "peace, justice and reconciliation," as an Episcopal News Service story noted.

In a further move away from complete delegation of The Episcopal Church's Christian-Muslim concerns to the NCCC for attention, the 1997 General Convention issued an endorsement of substantive Christian-Muslim dialogue. Six years later, General Convention 2003 would reaffirm this. However, we should note that the 1997 resolution favored a dialogue in which Christians and Muslims would be represented equally, and for which the "indigenous Christian communities" would be included in the Christian delegation. It also urged appropriate ecumenical bodies to address patterns of discrimination against minorities. Together, this would seem to indicate that General Convention 1997 was thinking more toward Christian-Muslim conversation in Muslim-majority contexts around the world than it was about Christian-Muslim relations in the US.

When speaking to the ISNA convention-goers in 2004, the Presiding Bishop's Deputy Ecumenical and Interreligious Relations had, as we saw, described The Episcopal Church as interested in robust dialogue with Muslims on matters of consequence. "However, truth be told," he admitted to his audience, "it has only been since the horrifying events of September 11, 2001, that we have begun to live up to those noble ideals." The Episcopal Church's official teachings in the immediate aftermath of the 9/11 attacks are our next concern.

On Waging Reconciliation

As we learned in the previous chapter, *Guidelines for Christian-Jewish Relations for Use in The Episcopal Church* has been in place since 1988. The Episcopal Church has an officially endorsed course of action for thinking theologically about, and behaving toward Judaism and Jews. However, no guidelines have been carefully developed, ratified by General Convention, and systematically promulgated for thinking theologically about and behaving toward Islam and Muslims.[3] One might well argue that The Episcopal Church's *Principles for Interfaith Dialogue* (1994) and the National Council of Churches' Policy Statement, *Interfaith Relations and the Churches* (1999) provide all the guidance necessary—that "interfaith dialogue" and "interfaith relations" includes

Episcopal-Muslim engagement of whatever sort. Yet, the series of General Convention calls for specific action on Episcopal-Muslim concerns suggests that Episcopalians (at least in some quarters) were eager for help in that regard. In the fall of 2001, the need for principles and guidelines became urgent.

The 9/11 attacks provoked a number of responses which can be construed as The Episcopal Church's teaching on Islam and Episcopal-Muslim relations. By nightfall, then Presiding Bishop and Primate Frank T. Griswold had issued a pastoral letter which stated, in part:

> The events of this morning…make me keenly aware that violence knows no boundaries and the security is an illusion….Many are speaking of revenge. Never has it been clearer to me than in this moment that people of faith, in virtue of the Gospel and the mission of the Church, are called to be about peace and the transformation of the human heart, beginning with our own. I am not immune to emotions of rage and revenge, but I know that acting on them only perpetuates the very violence I pray will be dissipated and overcome….
>
> Yes, those responsible must be found and punished for their evil and disregard for human life, but through the heart of this violence we are called to another way. May our response be to engage with all our hearts and minds and strength in God's project of transforming the world into a garden, a place of peace where swords can become plowshares and spears are changed into pruning hooks.[4]

By September 20th, Griswold had requested Episcopal Church "bishops and diocesan ecumenical officers to promote contacts with Muslim neighbors," pointing out that Sikhs and non-Muslim Arabs might also be feeling vulnerable. "American Muslims, Arabs, and Sikhs are suffering what they call double anguish at this time," he explained:

> …the heart-wrenching pain of the loss of loved-ones coupled with the deep hurt brought by finding themselves the victims of generalized blame through ignorance and stereotyping. Jesus said, 'Love your neighbor as yourself,' but to love our neighbor we must know our neighbor. We would urge you to take new (or renewed) steps toward interfaith and intercultural education.[5]

At St. Paul's Cathedral, Burlington, Vermont, on 21 September 2001, Griswold preached on "My joy is gone, grief is upon me, my heart is sick" (Jer. 8:18) —a passage from one of the lessons appointed for the Sixteenth Sunday after Pentecost.[6] Several points made in this sermon are worth highlighting:

- Lamentation is an appropriate mode of speech for Christians, an appropriate mode of address before God.

- As Christians, service to others should be "our fundamental orientation".

- In suggesting that, "If our life is ordered to God, we find ourselves caught up in God's mercy and compassion," Griswold teaches that a characteristic (even definitive) theological assertion of Muslims—who do everything "in the name of God: the Compassionate, the Merciful"—is native to Christian theology as well.[7] In fact, he teaches, drawing on the wisdom of the Early Church, that those who would draw near to God, who would strive to be Christ-like, will seek the cultivation of "a merciful and compassionate heart," aware that such cultivation "is the consequence of Christ being formed in us, our being conformed to Christ" through baptism and regular participation in the Eucharist.

- Christians are to incarnate "God's all-embracing compassion" in corporate, as well as our personal, lives—which requires discipline, sacrifice, and the reordering of interests. But, this discipline, sacrifice, and reordering is worthwhile, because "the way of compassion transfigures and heals not simply those to whom it is directed, but those who practice it."

- "God's project…is one of reconciliation;" so should be ours.

- Reconciliation's "active principle" is "God's compassion, God's mercy, God's loving kindness, God's fierce bonding love."

- Reconciliation is defined as "the gathering up of all things into a unity in which difference is both honored and reconciled in the fullness of God's ever creative imagination."

- Finally, healing is better sought and achieved through service and sharing than through revenge and retaliation.[8]

Sermons of Presiding Bishops are indeed a source of the Church's teaching. But, they rank below pastoral letters from that office; and in general, they are promulgated less broadly. That this particular sermon was indeed broadcast as an Episcopal News Service press release means that is was in fact offered as a theological lesson to and by The Episcopal Church.

At least as significant to the instructional power of this sermon, however, is the larger context in which it was preached: during a week-long meeting of the House of Bishops. This was a regularly scheduled meeting; the agenda—a multi-directional examination of *God's Mission in a Global Communion of Difference*—had been set months before the 9/11 attacks on the United States. During the course of the week, seven formal expert presentations were made. As Griswold saw it, all of presentations and conversations during this week were meant to help the bishops and their spouses consider the meaning of being "reconcilers as a church and as a province in the Anglican Communion."[9]

Before adjourning, the bishops prepared another significant teaching: *On Waging Reconciliation*—a Pastoral Letter from the entire House of Bishops, issued on their behalf by the Office of the Presiding Bishop on 26 September 2001.[10] The rhetoric of *On Waging Reconciliation* is strikingly similar to the sermon delivered to the bishops a few days earlier.

The Episcopal Church has been a multinational body for decades. The present Presiding Bishop, Katharine Jefferts Schori, stresses this; General Convention has eschewed the use of the shorthand identifier ECUSA. However, *On Waging Reconciliation* seems in many ways (and unapologetically) to have been penned by and for Americans. When it speaks of "our nation," "our military chaplains," and "our Muslim brothers and sisters who are rendered vulnerable in this time of fear and recrimination," it quite clearly means the USA (as did Griswold in his at least half-dozen uses of "our nation" or a similar construct in his sermon of 21 September 2001). To note this is not to say it should have been otherwise; it is merely to point out that it was a characteristic of The Episcopal Church's way of thinking and talking about itself at the beginning of the 21st century.

Reconciliation, as the title indicates, is the primary theological theme—developed in incarnational and soteriological terms—of the House of Bishops' Pastoral Letter. Drawing on the Book of Common Prayer, supplication is made "for our enemies, and those who wish us harm; and for all whom we have injured or offended." Assuredly, this letter takes some cues from the statement issued by Griswold on the afternoon of the attacks. Noting that the urge for revenge was understandable, he had asserted "...people of faith, in virtue of the Gospel and the mission of the Church, are called to be about peace and the transformation of the human heart, beginning with our own."[11] Thus the thinking in the Presiding Bishop's 9/11/01 statement, his sermon of 9/21/01, and the House of Bishops' pastoral letter of 9/26/01 are very much in line with that of advocates of conflict-transformation and just-peacemaking.[12]

As is true of anything issued by the House of Bishops, *On Waging Reconciliation* yielded a range of responses from Episcopalians. It also provoked a range of responses in the secular press—and that is far less typical for pastoral letters from the House of Bishops. Negativity toward the statement began with distaste for the title: it seemed an odd construct; *war* is what is waged, after all! Yet, it is quite clear that, for some decades, the term *waging* had already been in use to mean "a campaign for something." A related phrase, "waging peace," was already a fixture in the conflict transformation paradigm. It is said to have been coined in the 1950s by peace activist Warren Wells, in a letter to President Dwight D. Eisenhower. By 1984, it had become the title of a booklet-series produced by the Nuclear Age Peace Foundation.

A related complaint was that the title, indeed the whole statement, is obtuse: what on earth does "waging reconciliation" mean, after all? Again, the field of conflict transformation offers many sound methodologies. These were not spelled out; nor does it seem essential that they should have been in a short statement attempting to be at least as poetic as practical.

But the poetic rhetoric was an element in raising the hackles of naysayers, too. Absolute clarity should have been the bishops' goal, it was said, especially in denouncing the evil behind the attacks—which detractors either felt was not recognized at all, or was denounced all too vaguely. In a similar vein, the bishops' response was called weak, morally relativistic, mere Vietnam-era anti-war sentiment—when underscoring the US government's God-given right to punish the perpetrator would have been more appropriate (and what, the critics asserted or implied) people in the pew needed to hear.

Others, however, found *On Waging Reconciliation* theologically sound. It may be described as implicitly (rather than overtly) Trinitarian, radically incarnational, and soteriologically and eschatologically inclusive—rooted in an understanding that God is at work in all of creation, thus a conviction that God's gracious love is extended beyond the Christian community. Scott Becker, pastor of Seattle's Bethany Community Church, responded directly to the document's detractors via an article published by *The Seattle Times*. In it he outlined three ways in which *On Waging Reconciliation* demonstrated commitment by the House of Bishops to "non-negotiables" long a part of Christian moral theology: commitment to the mandate not to kill, recognizing the corollary that governments—while they may rightly choose violence for the sake of justice—are to be held accountable for how they make use of that option; conviction that Christians are to pray for their enemies, and also to engage in humble self-examination—thus mitigating the power of the enemy to provoke us to evil; and, commitment to reconciliation. As Becker went on to point out, reconciliation has become confused with "making nice", when in fact it is to the contrary a difficult process involving listening, confrontation, and active engagement; a process involving repentance, forgiveness, and truth-telling.[13]

In considering the theology of *On Waging Reconciliation*, it is interesting to know that it was developed during a colloquium which had convened in a secular space (a hotel banquet hall) transformed by the addition of an altar. Above the makeshift altar had hung a crucifix—the work of an artist then-anonymous, now known to be Geralyn Wolf, Bishop of Rhode Island. She had crafted the piece out of discarded wood scraps she had collected from a construction site in Lower Manhattan she had visited (ironically) on September 8th. She had adorned the Jesus-figure with a tool belt holding five nails (representing the crucified Christ's five wounds), and had placed a hammer in his right hand. The cross's horizontal bar bore the inscription *Construire de nuevo mi mundo* (Rebuild the world in me)—that is, as missiologist Ian Douglas explained at the time, "Rebuild the world in Jesus from the debris and broken pieces of our lives."[14] The pastoral letter *On Waging Reconciliation* is informed by this icon. Where other voices were calling for vengeance, *On Waging Reconciliation* called for radical peacemaking, motivated profoundly by a doctrine of radical incarnation.

Rarely has the attention of The Episcopal Church's Executive Council been more focused on interreligious concerns, and the theology necessary to address them, than during its meeting in mid-October 2001. As was explained in this book's Introduction, the Executive Council meets frequently between General Conventions, and its actions rank just below those of General Convention as a source of church teaching. Action during its October 2001 session began with extension of "profoundest condolences" to those most directly affected by the 9/11 attacks. It continued with praise of the Presiding Bishop's assertion that day, "that the mission of the Church is about 'peace and the transformation of the human heart, beginning with our own;'" with applause for personnel from The Episcopal Church Center, the Seaman's Institute, Trinity Wall Street and St. Paul's Chapel, and the General Theological Seminary "for being the body of Christ in New York City in the days following the attacks;" and with commendation of the House of Bishops "for its commitment to develop clear steps, personally and as a community of faith, in order to 'wage reconciliation'"—an allusion to the bishops' pastoral letter of 26 September 2001.[15]

The Executive Council then formally called upon the entirety of The Episcopal Church "to engage in local inter-faith dialogues among peoples of the three Abrahamic faiths with resources developed by the office of Ecumenical and Interfaith Relations, condemning in the strongest terms all actions by any groups that pervert the true values of Islam, Judaism and Christianity, especially the core belief of non-violence as expressed in salaam, shalom and peace, noting that such interfaith dialogue can help reduce incidents seen in recent weeks of backlash violence against Muslims, Sikhs, Hindus and others."

As the list of resolutions continued, the Executive Council affirmed the US President's leadership, during these first weeks after the attacks, but at the same time cautioned against responding to the attacks with war—urging instead the use of conflict-transformation and peace-building strategies. It welcomed President Bush's call for Palestinian Statehood, framing its support for the renewal of the Israeli-Palestinians peace process in terms of taking "direct action against terrorism." It called for protection of constitutional rights and civil liberties, avoidance of racial and ethnic profiling, care for the rights of legitimate asylum-seekers, and continuation of local ministries of hospitality to all refugees and immigrants. Resounding throughout this series of Executive Committee actions is the baptismal promise to "strive for justice and peace among all people, and respect the dignity of every human being," which Episcopalians reaffirm throughout the liturgical year.

Renewing Our Pledge

In ensuing years, The Episcopal Church did wage reconciliation in a number of ways. New or renewed interest in study of Islam, engagement with Muslims, or closer attention to theologies of religious diversity was demonstrated at the multi-national, diocesan, deanery, and parish levels. Several Episcopal seminaries offered courses or workshops on Islam and Christian-Muslim relations. At its June 2005 meeting, the Executive Council went on record as deploring "the desecration of any religious sacred text or space and calls upon all people of faith to respect religious diversity and never to defame or abuse that which is considered holy by others." Certainly, one motivation for this action was concern for the outrage (sometimes violent, even deadly) which had erupted in many parts of the world in reaction to news reports of the desecration of copies of the Qur'ān at the Guantanamo Bay detention center. The US had suffered a spate of mosque desecrations during the winter and spring of 2005—Boca Raton, Florida (February); Fort Collins, Colorado (April); Adelanto, California (June)—and this may also have been on the mind of the council. Perhaps the Executive Council's teaching was of some help to Episcopalians when, in Fall 2005, the so-called "Danish cartoon controversy" broke out.

Autumn 2007 brought a challenge of a different sort, and with it a different opportunity for the waging of reconciliation. If the convening of the World's Parliament of Religions (1893) and the Vatican's promulgation of *Nostra Aetate* (Declaration on the Relation of the Church with Non-Christian Religions, 1965) are landmarks in the establishment of the modern interfaith movement, arguably another such landmark is *A Common Word Between Us and You*. This call for dialogue was issued in November 2007 by 138 distinguished Muslim religious leaders, each significant in stature and influence, together embodying the breadth of Islam, geographically and otherwise. Thus *A Common Word* rightly can be said to represent the consensus of the *ummah* (the entirety of the Muslim community) in a manner accomplished only rarely since the time of the Prophet Muhammad.[16]

A Common Word is a lengthy document. In short, it asserts that, since the religion-communities of Muslims and Christians comprise more than half of the world's population, world peace depends on peace between them. The basis for that peace already exists in the Biblical and Qur'ānic mandates to love God and neighbor.[17]

The impetus for the penning of this document were remarks included by Pope Benedict XVI in a lecture he gave at the University of Regensburg (Germany) on 12 September 2006. In light of these remarks, a letter calling for dialogue was signed by thirty-eight Muslim leaders and sent to the pope in mid-October. When this request received no response, a broader approach was taken. *A Common Word* was addressed to "Leaders of Christian Churches, everywhere;" twenty-eight international Christian leaders were addressed by name.

A copy was hand-delivered to Archbishop Rowan Williams at Lambeth Palace on 11 October by one of the signatories. His initial response was immediate and warm-hearted, calling the theological basis of *A Common Word* "indicative of the kind of relationship for which we yearn in all parts of the world, and especially where Christians and Muslims live together." Noting that the emphasis placed by *A Common Word* on the fundamental importance of belief in the unity of God and love of neighbor is welcome, he went on to say that "the letter rightly makes it clear that these are scriptural foundations equally for Jews, Christians, and for Muslims, and are the basis for justice and peace in the world."[18]

In early 2008, I received nearly simultaneous requests—one from the office of the Anglican Communion Network of Inter Faith Concerns (NIFCON), another from The Episcopal Church's Office of Ecumenical and Interreligious Relations (OEIR)—for input into the process of crafting the lengthy, formal response to *A Common Word* to be issued by the Archbishop of Canterbury later that year. After a brief consultation, all agreed that I would write a formal response to *A Common Word* on behalf of The Episcopal Church—and would do so quickly. The text would be edited and approved by the office of the Presiding Bishop before submission to NIFCON. From there, it would be forwarded to the Archbishop's office, to be stirred into the mix of ideas received from around the Anglican Communion. At the same time, OEIR would make it available for use by Episcopalians seeking better understanding of *A Common Word*.

My effort to respond to *A Common Word* was undertaken with awareness that, already, the Yale Center for Faith & Culture had brought together a diverse gathering of Christian scholars, leaders, and activists. They had penned *Loving God and Neighbor Together: A Christian Response to A Common Word Between Us and You*; and had published it and the names of its 300 signatories (among them a number of Episcopalians) as a full-page ad in the 18 November 2007 edition of *The New York Times*.[19] The Yale Response characterizes *A Common Word* as offering "a Muslim hand of conviviality and cooperation…to Christians worldwide," asks (on biblical grounds) forgiveness for past misdeeds by Christians against Muslims, and praises the insight and courage of the authors of *A Common Word* in having identified the common ground between the two traditions in "something absolutely central to both" (not "marginal" to either, nor "merely important to each") as deeply insightful and courageous.

My attempt took note of the tone and content of the Yale Response and the praise and criticism it had elicited. As well, I considered other official and popular responses to *A Common Word* which had been issued by this point. Negative opinions typically asserted that assent to *A Common Word's* invitation would entail comprise of (even capitulation on) core Christian doctrines. The Episcopal response endeavored therefore to demonstrate that one could respond to this pan-Muslim request for dialogue in the affirmative *because* of (not in spite of) Christian conviction. It strove to meet the scriptural evidence mounted in *A Common Word* with scriptural evidence of its own. It sought to make a case consonant with prior Episcopal Church and Anglican Communion official teachings on Christian-Muslim relations.

The resulting document (the text for which is in the Appendix) is entitled *Renewing Our Pledge*. It is addressed outwardly, but with the intention that it would be read and taught in-house. That is, *Renewing Our Pledge* was written with multiple audiences in mind: Muslims (those who signed *A Common Word*, and their constituents), yes; but also, the Archbishop of Canterbury and his staff, the Presiding Bishop's Deputy and Associate Deputy for Ecumenical and Interreligious Relations, and the Diocesan Ecumenical and Interreligious Officers of The Episcopal Church.

Renewing Our Pledge differs from many of the documents considered in this book in that it is an example of The Episcopal Church's teaching only indirectly. While it benefits from input from the Presiding Bishop's Deputy and Assistant Deputy for Ecumenical and Interreligious Relations (and was promulgated from that office), the need to meet a Lambeth Palace deadline did not allow the document to be refined and approved through other channels such as the Standing Commission on Ecumenical and Interfaith Relations.

For several years, *Renewing Our Pledge* was made available on The Episcopal Church's website as a teaching resource. It was the basis for an Episcopal-Muslim Relations Committee workshop during the fall 2008 convention of the Diocese of New York. It was the topic of a lecture I gave at the 2009 annual meeting of Episcopal Diocesan Ecumenical and Interfaith Officers, an element in my daily presentations for the 2009 National Workshop on Christian Unity, and a primary focus of workshops held in the Diocese of Chicago in fall 2010. It has been included in the assigned or recommended reading for courses taught by me and others at General Seminary, New York Theological Seminary, Ecumenical Theological Seminary (Detroit), Hartford Seminary, and The College of Idaho—perhaps elsewhere. It has been proven a useful tool in conveying the significance of *A Common Word* as a pan-Muslim dialogical initiative, and in encouraging Christians to formulate their own responses to it.

But as did *On Waging Reconciliation*, its parent document in a sense, *Renewing Our Pledge* has garnered complaints. As had several previous Anglican and Episcopal interreligious-relations documents, it draws a warrant from the Ninth Commandment, which "orders us not to bear false witness against our neighbor (Exodus 20:16)." It goes on to note that "we are hard pressed to bear accurate witness to the religion of our neighbors if we have little sense of what their religion is about. Bearing truthful witness regarding our neighbor includes what we say about their religions' beliefs and practices." Critics have taken exception to this line of thinking, saying that it misstates (or at least, mis-implies) what the Ninth Commandment demands. The Commandment does not require us to learn anything about Islam or Muslims, they counter. It simply demands that we take care not to spread falsehood—thus that we not testify unless we are willing to take responsibility for the truthfulness of our statements. Accordingly, the Ninth Commandment puts no pressure on us to learn anything about our neighbor's faith; it only expects us to keep silent if we cannot vouch for the truthfulness of what we say.

Some have said that *Renewing Our Pledge* should be more skeptical of *A Common Word's* claims. For example, say those making this critique, the hadith (tradition of the Prophet) to which *A Common Word* points in its assertion of neighbor-love as a core Islamic principle has been interpreted most often by Muslims throughout history as referring only to the Muslim neighbor. Those who are firm in their skepticism are unlikely to accept that the esteemed signatories of *A Common Word* have the ability to offer a different authoritative exegesis.

Further, skeptics have asserted that *Renewing Our Pledge* should have responded as they would have responded themselves to *A Common Word*: we accept your invitation to talk—but only if the agenda begins with a clarification of basic human rights, including the rights of Christian minorities and the freedom for Muslims to convert to a different religion.

But again, the original motivation behind *Renewing Our Pledge* was the opportunity to participate in the process which would lead to an extended response to *A Common Word* by the Archbishop of Canterbury as one of its named addressees. That document, *A Common Word for the Common Good*, was released on 14 July 2008; it is addressed "To the Muslim Religious Leaders and Scholars who have signed *A Common Word Between Us and You* and to Muslim brothers and sisters everywhere," and acknowledges that the spirit of the missive to which it is responding is "hospitable and friendly" and helpfully generous in intention. The full text of *A Common Word for the Common Good* is too lengthy to include here. A digest of its major points will, however, demonstrate that it is as well an excellent instructional resource.[20]

Rowan Williams sees in *A Common Word* a modest, "realistically hopeful recognition that the ways in which we as Christians and Muslims speak about God and humanity are not simply mutually unintelligible systems." To him, the document's use of "perhaps" twice in a key paragraph suggests an allowance for further discussion within and between our two communities. He identifies in the original document emerge five themes for further exploration:

- Our respective understandings of love and praise of God;
- Practical implications of love of neighbor;
- Attention (through studying together) to how each community uses its sacred texts;
- Engagement "with each other without anxiety…[or] mutual fear and suspicion;"
- Exploration of "a common awareness of responsibility before God," in light of our real and serious differences, and in faithfulness to our respective convictions;

Having then expanded at length on each theme, Williams outlines three imperatives implied by *A Common Word's* "powerful call to dialogue and collaboration":

- Strengthening of "grass-roots partnerships and programmes;"
- Intensification of formal dialogue and study such as he had been facilitating since 2003 through the Building Bridges Seminar initiative;
- Deepening of appreciation "for each other's religious practice and experience."

Given that Christian-Muslim encounter has the potential to take a variety of forms, Williams identifies three primary outcomes worth seeking:

- Maintaining and strengthening current Christian-Muslim engagement.
- Finding ways for honest exploration of differences and convergences between Christians and Muslims.
- Ensuring that high-level dialogue has relevance and influence at the local level.

Toward these ends, he delineates three priorities: education about one another (for which, he says, the need is urgent in both traditions); "opportunities for lived encounter with people of different faiths, both within and across national boundaries, need to be multiplied and developed in an atmosphere of trust and respect;" and, sustained commitment to the dialogical process, which has the potential to nurture "affection, respect, collegiality and friendship."

Marking a Decade

As the tenth anniversary of the September 11th attacks loomed, Sharon Ely Pearson compiled *Remembering a Time That Changed US* [sic], an anthology of worship and educational resources—among them a prayer composed by Frank Griswold. It is addressed to "God the compassionate one," and is offered in the name of Jesus, the reconciler who draws all things to himself.[21] Theologically, this prayer is consonant with the inclusive eschatology of *On Waging Reconciliation* (2001). It strives to be pastoral to insiders, while signaling "openheartedness-to-others" to outsiders. Not surprisingly, as had happened in 2001, this offering had its detractors, who criticized it along similar lines: its text was deemed inscrutable, vapidly liberal, even anti-American; particularly, it was disparaged for opening with a turn of phrase which sounded (to its critics) more Qur'ānic than biblical.

Indeed, many Episcopalians remain deeply uncomfortable with Islam. As Rowan Williams has noted, the differences between Christianity and Islam are real and serious. Similarities abound; but Muslims and Christians aplenty are not ready to see, let alone celebrate, this. However, what The Episcopal Church teaches, as discerned from the items presented in this chapter, is that whatever Episcopalians may think about the religion of Islam, the obligation to be the good neighbor to Muslims still obtains. If they act on this obligation, we have reason to hope that the results will be positive. In their *American Grace: How Religion Divides and Unites Us*, sociologists Putnam and Campbell argue on the basis of social contact theory that "having a religiously diverse social network leads to a more positive assessment of specific religious groups, particularly those with low thermometer scores;" that "religiously diverse social networks do indeed have a positive effect on interreligious acceptance."[22] In his September 2011 policy brief, *Malleable Stereotypes: How Media Is Improving the Image of American Muslims,* researcher Daniel Tutt notes that social psychology studies indicate "a steady and sustained introduction of positive images sustained over time can change stereotypes."[23]

Dialogue is one method of introducing steady and sustained positive images. The Anglican Communion has its own model to offer: the Building Bridges Seminar. Founded in January 2002 by the Archbishop of Canterbury, it was sustained through mid-2012 as a project of Lambeth Palace. Georgetown University, which has helped support the seminars since 2004, has accepted Rowan Williams' invitation to take over stewardship of the seminars, and intends to continue the Anglican involvement in the series. This annual gathering brings together a diverse roster of some twenty to forty Christian and Muslim scholars and leaders for what Rowan Williams has called "appreciative conversation." Participants are called to three full days of deliberation, each day addressing a particular theme related to the year's overarching topic by means of pairs of public lectures, closed plenary sessions, and work in pre-assigned small groups. Most years, the core activity has been intense discussion of pre-selected pairs of Bible and Qur'ān texts, but other writings have also been studied collaboratively. Difficult texts, themes, and issues have indeed been tackled.

The Building Bridges Seminar is replicable. A sustained, top-level dialogue sponsored by The Episcopal Church and using the Building Bridges model could be both interesting and productive. However, as I have argued for many years, the Building Bridges model could also be employed on more local levels. Digests of the first six seminars have been published as books; others are forthcoming. Several of these are now available as PDFs for free download on the Berkley Center website, as is much of the material sent to participants for their pre-seminar preparation.[24] In due course, the remaining seminar digests will also be released. Muslim and Christian leaders thus have ready access to a program by which members of their congregations could work together quite fruitfully over time—perhaps in weekend retreats; perhaps by meeting weekly or monthly.[25] Exploring common words between us is thus both process and goal.

In its report to General Convention 1991, the Standing Commission on Peace's Middle East Task Force had lamented that—whereas, since the 1970s, The Episcopal Church had expended major effort on bettering Christian-Jewish relations, "no comparable effort has been made to relate to the Muslim world."[26] As a way forward, it reiterated its previous calls for more parish-education resources, and for "courses in Muslim theology" in Episcopal seminaries. Since 1991, The Episcopal Church has made progress in the arena of Christian-Muslim concerns; there is room for much more.

Notes

1. *Episcopal Interfaith Officer Addresses Muslim Convention,* Episcopal News Service 070904–1 (7 September 2004).

2. 1979-D133 "Devise a Means for the Church to Initiate Conversations With Islam."

3. An exception might be raised. The Interfaith Education Initiative, which was funded by Episcopal Relief and Development from January 2002 through December 2004, created many useful items, assembled many from other sources. These materials were made available through an educational website which Diocesan Ecumenical and Interfaith Officers were encouraged to promote. Included was much information on Islam and Christian-Muslim relations. However, General Convention has never endorsed a set of principles or guidelines, or a theological position, or specific teaching materials on Christian-Muslim relations.

4. *'We Are Called to Another Way': Presiding Bishop Griswold on the September 11 Attacks,* Episcopal News Service 2001–239 (11 September 2001).

5. Jan Nunley, *Episcopalians Begin to Battle "Backlash Violence" Against Muslim Neighbors,* Episcopal News Service 2001–264 (20 September 2001).

6. Readings for the Sixteenth Sunday After Pentecost, Year C (Revised Common Lectionary): Jeremiah 8:18–9:1; 1 Timothy 2:1–7; Luke 16:1–13.

7. For a biblical instance, see James 5.11: "and you have seen the purpose of the Lord, how the Lord is compassionate and merciful."

8. The full text of Griswold's 9/21/2001 sermon is provided in the Appendix.

9. The theme for this meeting was derived from a June 2001 retreat made by Griswold and several theologians and missiologists. See *Bishops Call 'Waging Reconciliation' the Answer to Globalization, Terrorism.* Episcopal News Service 2001–277 (28 September 2001). Texts for the seven formal expert presentations made during the weeklong meeting are the core content for *Waging Reconciliation: God's Mission in a Time of Globalization and Crisis,* ed. Ian T. Douglas (New York: Church Publishing, 2002).

10. The text of *On Waging Reconciliation* is provided in the Appendix.

11. Griswold's sermon on 9/21/2001.

12. The just peacemaking paradigm, as developed and advocated by Glenn H. Stassen, in collaboration with a team of Christian ethicists, international relations scholars, conflict resolution specialists, theologians, biblical scholars, and activists. Describing itself as a third option between just war theory and pacifism, it promotes ten peacemaking practices, each with a biblical basis. Stassen published a short explanation, *Just Peacemaking: Ten Practices for Abolishing War,* in 1998; it is now available at http://documents.fuller.edu/sot/faculty/stassen/cp_content/homepage/homepage.htm. For the latest book-length treatment of this paradigm, see Glen H. Stassen, ed., *Just Peacemaking: The New Paradigm for the Ethics of War and Peace* (Cleveland, Ohio: Pilgrim Press, 2008).

13. Scott Becker, "Responding to Violence with Wisdom and Morality," *The Seattle Times* (26 October 2001). http://community.seattletimes.nwsource.com/archive/?date=20011026&slug=becker26. Last accessed: 5 July 2012.

14. Ian T. Douglas, ed., *Waging Reconciliation: God's Mission in a Time of Globalization and Crisis* (New York: Church Publishing, Inc. 2002), xiii. In addition to helpful scene-setting by the editor, this book contains all seven lectures presented during the meeting of the House of Bishops in Burlington, Vermont, September 2001.

15. *Executive Council Minutes*, Oct. 15–19, 2001, Jacksonville, Florida, 7–9.

16. Ingrid Mattson, who (as President of the Islamic Society of North America) was one of the original signatories to *A Common Word*, made this point during a course she and I co-taught at Hartford Seminary in June 2010.

17. The full text of *A Common Word Between Us and You* is available at www.acommonword.com

18. For a press report on Rowan Williams' first response to *A Common Word*, issued on 11 October 2007 (the same day on which he received his official copy), see http://www.archbishopofcanterbury.org/articles.php/1148/archbishops-response-to-a-common-word. Last accessed: 6 July 2012.

19. For a PDF of *Loving God and Neighbor Together* as it appeared in *The New York Times*, see: http://www.acommonword.com/lib/downloads/fullpageadbold18.pdf. Last accessed: 6 July 2012.

20. For the full text of *A Common Word for the Common Good*, see http://www.archbishopofcanterbury.org/articles.php/1107/a-common-word-for-the-common-good (A download button for MS Word can be found on the screen's right). Last accessed: 6 July 2012.

21. Sharon Ely Pearson, ed., *Remembering a Time that Changed US: Worship & Education Resources for the 10th Anniversary of 9/11* (New York: Church Publishing, 2011), 1.

22. Robert D. Putnam and David E. Campbell, *American Grace: How Religion Divides and Unites Us* (New York: Simon & Schuster, 2010), 526–27; see also the remainder of their discussion.

23. Daniel Tutt, "Malleable Stereotypes: How Media is Improving the Image of American Muslims," *Institute for Social Policy and Understanding Policy Brief #48* (September 2011).

24. See http://berkleycenter.georgetown.edu/resources/networks/building_bridges.

25. I make this point in "Appreciative Conversation: The Archbishop of Canterbury's 'Building Bridges' Seminars", available since May 2010 at http://berkleycenter.georgetown.edu/resources/networks/building_bridges.

26. *The Blue Book* 1991, 412.

V
RELATING MULTIRELIGIOUSLY
LOCATING AND JUSTIFYING INTERFAITH RELATIONS

"If it is the task of Christian theological reflection to be as all-embracing as possible in its desire to comprehend the religious dimensions of our being human," says theologian Paul Hedges, "then the very fact of religious plurality surely cries out for interpretation."[1] As we saw in Chapter Two, The Episcopal Church is a signatory to *Interfaith Relations and the Churches*, adopted in 1999 by the National Council of the Churches of Christ in the U.S.A. [NCCC] as its Policy Statement on that matter. That policy is still in place. Nevertheless, during the first years of the 21st century, The Episcopal Church—a multinational entity primarily situated in (and most often identified with) the US—decided to attend to and to interpret religious manyness with a theological rationale of its own.

Locating the Work

The decision to craft an interreligious relations rationale for the Church begs an important question: Exactly whose responsibility is such a task? The answer of location is not unremoved from theology.

Somewhat paradoxically, throughout most of its history, The Episcopal Church has prefkerred to work ecumenically on interreligious matters, yet has been reluctant to add interreligious concerns to the portfolio of its own official structure for ecumenical work. The argument given to the 1973 General Convention by the Joint Commission on Ecumenical Relations is representative. In its report that year, the Commission asserted:

> ...*theological relationships* between Judaism and Christianity are not the only focus of concern in relationships between Jews and Christians. The problems arising from the Middle East crisis; difficulties of Jews in Soviet Russia; the issues of anti-Semitism, both at home and abroad; and many other social and political problems are matters with which The Episcopal Church must deal. *Many of these issues are outside the special ability of a Commission primarily concerned with overcoming divisions among Churches in the U.S.A.* [i.e. the Ecumenical Commission].[2]

The added emphasis is mine. This report is evidence of a question with which The Episcopal Church wrestled for more than a quarter-century: Which office and Standing Commission is the most appropriate location for The Episcopal Church's official interreligious work?

Was interreligious relations properly the domain of the ecumenical office? The task of that office had always been to explore and facilitate bridge-building between The Episcopal Church and other Christian denominations and branches. Such bridge-building is founded on Jesus' prayer that "they all may be one" (John 17:21). The goal of Christian ecumenism was (and remains) full communion among the churches. But the goal of interreligious relations was different: the mutual flourishing of diverse religion-communities, *yes*; something approximating full communion, *no*.

Or, were interreligious concerns the purview of the mission office? If so, interreligious work would be motivated primarily by the Great Commission—by an effort to fulfill Jesus' mandate to "make disciples of all the nations" (Matthew 28:18–20). The 1958 General Convention had asserted that "...the call to the missionary outreach of the Church confronts today a revolutionary and changing world—one in which resurgent non-Christian religions are offering new challenges to the Gospel."[3] However, it then issued a formal call for action by the NCCC in "leading this Church into greater understanding, support and service in its world-wide mission."

Or, should interreligious concerns be located in the office of Peace and Justice? The 1973 report excerpted above implies as much. In fact, in reporting on an "Interfaith Agenda" for The Episcopal Church for the period 1996–2001, the Presiding Bishop's Advisory Committee on Interfaith Relations had rightly noted that

> ...in both the pluralistic society of the United States and on the international scene, the Interfaith dimension is rapidly growing with major Peace and Justice implications as well as the spiritual level of apparent religions in conflict. With due recognition of the significance of this changing scene, this church can take relatively simple steps during the next triennium to be better prepared for this development than it will be if the present approach continues unchanged.[4]

Locating interfaith work in the Peace and Justice Office would surely be in concert with what became (in 1979) the Baptismal Covenant's mandate to "strive for justice and peace among all people, and respect the dignity of every human being."

In 1991, the General Convention instructed The Episcopal Church's Standing Commission on Structure to "prepare a recommendation for policy oversight of interfaith dialogue."[5] General Convention provided a formal decision on the matter in 2003.

General Convention 2003 was the first such meeting of The Episcopal Church following the 9/11/01 attacks. Interreligious concerns were included in an "Evening of Conversations"—simultaneous presentations of several topics. The discussion on "war and peace" (which included some Christian-Muslim relations activists among its panelists) drew a larger audience than the presentation (which I moderated) on how Christians, Jews and Muslims might work creatively for reconciliation in the world as it is today.

The Standing Commission on Ecumenical Relations [SCER] report to the 2003 convention asserted the urgent necessity for The Episcopal Church itself to be about the business of interreligious relations, saying: "We are committed to establishing our own sustained educational and dialogical work in this regard on foundations of equitable and realistic respect for human rights." However, it also underscored the fact that this commission's resources and personnel were inadequate to the task of overseeing both inter-Christian and interfaith work. "In light of the pressing world challenges that bear upon interfaith understanding, and the realities of supporting interfaith work in ways that sustain its energy and purpose," the SCER announced its intention to propose to the next General Convention (2006) that a full-time Associate Deputy for Interfaith Relations be added to the Office of Ecumenical Relations. (Sadly, no such proposal was forthcoming.)[6]

And, after years of discussion, General Convention 2003 amended the Canons of The Episcopal Church "to include the word 'interreligious' as part of the name and duties of the Standing Commission on Ecumenical Relations." Whether to use the word "interreligious" rather than "interfaith" received intense consideration. The prevailing argument was that "religion" is the broader, more inclusive term than "faith." Be that as it may, this action stipulated where official oversight of such work would be located going forward. Where interreligious concerns had been in tangential relationship to this commission's agenda, they were now placed firmly in its portfolio. With a home for this work having been settled upon, the next step was to establish a canonical theological basis for The Episcopal Church's involvement in interreligious relations. This would be accomplished with the adoption of the *Theological Statement on Interreligious Relations* by General Convention in 2009.

Missiology and the Rationale for Interreligious Dialogue

The 2009 *Theological Statement*, as the text itself acknowledges, is but the most recent step (albeit quite a hearty one) in The Episcopal Church's development of a theology of religious manyness. Certainly this cannot be seen as entirely separate from developments in missiology. As missiologist Ian Douglas reminds us, the first two decades of the twentieth century saw the most dramatic expansion of Episcopal foreign mission activity before or since. By 1919, Douglas notes, "American Episcopalian missionaries were serving overseas in twelve foreign and five extra-continental missionary districts of The Episcopal Church."[7]

Constitutionally, The Episcopal Church is the Domestic and Foreign Missionary Society. Every Episcopalian is a member of that Society by virtue of baptism. Because of this, Douglas explains, from 1835 to 1985 (or thereabouts), "The Episcopal Church would say that mission and the church are inseparable. To be an Episcopalian is to be involved in mission. The church is mission."[8]

Much more could be said about The Episcopal Church's theology of mission during the second half of the 20th century. It will suffice for the moment, however, to note that release of Titus Presler's *Horizons of Mission* in 2001 marked the first time a volume specifically on mission had been included in the succession of the *Church's Teaching Series* of books for lay persons, beginning in the 1950s. This book set the stage for The Episcopal Church's next major theologizing and strategizing about mission; in turn, that had direct impact on the development of an *apologia* for The Episcopal Church's participation in interreligious relations work.

A modest but important step toward a rationale for interreligious relations was take in 1991, at the beginning of The Episcopal Church's Decade of Evangelism. That year, General Convention passed a resolution submitted jointly by the still rather new Presiding Bishop's Committee on Christian-Jewish Relations and the Standing Commission on Evangelism. The resolution affirmed The Episcopal Church's commitment to the unique Christian message about God's self-revelation through Jesus, but at the same time "recognizing that the gospel in a pluralist society requires us to be aware of the significance of God's self-revelation outside the church." Again affirming Christian witness, General Convention asserted its recognition "that God's activity in the world is not confined to the church;" therefore, the Convention affirmed its "willingness to listen carefully to and learn humbly from those whose perception of God's mystery differs from our own."[9] The theological generosity of this resolution echoed the spirit and recalled the language of the Lambeth 1988 document, *Christ and People of Other Faiths*. In a lecture given in 1992, Marilyn Salmon noted that Jay Rock, then director of Christian-Jewish Relations for the NCCC, was impressed by this action of The Episcopal Church. His congratulatory message was accompanied by his observation that the General Convention resolution had stated "a theological position that not all of our churches [i.e. member communions of the NCCC] are willing to articulate publicly." Salmon's notes also indicate the receipt of a note from a representative of the Jewish Congress which said, "I am impressed with these words."[10] Clearly, one purpose of this resolution was to reiterate and strengthen the notion of the compatibility of witness and dialogue.

In 2003, the Standing Commission on World Mission brought a "Mission Vision Statement" to General Convention. Entitled *Companions in Transformation: The Episcopal Church's World Mission in a New Century,*[11] the actual writing of the text was accomplished by a team comprising Titus Presler, Willis Jenkins (now on the faculty of Yale Divinity School), and Helena Mbele-Mbong (of the Convocation of Episcopal Churches in Europe). "Our discussions were long and probing," Mbele-Mbong told me in a recent exchange. "We spent a lot of time thinking about the meaning and implications of our ideas and the words and phrases we used as we put together the chapters," she recalls. Titus Presler, the principal author, recalls that the SCWM as a whole contributed "lots of good suggestions both general and specific." As its Preface states, the document also reflects thorough consultation with the world mission community of the time as a whole.

As the Introduction to *Companions in Transformation* explains, the document was offered as an example of the sort of "reflection on the past, discernment in the present, and vision for the future" necessary to guide the Church forward to the year 2020. Among the reasons for issuing such a formal statement at that particular time (2003), was the fact that the events of and following 11 September "prompted reflection about interreligious relations and the projection of US presence abroad."

The body of *Companions in Transformation* has five sections:

- Theological Basis: God is on Mission in Christ;

- An Ethos for Mission: God's People are Companions in Mission;

- The Context for Mission: World Crisis and Mission Integrity;

- Modes of Mission: Incarnate Presence in a World Community;

- Resources for World Mission: Equipping the Church for the 21st Century.

The organizational principle of Section II, *An Ethos for Mission*, is of special interest. Here are laid out seven marks of "missionary character" which are "important at all levels of the church," all deriving from the "central characteristic" of *companionship*. Given the literal meaning of companions as "those who share bread together," the missionary is witness, pilgrim, servant, prophet, ambassador, host, and sacrament.

This last mark of the missionary is founded in the radical incarnationalism typical of classically Anglican theology. A sacrament is an outward and visible sign of inward and spiritual grace; a missionary is one who embodies Christ and is a sign of God's mission and global presence. Presler writes in these terms in his *Horizons in Mission* (2001), where he argues that incarnational theology says that God is up to something in the world.

> God calls us to engage the world expecting to glimpse something of what God is doing and how we can participate. That is as true of our encounter with other religions as it is of our encounter with anything else....The expectancy is incarnational in the sense that interreligious encounters are not encounters with other religions but with other people....Incarnational expectancy also means that we are eager for what God may be doing in and through ourselves. An interreligious encounter is a full encounter only if all participants share their sense of the divine.[12]

As we shall see, these marks of missionary activity would have direct influence on the framing of The Episcopal Church's interreligious relations rationale. Also of interest is the sub-section "Mission in the Conflicts of Religions and Peoples" (a part of Section III, *The Context for Mission*), which brought the intersection between mission, peace-and-justice advocacy, and interreligious relations efforts into focus:

> Inquiry, exploration and dialogue are crucial in conflicts among religious groups....[I]t is missionaries who are called to catalyze the encounters that can lead individuals and groups from animosity to appreciative listening....Undertaking common mission is central in inter-religious understanding. Rather than competing, religions must stand together in solidarity with all who are suffering and witness to the dignity of every human being. In these ways, missionary presence becomes a courageous mode of peacemaking in a violent world.[13]

This section's summary includes a citation of the call "to self-examination and repentance" as found in *On Waging Reconciliation*, the Pastoral Letter from the House of Bishops discussed at length in the previous chapter.

The *Mission Vision Statement* returns to interreligious relations themes in the fifth sub-section of Section IV, *Modes of Mission: Incarnate Presence in a World Community*. It endorses dialogue and interfaith collaboration, saying:

> With ecumenical and interfaith groups, initiatives to encourage contact and dialogue are imperative for reconciliation amid today's heightened tensions among religions, especially between Islam and Christianity. With all, God is calling us to join hands and speak out when religious freedom is curtailed and when the social, environmental, economic, or political welfare of communities is damaged....*The Commission calls on all Episcopal mission groups to undertake intentional group reflection on the impact their work has on inter-religious relationship in the geographical areas they serve.*[14]

The emphasis in the text is part of the original document, the concluding section of which is "A Doxology" celebrating the confidence with which the foregoing vision of mission is embraced.

Companions in Transformation was published as a booklet; it has also been made available as a downloadable document on the website of The Episcopal Church. A Study Guide was also developed, and remains available online. It includes plans for single-session or multi-session forums on the *Mission Vision Statement*, with section-by-section suggestions for preparation and discussion. The Study Guide concludes with a request for feedback to the Standing Commission on World Mission. It also provides a list of short documentaries by and about Episcopal Church missionaries.[15]

In his more recent book, *Going Global With God* (2010), Presler asserts a "functional definition" of mission as "ministry in the dimension of difference." Explaining further he says: "...difference is the terrain of mission. Disconcerting and magnetic, difference both draws and challenges. Difference stimulates, and paradoxically it can comfort as well. Through difference comes insight into religious experience, insight into God." In terms reminiscent of the neighbor-christology of Thomas Breidenthal (which figured in Chapter Three), Presler makes three observations with particular implications for interfaith work. The first is that "current emphases on mutuality in partnership and companionship suggest that difference should be explored and embraced in community rather than accentuated by competition and effaced by domination." The second is that "the other who is different" is the "frontier over which the journey of understanding is both outward and inward, both receptive and reflexive." His third is that "difference, in sum, is foundation in human experience, which includes our religious experience."[16]

Given the mid-20th century presumption on both sides of the North Atlantic, that "the influence of religion would fade with the intellectual and social impact of Darwinian evolution, Freudian psychology, Marxist communism and market consumerism," the fact that interreligious relations are a major source of tension in the 21st-century interreligious conflict has caught many off-guard, Presler contends. As he sees it, reconciliation is at the core of a way forward—"beyond tolerance and mutual coexistence." He affirms dialogue as a "long cherished approach in ecumenical and interreligious relations," noting that "mutual learning and discussion of points of contact and conflict are essential between people of different religions."[17]

Interreligious Relations Statement
(2006)

The 2001–2004 triennium was the first during which a single commission had formal oversight of both the interreligious relations and the ecumenical relations of The Episcopal Church. The newly re-named Standing Commission on Ecumenical and Interreligious Relations [SCEIR] included clergy and laypersons with particular interreligious relations experience.[18] When it met in April 2005, it heard from representatives of several ecumenical partners including the NCCC, the US Conference of Catholic Bishops, and the Evangelical Lutheran Church in America, about their approaches to interreligious work. The commission also received input from experts on the theology of interreligious relations and discussed at length interreligious-relations convergences with and divergences from ecumenism. Still believing in the wisdom of working ecumenically on interreligious matters, as had often been asserted in the past, but now also realizing that The Episcopal Church brings its own strengths to the enterprise, the commission was determined to draw up an interreligious relations strategy—a process already underway because of this meeting.

Daniel Appleyard, then rector of Christ Episcopal Church (Dearborn, Michigan) was appointed to this commission in 2003, just as it received its mandate to engage in Interfaith/Interreligious Relations. He was responsible for preparing presentations on why it was imperative to include that work in the portfolio of Ecumenical Relations as a Standing Committee in The Episcopal Church. He became, therefore, a leader in formulating a theological rationale; with Thomas Ferguson, then Associate Deputy for Ecumenical Relations, he penned the first draft.

The process of authoring the 2006 Interreligious Relations Statement, says Appleyard, was informed by his many conversations with Clare Amos (then coordinator of the Anglican Communion Network of Inter Faith Concerns) and with me (NIFCON's North American staff assistant). One fruit of this relationship was that he encouraged use of the Lambeth 1988 resolution from which had come NIFCON's founding as a model—a notion also advocated by Ferguson. The resolution, "On the Topic of Ecumenical Relations and Establishing a Basis for Interreligious Dialogue," which offered a succinct statement of The Episcopal Church's basis for engaging in interreligious dialogue was brought to General Convention in 2006. As revised and approved by the House of Bishops, it read:

> We affirm the foundational Gospel proclamation that "Jesus is Lord" (1 Cor. 12:3), and therefore we affirm the centrality of Jesus' Summary of God's Law: to love the Lord our God with all our hearts, with all our souls, and with all our minds, and to love our

neighbor as ourselves (Mark 12:29–31; BCP, Catechism, page 851). For this reason we
reach out in love and genuine openness to know and to understand those of other faiths.

Therefore we commend to all our members dialogue for building relationships, the sharing of information, religious education, and celebration with people of other religions as part of Christian life, with the understanding that:

1. dialogue begins when people meet each other

2. dialogue depends upon mutual understanding, mutual respect and mutual trust

3. dialogue makes it possible to share in service to the community

4. dialogue is a medium of authentic witness by all parties and not an opportunity for proselytizing

We believe that such dialogue may be a contribution toward helping people of different religions grow in mutual understanding and make common cause in peacemaking, social justice, and religious liberty.

We further commend that dioceses, parishes, and other organizations of The Episcopal Church initiate such dialogue in partnership with other Christian Churches and in consultation with other provinces of the Communion, where appropriate.[19]

In the end, when time came for General Convention 2006 to adjourn, this resolution had not yet been taken up by the House of Deputies. SCEIR took this as an opportunity to develop a more robust document to present to General Convention in 2009.

Theological Statement on Interreligious Relations (2009)

With the Chicago Quadrilateral, a declaration of the House of Bishops in 1886, The Episcopal Church set forth the basis on which it participates in ecumenical conversations to this day: the Holy Scriptures as the revealed Word of God; the Apostles' and Nicene Creeds as the sufficient statement of Christian faith; the Sacraments of Baptism and Communion; and the historic episcopate, locally adapted. The Episcopal Church can work toward full communion with other churches who affirm these same four items. As had been the case in 2006, the intent in writing *Theological Statement on Interreligious Relations* (2009) was to do the same for the interfaith arena: to articulate a theological basis for The Episcopal Church's participation in interfaith dialogue.[20]

Daniel Appleyard chaired the SCEIR Interreligious Relations Subcommittee during the 2007–2009 triennium, thus was chair of the committee responsible for drafting a theological rationale for interfaith engagement. It had been his idea to reference the Chicago Quadrilateral in conceiving an interreligious relations rationale. In conversations with me, he explained that the goal was to produce a document of substance, but readable by non-specialists. The result might be seen as a primer on theology of religious manyness and interfaith dialogue. The result does not break new ground; it does try to be accessible.

When producing formal documents, The Episcopal Church's method can be confusing, Appleyard admits. "It's a process which tries to gather voices," he explains. Lots of voices contributed to the crafting of the *Theological Statement* (2009); the many had then to be massaged into a single tone. The legislative process invites last-minute revision, with little time to produce or maintain elegant prose. "It involves dislocation and coordination—but, sometimes, synchronicity happens! It is not always coherent, but it can be delightful. There are moments of frustration, but also moments of epiphany." And, he says firmly, it is often more important to have a document which is "clunky," but is endorsed and ready for use by the Church, than to have no document at all.

Indeed, the 2009 document was subjected to dramatic revision during General Convention itself. During a Legislative Committee meeting, Tiffany Israel, First Lay Alternate Delegate for the Convocation of Episcopal Churches in Europe, was given the floor. A scholar of ecclesiology, Israel commended the document's content on the whole. However, she had several serious misgivings. Certain sections were weak; certain themes (she mentioned Incarnation, Creation, Trinity) were omitted or underdeveloped. Most especially, she had deep concern about the section on soteriology. It was vague, she asserted at the time. This was a paper on *why* The Episcopal Church engages, and *what* The Episcopal Church brings to this engagement, she argued. If a section on soteriology was to be part of such a paper, then it ought to be authentic, bold, and clear. "If we mean to say that interreligious relations is good," she declared, "then we need to be willing to say who we are."

A heated debate followed. With The Episcopal Church, she notes, "we're not only dealing with other traditions; we have internal interreligious dialogue! As Anglicans, we hold *difference* together; we understand how hard this is." On the basis of this discussion, SCEIR decided to revise the document. Pierre Whalon, Bishop of the Convocation of Episcopal Churches in Europe, was a member of the subcommittee which prepared the original document. He took the lead in putting the document through a rigorous, extensive, if hurried, rewrite. Assisting him in this nightlong effort were four others, Israel among them. Many paragraphs remained untouched. Several small changes were made. For example, in paragraph 19, the opening word "Traditionally" was replaced with

"Historically." In paragraph 10, which references the attacks of 9/11/01, the original final sentence was awkward in its attempt to condemn backlash incidents against American Muslims and Arabs. The new ending is less specific, but by speaking more generally it is actually more pastoral. The advice it offers extends beyond the US context—a move recollecting that The Episcopal Church is multinational.

Two other changes are much bolder. The Introduction has been given a new opening paragraph, followed by material retrieved from the document submitted in 2006. Section V has been given a new title: where it had been "Soteriology and Interreligious Relations," it was now "Salvation in Christ…;" and, its seven paragraphs were rewritten almost entirely. Without doubt, the section is now stronger, clearer, and "more orthodox"—says Whalon. It includes more quotation of scripture than had the original version. The rhetoric of the whole is now more consistent.

As endorsed by General Convention, *Theological Statement on Interreligious Relations* has six sections. Section I, labeled *Introduction*, begins: "We affirm the foundational Gospel proclamation that 'Jesus is Lord' (I Corinthians 12:3 NRSV), and therefore [we affirm the] Summary of God's Law: 'love the Lord your God with all your hearts, with all your souls, and with all your minds, and…love your neighbor as yourself' (Mark 12:29–31)." The decision to begin by quoting a Bible passage was quite strategic. Explicit biblical references might fend off some criticism from more theologically conservative quarters. But then, drawing upon Scripture is hardly an un-Episcopalian thing to do; the same passage figures in the Book of Common Prayer Catechism.

The *Introduction* emphasizes the necessity to ground The Episcopal Church's multifaith relationships in "thoughtful exploration of and reflection on the appropriate ways to profess Christianity." It is, the statement insists, *because of* our embrace of the "foundational Gospel proclamation that 'Jesus is Lord' (1 Cor. 12:3)," *because* we take Jesus' Summary of the Law seriously, that Episcopalians "reach out in love" and are genuinely open to knowing and understanding people whose religious convictions differ from theirs. It is on this basis that dialogue is commended to Episcopalians "for building relationships, the sharing of information, religious education, and celebration with people of other religions.

Some critics find what is being advocated here to be impossibly unspecific. Dialogue is commended "for building relationships." They ask: What kind of relationships do the document's authors see dialogue able to build? With whom? For what outcomes? It commends "dialogue for…the sharing of information." What kind of information? For what purpose? It commends "dialogue for…religious education." What is meant by this? Sunday School? Adult Forums? Seminaries?

Section I also includes (with slight adaptation, and without heading or attribution) the four basic principles of dialogue ("dialogue begins when people meet each other," etc.) articulated in 1981 by the British Council of Churches, now known as Churches Together in Britain and Ireland. These principles were popularized in the early 1980s by means of an inexpensive BCC booklet, *Relations with People of Other Faiths: Guidelines for Dialogue in Britain*. Their roots are much older and more global, says Paul Weller, who had been a member of the committee responsible for preparing the BCC booklet. In a January 2009 lecture, he explained that "a lot of the thinking that lay behind what eventually became these four principles of dialogue, used as an educative resource among Christians in the UK, came out of the experience of minority Christian groups in the two-thirds world" in the 1960s and 1970s.[21]

Some critics call this four-point formula trite; others call it problematic. They have no quarrel with the first point: meeting *is* mere encounter; but without meeting in the first place, no dialogue can ever happen. But Point 2 is challenged: it asserts that "dialogue depends on" these things; should it not rather "promote" them? If one needs mutual understanding in advance of a dialogue, one has severely limited who can participate. Point 3 is also vague, the complaint continues. *What* about dialogue makes service possible? Doesn't this change with the context? *What* makes people who ordinarily barely speak to each other be willing to join hands in addressing a calamity? What makes *that* possible? And while for some, Point 4 will sound trite, for others it will sound prejudiced. Why use this word *proselytizing*? How is it different from evangelism? In sum, is not dialogue rather a process that can foster mutual understanding, mutual respect, mutual trust, collaborative service, and authentic witness?

Be all of that as it may, embrace of this formula situates The Episcopal Church's teaching within a half-century of ecumenical proclamation about dialogue. It also issues an implicit reminder from the outset that dialogue is never "between religions;" it is between people with religious convictions. It implies as well that dialogue is more than a single encounter, and that interfaith dialogue can be an authentically Christian undertaking.

Section II (Historical Context) notes the various modes of Episcopal Church interreligious engagement. These include numerous local efforts (diocesan, congregational, individual); ecumenical efforts, particularly through the National Council of the Churches of Christ in the USA; international efforts through the Anglican Communion Office, including active participation in the Network of Inter Faith Concerns of the Anglican Communion [NIFCON]; the

Presiding Bishop's own particular initiatives; and the work of task forces such as the current Standing Commission on Ecumenical and Interreligious Relations.

In providing some of the history of Episcopalians' interreligious work, the Statement also acknowledges its debt to earlier major documents. First among them is the Vatican's *Nostra Aetate* (1965), which—as was explained in Chapter One, and as *Theological Statement* (2009) puts it—"helped to inaugurate a new era of dialogue between Christians and those of other religions." Theologically, *Nostra Aetate* is informed by consideration of the usual questions concerning the nature of human existence. While maintaining a christological focus, *Nostra Aetate* not only expresses "profound respect" for persons living faithful lives within other religious traditions, it goes further to urge Christians to act positively to preserve and even promote "all that is good in other religions." It calls for "humane collaboration" at the least, and dialogue at best. *Nostra Aetate* was controversial. Repercussions were generated primarily by its pairing a brief, warm-hearted avowal of "respect and reverence toward Islam," with a longer, more complicated statement on Judaism eschewing all forms of anti-Semitism. *Theological Statement* (2009) follows on all of this. "The lesson of *Nostra Aetate*—and of early church thinkers like Clement and Origen—is to keep your integrity; avoid syncretism," Pierre Whalon said during one of our conversations. "Engage, but engage so that your neighbor can *hear* you."

Of the explicit teachings on interreligious matters emanating from or written in preparation for the Anglican Communion's Lambeth Conferences, two are particularly eloquent: *Christ and People of Other Faiths* (from Lambeth 1988, discussed in Chapter One); and, *Generous Love: the truth of the Gospel and the call to dialogue—An Anglican theology of inter faith relations*, prepared by NIFCON in anticipation of Lambeth 2008.[22] *Theological Statement* (2009) applauds the Lambeth 1988 material for "commending dialogue with people of other faiths as part of Christian discipleship and mission" and for providing the useful document *Jews, Christians, and Muslims: The Way of Dialogue*. As will be recalled from the close reading given it in Chapter One, this material includes the same fourfold principles of dialogue formula developed by the British Council of Churches which figures now in the Introduction to *Theological Statement* (2009). In addition to putting forth principles behind and guidelines for dialogue, Lambeth 1988 provided an in-depth Anglican theology of the Other-than-Christian which is biblical, Trinitarian, and Incarnational. While they did not quote Lambeth 1988, the authors of *Theological Statement* (2009) most certainly took note of its ideas.

Generous Love was issued by NIFCON on 7 February 2008. This treatise of some 5400 words strives to provide a distinctly Anglican theological foundation for interfaith relations, so that (as the news release accompanying it explained) "the pressing need for serious engagement and understanding" is met from within Christian faith, rather than "out of political expediency or to suit the current trend."[23] Its first section, *Beginning with God*, identifies the "voice" of the document as "members of the Church of the Triune God," signalling that this will be a thoroughly Trinitarian argument throughout. The document's susequent sections are dedicated to the following themes:

- Our Contemporary Context and Our Anglican Heritage;

- Shaping Anglican Insights: Reading the Scriptures;

- Shaping Anglican Insights: Tradition and Reason;

- Celebrating the Presence of Christ's Body;

- Communicating the Energy of the Spirit;

- Practicing the Embassy and Hospitality of God.

Generous Love closes with a section entitled, "Sending and Abiding," in which it asserts that in the mutuality of interfaith encounter, "we can experience God's gracious presence in a new way." It commends *Dabru Emet* and *A Common Word*, statements "produced respectively by international groups of Jewish and Muslim scholars" as examples of "new readiness on the part of scholars and leaders of other faiths across the world to engage seriously at a theological level with the Christian faith."

Pierre Whalon served on the writing teams for both *Generous Love* and *Theological Statement* (2009), so carried sensibilities of the first document to the second. This bridge is interesting for another reason. Of The Episcopal Church interfaith documents examined in this study, *Theological Statement* (2009) most explicitly demonstrates Episcopal Church awareness of itself as multinational. The presence of the Bishop of the Convocation of Episcopal Churches in Europe on the writing team underscores this awareness.

Generous Love is foundational to *Theological Statement* (2009), Whalon told me. In writing it, "we didn't try to improve on *Generous Love*." As Daniel Appleyard recalls, one important lesson the committee took from *Generous Love* was its abundant use of scripture in making points. Being more overtly biblical seemed to have become more necessary of late, he noted.

Where *Generous Love* provided an underlay for *Theological Statement* (2009), another Anglican Communion document played a more obvious role. "Relations with Other World Religions" comprises Section F of the Lambeth Conference 2008 *Indaba Reflections*.[24] A Zulu term, *indaba* refers to a meeting on an important concern, during which mutual listening and engagement makes it possible for consensus to emerge for the common good. Thus it has been embraced by the Lambeth Conference as a method of a way of considering challenges facing the Anglican Communion. It is significant that "Relations with Other World Religions" was deemed a concern off sufficient importance to merit address by this method. Theological Statement (2009) commends Indaba Reflections (2008); it also draws on it directly in Section II, when making a point about variation in interfaith dialogue contexts worldwide—and again, as we shall see in Section V.

Section III continues a theme introduced in Section II: the profound changes in interreligious relations context, activity, and dynamics—not only in the US, but throughout the Anglican Communion—wrought by the terrorist attacks of September 11, 2001. What is left unsaid is that subsequent US foreign policy has contributed to these changes. Gwynne Guibord, of the Diocese of Los Angeles, was the principle author of this section. Whalon calls it "the most 'American' of the whole document;" adding, in the spirit of Guibord's writing, "9/11 really is a hinge-date worldwide. The world really did change."

In fact, Section III describes, in rather dismal terms, the current dialogical context as one in which "[b]orders and boundaries are fluid, easily fractured, and unstable," one in which the view from space is simultaneous with the view from personal computer screen; one in which nothing is now truly "distant".

This section is provocative, counter some readers. Episcopalians are this document's primary audience; what agenda is being put forward in telling Episcopalians this? This is a "value-laden" list of woes, one reader commented. "What about growing secularism? Why isn't the rise of secular ideologies on this list of problems? Why not mention "prejudice in its various forms" in this catalogue?" The answer is implied in paragraph 10: the 9/11/01 attacks were still driving theological reflection as this document took shape.

In the remaining two paragraphs of this section, The Episcopal Church acknowledges the multireligiousness of, and its own interconnectedness with, its neighbors. Further, it recognizes that, "[t]hroughout the world, people of different religions can be seen searching for compatible if not common ways toward justice, peace and sustainable life." Shifting to a positive tone, the section concludes by noting that The Episcopal Church's "theological and ecclesial heritage offers significant resources for participating" in such efforts.

In Section IV, the Statement lays out particularly Anglican and Episcopal resources for interreligious dialogue. While a committee effort, it draws heavily on material Whalon wrote in 2005. "This section affirms that 'we are our past'," he says, "and reminds us that we have endless resources." Among these is the thinking of Richard Hooker, whose *Of the Laws of Ecclesiastical Polity* is the classic Anglican explanation of the relationship between religion and society. Of relevance to interreligious-relations work is his description of the "way of salvation"—that is, the Christian moral vision—as having three ultimately inseparable dimensions of faith, hope, and love. *Theological Statement* (2009) cites his teaching on the integral interrelationship of scripture, tradition, and reason. Kurt Dunkle, a delegate to the 2009 General Convention, told me how he found it interesting that revisions of the *Theological Statement* "purposefully omitted the Wesleyan concept of 'experience' which the earlier draft had included, thereby expressly refusing to create a fourth leg to the traditional three-legged Hooker stool."

Accordingly, the Statement affirms Scripture as source of "the *invitation* and the *direction* to engage with people of other religions." But another aspect of Anglican identity with implications for interreligious dialogue is latent here. As Presiding Bishop Katharine Jefferts Schori puts it, a particular understanding of authority is essential to the Episcopalian self-definition:

> We claim three strands of inspired authority—Hooker's definition of scripture, reason, and tradition. As Episcopalians, we also affirm the importance of a dispersed authority that's not vested in one particular prelate—or indeed in prelates alone....That multifaceted understanding of authority leads toward a baptismal sense of authorization and ministerial empowerment—in very concrete terms, not just in the abstract.[25]

During its discussion of scripture and reason, the document asserts (in paragraph 15) that "Because of our faith in the incarnation of God in Jesus Christ, we expect to meet God in our neighbor, whom God commands us to love as we love ourselves (Mark 12:29–31)." This is not a valid syllogism, one observer said to me. "To say, 'Because of our faith...we expect' is to make a huge theological leap! Does this mean we are expecting to see more of God in our neighbor than we see in scripture? It is problematic to look for further insight about the nature of God by looking at a neighbor of another faith."

Section V takes up, rather robustly, the matter of unique truth claims—particularly the Christian belief in salvation through Jesus Christ. Pointing to the historic creeds (Nicene and Apostolic) and the liturgy for evidence, this section asserts that "[s]ince God has chosen to share our life, we affirm that God is intensely concerned about every human life." (Emphasis mine.) "Episcopalians have a particular appreciation of this teaching," the Statement asserts, "in that we believe that the coming of God in Christ has already begun to transform all of creation." This claim seems to have in mind what is sometimes called Anglican radical incarnationalism—the notion that even if humanity had not sinned, God would still have become flesh; the divine-human relationship is profoundly familiar, and God's desire to be with us as we are is deep. Though not original with Anglicans, it is still characteristic.[26]

Having explained the role of the cross, the meaning of resurrection, and the notion of incorporation into the Body of Christ via baptism, the Statement insists that Christian truth claims are not barriers to interreligious dialogue. Quoting from Lambeth 2008 *Indaba Reflections*, it explains that the "purpose of dialogue is not compromise, but growth in trust and understanding of each other's faith and traditions. Effective and meaningful dialogue will only take place where there is gentleness, honesty and integrity. In all of this, we affirm that Christianity needs to be lived and presented as 'a way of life', rather than a static set of beliefs."[27]

Citing a promise Episcopalians make (and reaffirm regularly) through the Baptismal Covenant, the Statement notes that to claim "Jesus as the Way... requires us to 'respect the dignity of every human being'." It goes on to explain: "In mutual encounters and shared ascetic, devotional, ethical, and prophetic witness, we dare to hope that God will reveal new and enriching glimpses of a reconciled humanity." Some critics wish the Statement had said more here. They point out that situations are plentiful in which the "shared ascetic, devotional, ethical, and prophetic witness" it specifies may actually be dangerous for all concerned—at least for novices. As one reader put it, these experiences are better seen as fruit, rather than as a means, of dialogue.

Section VI offers a paradigm for continued involvement by Episcopalians in mission and evangelism, while simultaneously engaging authentically in interreligious dialogue. In terms quite similar to the 1999 NCCC Policy Statement on interreligious relations, paragraph 30 acknowledges that Episcopalians will not be of one mind on how best to practice neighbor-love. Some will give pride of place to evangelization, while others are more concerned with matters of "justice and mutual respect." Given the foundational biblical mandate to love our neighbor, the Statement appropriates, as a way forward, the theology of companionship articulated in *Companions in Transformation* (2003), the Mission Vision Statement introduced above.[28]

In hearty agreement with the position advocated therein, that authentic Christian witness is compatible with interreligious dialogue, the *Theological Statement* takes the Mission Vision Statement's seven modes of companionship, redefining them as "ways" of interreligious "companionship and partnership" toward the common "social, environmental, economic, or political welfare." That is, Episcopalians may be in companionship with interreligious partners as witness, pilgrim, servant, prophet, ambassador, host, or sacrament. Emphasizing the sacramental in interreligious relationship, the *Theological Statement* asserts, helps Episcopalians "retain an incarnational focus on people, relationships, and community, where God truly lives and where the most lasting impacts are made." The missiology at work here resonates with The Episcopal Church's shift from *missio ecclesia* to *missio dei* documented by Ian Douglas in his acclaimed missiological history of The Episcopal Church.[29]

In paragraph 32, the *Theological Statement* declares: "We believe that religions must stand together in solidarity with all who are suffering and witness to the dignity of every human being." Here it has painted with much too broad a stroke. It is calling for a logical impossibility: "religions" cannot stand together; only their adherents can. Since almost every religion is internally diverse—an enormous umbrella under which we find a staggering number of persons along a gamut of commitment to that religion's normative beliefs and practices, and even a larger number of opinions as to what those norms really are. One has only to try to offer a succinct explanation of the mosaic called up by the label "Christianity" to see what is at stake here. Better to have said something like, "We believe that persons of widely diverse religious convictions can be found who are willing to stand with us in solidarity....We pledge our willingness to stand with them."

The rationale concludes with a reminder that, presently, "Christianity lives and serves in a global setting in which all of God's human creation is challenged to find common ground *for our mutual flourishing.*" (Emphasis mine.) Just as the 1886 Chicago Quadrilateral outlines what is essential to The Episcopal Church's ecumenical engagement, so the *Theological Statement* seeks to articulate principles "for authentic interreligious relations and dialogue" in for the 21st century. Thus it highlights "three particular Episcopal gifts to [this] ongoing process:" a "comprehensive way of thinking by which we balance Scripture, tradition and reason in relationship building;" an incarnational theology centered "on the Crucified One who leads us to a place of self-emptying, forgiveness and reconciliation;" and a "practice of focusing mission in terms of service, companionship, and partnership between people as demonstrative of God's embrace of human life."

What is striking here is that, whereas the Chicago Quadrilateral is a list of four understandings which must be present *on the other side of the table* before meaningful dialogue can occur, the *Theological Statement* (2009) outlines only what The Episcopal Church pledges to bring to the exchange. The differnece between these projects is a difference of ends: Whereas the goal of ecumenism is full communion, the goal of interreligious dialogue is companionship.

Noting that Martin Luther King, Jr., "foresaw a time when *as one* all human beings of every religion would have to learn to choose 'a non-violent coexistence' over a 'violent co-annihilation,'" the Statement asserts that "interreligious relations are no longer about competing religions but about mutual demonstrations of Love Incarnate." In fact, the last word is given to Martin Luther King (whose life and ministry The Episcopal Church honors annually), by excerpting a 1967 sermon in which he asserted that 1John 4 sums up a "Hindu-Muslim-Christian-Jewish-Buddhist belief about human reality"—that "Love is the key that unlocks the door which leads to ultimate reality."[30]

Some have asked, Why end with such a highly problematic quote? That "love is the key" is not true of all worldviews; this is not a universal belief! Only *some* religions teach that "love…unlocks the door to ultimate reality." MLK is hardly an expert on the world's religions, such critics complain. Ah, but others may counter, MLK travelled to India in 1959. He visited Mahatma Gandhi's birthplace. He was influenced profoundly by the principle of *ahimsa* (non-harming)—core to Jainism, and embraced by many Hindus—which had informed Gandhi's nonviolent resistance strategies. And, meditation on and cultivation of loving-kindness is a significant practice in the Theravadin and Tibetan Buddhist traditions. We could go on. MLK knew *something* about other religions.

Yet, even if we were to agree that MLK's effusive exclamation makes for an odd ending to an Episcopal Church rationale, we can still celebrate this first-ever explicit mention of Hinduism and Buddhism in a document on interreligious relations adopted by The Episcopal Church's General Convention. Lest one think that the document closes on too "American" a note, Pierre Whalon, Bishop of the Convocation of Episcopal Churches of Europe, is unconcerned: "MLK has become universal," he notes. "The Episcopal Church stretches from Taiwan to Austria," he often notes. How does Theological Statement (2009) reflect or address the concerns of the Church of Taiwan? This is an important question to ask. "Taiwan's concern is with Buddhism," Whalon points out; "Taiwan is not so interested in Islam. This document is looking beyond the Abrahamic. It tells us how to, and that we should, deal hospitably with our Hindu or Buddhist neighbors."

Toward Credibility and Applicability

Theological Statement (2009) references a *missiological* document, but it is itself a rationale for participation in what is often called the "modern interfaith movement"—defined in Chapter One above. It has canonical weight; it is The Episcopal Church's teaching on this matter. Kurt Dunkle, who practiced law for many years before becoming a priest, brings an attorney's perspective to this document of the Church. In a conversation with me, he explained:

> In American jurisprudence, a 'treaty' with another country is considered the 'supreme law of the land.' In the hierarchy of how laws are applied, all others—federal, state and local—are subordinate to a treaty with another country. Our founding fathers believed that what we tell others—that is, foreigners—through our treaties, must have attached to them the highest degree of credibility and applicability. This assurance is that we will subordinate even our own domestic laws to the treaty we are offering the foreigner. In other words, through our treaties we are saying to our counterparties, "this is so important that we intend to live by it even when we want to pass self-governing internal laws which may be in conflict; we expect the same out of you, too!"

In interfaith dialogue, there is a rough equivalency to this concept of 'treaties.' When contemplating a deeper relationship with another expression of faith, what we tell others about ourselves should have a similar superior degree of credibility and applicability. When we begin to discuss our own faith, our statements should be treaty-like in import. In interfaith statements, we should only describe those tenants of our faith upon which we are bound, even to the exclusion of our own wayward laws and practices.

In The Episcopal Church, Resolution 2009-A074 regarding Interfaith Dialogue is such a statement. Similar to the four statements of ecclesial polity 'essential to the restoration of unity among the divided branches of Christendom' in the Chicago-Lambeth Quadrilateral of 1886 and 1888, The Episcopal Church's resolution 2009-A074 sets forth those essentials of our unique interpretation of God in Jesus Christ. No doubt *our* founding fathers, too, would urge that we be bound by the declarations of 2009-A074 as the 'supreme law of the land' of The Episcopal Church. As others will be relying upon our self-disclosure of our essentials of faith in Jesus, our own domestic law-making and practice in our use of scripture, reason and tradition[1] must conform with 2009-A074. Only through our internal fidelity to what we tell outsiders will our words have dignity.

As an official teaching, the *Theological Statement* (2009) is available on the website of The Episcopal Church, but only in English. This is problematic on two counts. First, the Diocese of Haiti is the largest diocese of The Episcopal Church—and it is francophone. Second, even if that were not the case, Church canons mandate that *all* official documents be translated into Spanish and French; if this particular document were to be translated into a third language, Whalon would recommend Mandarin. The statement has yet to be published in an engaging fashion. In advance of presentation of the *Theological Statement* to General Convention, an introductory document, *Frequently Asked Questions and Overview* was prepared. It is still available, but has not been updated to reflect changes to the document during General Convention. *Theological Statement on Interreligious Relations* (2009) would be better served now by a study guide of the sort developed for the NCCC Policy Statement: Interfaith Relations and the Churches—as was described in Chapter Two.

How well the *Theological Statement* (2009) document known in the Church? During the first three years following its adoption, it was put to use in various ways, mostly by those directly involved with authoring it. For example, in May 2010, Richard A. Burnett (rector of Trinity Episcopal Church (Columbus, Ohio) and a member of SCEIR, held a workshop on *Theological Statement* to the sisters of the Community of the Transfiguration in Cincinnati. As he explained in conversation with me in November 2011, this Order "runs a day school that is very pluralistic and interreligious in character." Having heard many people calling for a more robust interfaith experience in the daily life of the Church, he has used the *Theological Statement* in teaching his parish's

Formation and Explorers' classes, in order to help his congregants consider "essential faith statements for Episcopalians today."

In November 2011, Trinity Episcopal Church of Owensboro, Kentucky, held a forum on *Theological Statement* (2009) in conjunction with a weeklong Faith Fest which had a multireligious focus. The Episcopalians of the Tri-Faith Initiative (Omaha, Nebraska) studied it during Advent 2011, reported Tim Anderson, Canon for Episcopal Tri-Faith Ministries. Because of their unique depth of commitment to interfaith dialogue and cooperation, he explains, his congregants feel an urgency to deepen their understanding of their own faith: to be able to give account in no uncertain terms the authenticity of their interfaith efforts, and to be able answer questions about Christian doctrines of Incarnation and Trinity with confidence. The *Theological Statement* (2009), he contends, is a good resource for this.

In spite of these examples, the *Theological Statement* seems to have received rather little attention at the diocesan and congregational level during its first triennium in force. It is, of course, never to late to introduce or review it in parishes. How much attention did it received in Episcopal seminaries during its first three years? Whatever the answer, an encouraging sign came from Virginia Theological Seminary on 18 July 2012. A message posted that day on the VTS website celebrated General Convention 2012's commendation of *Theological Statement* (2009), explaining the document's relevance. It went on to announce interreligious education plans for the coming year and reiterated the seminary's commitment to interreligious dialogue as part of its educational mission.

SCEIR reported to General Convention 2012 that, during the triennium just concluding, it had "worked on implementation" of the 2009 General Convention actions. For the coming triennium, General Convention 2012 has reaffirmed "the commitment of The Episcopal Church to engage in interreligious relations." Once again, it has commended the *Theological Statement on Interreligious Relations* "to all dioceses, seminaries, congregations, and other organizations." It has encouraged "all members of the Church…to be involved actively and appropriately on every possible level in interreligious work such as, but not limited to, services, prayer groups, educational programs, community service, and study groups." Further, it has directed diocesan ecumenical and interreligious officers to "gather and report the interreligious practices in their respective dioceses" to SCEIR, so that its report in 2015 might be comprehensive.[31] If these findings can be disseminated from time to time by SCEIR in the interim, the potential for deepening the Church's involvement in interreligious relations and dialogue toward our mutual flourishing will assuredly be heightened.

As we saw in earlier chapters, The Episcopal Church has preferred to conduct interreligious relations ecumenically. Indeed, interfaith actions by ecumenical bodies have substance. The NCCC Policy Statement *Interfaith Relations and the Churches* (which was the focus of Chapter Two) is a useful document. However, in my experience, there are times when members of other religion-communities want to hear something more specific; they want to know what my particular branch of Christianity thinks. My students ask, What is The Episcopal Church's stance on religious manyness? The *Theological Statement* (2009) answers that question.

Notes

1. Paul Hedges, "A Reflection on Typologies: Negotiating a Fast-Moving Discussion," in *Christian Approaches to Other Faiths,* eds. Alan Race and Paul M. Hedges (London: SCM Press, 2008), 4.

2. *Journal of General Convention* 1973, 504–5.

3. *Journal of General Convention* 1958, 290.

4. *The Blue Book* 1997, 116.

5. Resolution 1991-A237. *Journal of General Convention*, 758.

6. *The Blue Book* 2003, 151.

7. Ian T. Douglas, *Fling Out The Banner! The National Church Ideal and the Foreign Mission of the Episcopal Church* (New York, New York: Church Hymnal Corporation, 1996), 83.

8. Douglas, 35

9. Resolution 1991-A060, "Reaffirm Commitment to Evangelism and Recognize Religious Pluralism." *Journal of General Convention*, 397.

10. The text for Marilyn Salmon's presentation can be found in the Center for Jewish-Christian Learning (St. Paul, Minnesota) 1992 Lecture Series, Vol. 7 (Spring 1992).

11. Published as *Companions in Transformation: The Episcopal Church's World Mission in a New Century* (Harrisburg, Pennsylvania: Morehouse, 2003).

12. Titus Presler, *Horizons of Mission* (Cambridge, Massachusetts: Cowley Publications, 2001), 123, 124.

13. *Companions in Transformation*, 16.

14. *Companions in Transformation,* 23. (Emphasis in the original.)

15. See http://www.tituspresler.com/global_mission/companions/index.html.

16. Titus Leonard Presler, *Going Global With God: Reconciling Mission in a World of Difference* (Morehouse, 2010), x, 58, 66.

17. Presler, *Going Global With God*, 78.

18. Previously, The Episcopal Church had the Presiding Bishop's Advisory Committee on Interfaith Relations (through 1997), and the Standing Commission on Ecumenical Relations (1997–2003). http://www.generalconvention.org/ccab/mandate/44.

19. Resolution 2006-A056, "On the Topic of Ecumenical Relations and Establishing a Basis for Interreligious Dialogue."

20. For the complete text of *Theological Statement* (2009) is provided in the Appendix.

21. For the complete text of Paul Weller's remarks, see http://www.dialoguesociety.org/download/Transcripts/Transcript-DS-Seminar-Four-Principles-of-Dialogue-Christian-Origins-by-Prof-Paul-Weller-090127.pdf. At the time of this lecture, Weller was Professor of Inter-Religious Relations, University of Derby, UK.

22. For the complete text of *Generous Love*, see http://nifcon.anglicancommunion.org/resources/generous_love/index.cfm.

23. http://nifcon.anglicancommunion.org/news/index.cfm/2008/2/7/NIFCON-launches-key-document.

24. *Lambeth Indaba: Capturing Conversations and Reflections from the Lambeth Conference 2008* (Lambeth Palace, London, 3 August 2008).

25. Katharine Jefferts Schori, *The Gospel in the Global Village: Seeking God's Dream of Shalom* (New York: Morehouse), 2009.

26. Urban T. Holmes III, *What is Anglicanism?* (Wilton, Connecticut: Morehouse-Barlow, 1982).

27. *Lambeth Indaba*, 89.

28. See particularly *Companions in Transformation* III.5, "Mission in the Conflicts of Religions and Peoples;" and IV.5, "Ecumenical and Inter-Faith Cooperation to Unify the Witness."

29. See Douglas.

30. This quotation of Martin Luther King, Jr. comes from his "Beyond Vietnam: A Time to Break Silence," a speech he gave to "Clergy and Laity Concerned" at The Riverside Church, New York City, 4 April 1967. King quotes 1 John 4:7–8, 12b to support his claim.

31. Resolution 2012-A035, "Commit to Continued Interreligious Engagement."

VI

INTERRELIGIOUS ECCLESIOLOGY

TOWARD OUR MUTUAL FLOURISHING

"Today Christianity lives and serves in a global setting in which all of God's human creation is challenged to find common ground for our mutual flourishing," notes The Episcopal Church's *Theological Statement on Interreligious Relations* (2009). Few would argue to the contrary. This reality has been assumed throughout our present study. In fact, as we saw in this book's Introduction, not just a few scholars would assert that, for Christians, the challenge of religious manyness is hardly a new state of affairs, hardly a new construction zone for theology. Rather, it is as old as Christianity itself. This chapter rehearses the grammar of thinking about this theological challenge systematically. It reviews the theological understanding latent in the interreligious-relations documents we have been scrutinizing—how theologies of manyness might categorize it, and what is distinctive about it. Finally, it considers what this may have to say about ecclesiology—about "being church" in the 21st century.

Religious Manyness—Making Meaning of the Fact

Veli-Matti Kärkkäinen defines Christian theology of religions as the attempt "to think theologically about what it means for Christians to live with people of other faiths and about the relationship of Christianity to other religions." (A Hindu theology of religions would do the same for Hinduism.) Kärkkäinen demonstrates the complexity of the Bible's teaching (in both Testaments) on the matter of Christianity's relationship to non-Christian religions. As well, he points out the "limited openness to other religions" held by certain great thinkers of the early Church.[1]

Similarly, Jesuit scholar Jacques Dupuis observes that both openness and negativity are apparent in early Church writers' assessments of aspects of the religions around them. Thus, he finds in early Church thought "an awareness of the universal and active presence of God through his Word, which is not without bearing on a theological evaluation of the religious traditions of the world."[2]

That a multireligious environment raises theological questions for Christians—this is not novel. However, these questions do seem more urgent in these early years of the 21st century. Globalization is one exacerbating factor, Kärkkäinen notes; the newfound ease of contact with and exchange between adherents of different religions—it almost goes without saying. As has been noted earlier in this discussion of The Episcopal Church's engagement with religious manyness, the patterns of emigration and immigration in the second half of the 20th century have caused new patterns of "nearness" (to return to a concept prominent in Thomas Briedenthal's thinking—prominent in Chapter Five). The new complexities of America's neighborhoods, as I have explained elsewhere, mean that in Flushing, New York, and Fremont, California—but also in Omaha, Nebraska, and Jacksonville, Florida—most of the world's religions are readily available for observation and encounter.[3] Kärkkäinen points to humanism and skepticism as two more key elements. But so is the rethinking of core Christian convictions—a process sparked by the Enlightenment which, as he describes it, has led to a shift away from dogmatic concerns, and toward "a new appreciation of the ethical life and love of neighbor as the essence of religion."[4] *Theology of religions* has wide usage as the label for the field of study out of which discussions like this come. Some prefer *theology of religious pluralism*. However, as we saw in this volume's Introduction, *pluralism's* potential for double meaning impedes its felicitousness—thus my preference for speaking of *theologies of religious manyness*.

As an academic discipline in its own right, what I am calling *theology of religious manyness* (effort to make theological sense of religious difference) is a rather recent development. Some point to the publication of John Farquhar's *The Crown of Hinduism* (1913) as its starting-point; others say it was launched by Ernst Troeltsch's essay, *The Place of Christianity Among the World Religions* (1923) and William Hocking's book *Rethinking Missions* (1932). I would point much earlier, to the great (if controversial) Anglican theologian Frederick Denison Maurice—a universal-salvationist, theologically. In his *The Religions of the World and their Relations to Christianity* (1847), Maurice expressed genuine interest in, and respect—even reverence—for each of the religions he examined and compared to Christian faith, going so far as to show what is positive, even helpful, in each. The opening of Vatican II in 1962 as the official Roman Catholic entry into this field. The World Council of Churches began to produce resources for Protestant theologies of religious manyness in 1974.[5] Since the 1980s, the stream of literature on the topic has been quite steady.

If religious manyness in itself can be bewildering, "the multiplicity and variety of [Christian] theologies of religions" can bewilder as well, notes Paul Knitter, speaking as one who has made his own significant contributions to this line of thought.[6] The mid-20th century brought the positing of systems by which to sort out the various positions taken by Christian theologians with regard to other worldviews. This sorting process is an ongoing exercise, in which theologians in the Anglican tradition have been major players.

Owen Thomas, an Episcopal priest and seminary professor, may well have devised the first formal system for sorting out theologies of religions.[7] In his *Attitudes Toward Other Religions*,[8] Thomas begins by outlining seven somewhat overlapping Christian positions on religious manyness:

a. *Truth/Falsehood:* Christianity is true; all other religions are false.

b. *Relativity:* All religions are adequate; the choice is a merely one of personal preference. (Thomas himself dismisses this as "simply not true to the facts about other religions.")[9]

c. *Essence:* All religions have something in common which allows us to call them "religion," i.e. they have the same core (which, according to some in this camp, Christianity manifests most purely and fully).

d. *Development/Fulfillment:* The history of religions has been progressive. Christianity is "religion" in its highest developmental stage (or even its final form). All other religions are "incomplete" or are examples of preliminary stage.

e. *Salvation History:* Since God is sovereign over all human history, all religions are somehow part of the "divine plan of salvation." However, Christianity is the way to "perfect salvation," thus all other religions are merely preparatory for it.

f. *Revelation/Sin:* Since God reveals Godself universally in creation, and in human reason and conscience, so all human beings have the possibility of responding positively to God's self-revelation. Many turn away, however. Religions other than Christianity are evidence of this turning-away. Into this category Thomas also places those who say: there are "the religions," on the one hand, and there is "Christianity," on the other; Christianity is not "a religion."

g. *New Departures* (i.e. positions which Thomas had noticed were emerging in the 1960s, and which did not fit well in any of his other categories): These include (1) the *Christian-presence* approach, which "expresses a way of meeting persons of other religions," but (at least as Thomas saw it in the 1960s) does not offer an interpretation of the fact of religious manyness: and, (2) the *Christian secularity* view, which defines *religion* pejoratively, thus is quite negative about *all* other religions—and about many aspects of Christianity as well.

Thomas then outlines ten theological positions with regard to other religions: Rationalism, Romanticism, Relativism, Exclusivism, Dialectic, Reconception, Tolerance, Dialogue, Catholicism, and Presence. He explains which of the attitudes in his paradigm each position draws upon, and illustrates each with excerpts from the writings of a noted Christian theologian, philosopher, or historian. Thus, *Relativism* is exemplified by Ernst Troeltsch (1865–1923). Friedrich Schleiermacher (1768–1834) is offered as an exemplar of *Romanticism*, which (with its emphasis on intuition, imagination, and God-consciousness) is an attitude toward religious manyness which draws from both "Essence" and "Development-Fulfillment" positions. In other words, the categories of the Thomas paradigm are somewhat like circles of a Venn diagram: they are distinct, but they often overlap; noticing the overlap can be fruitful.

In a recent conversation with me, Anglican priest and scholar Alan Race recalled that Owen Thomas's book was quite useful when it appeared, "and still is." However, in the main, the Thomas paradigm has lost whatever traction it once had. Why? Paul Hedges suggests two possibilities. Perhaps the Thomas model highlights differences in a way which tends to obscure similarities. Perhaps a seven-dimensional paradigm presents too many categories for today's discussion.[10]

Similarly, in an article for the journal *Buddhist-Christian Studies*, Terry Muck suggests that "Thomas's categories have not stuck…perhaps because they seem a mixture of apples and oranges, that is, a conglomeration of logical positions, emotive states, and simple demographics." Yet, Muck admits, "hodge-podge may be more true to the reality of the complex ways Christians relate to people of other faiths" than, for example, Alan Race's paradigm—to which we now come.[11]

In his *Christians and Religious Pluralism: Patterns in the Christian Theology of Religions* (1983), Alan Race introduced his own simpler, three-term paradigm by which to account for the various Christian theological approaches to other religions. This oft-cited typology offers Exclusivism, Inclusivism, and Pluralism as "three basic categories into which Christian responses to other faiths could be fitted,"[12] with soteriology as the driving concern. As it was put forth originally, *Exclusivism* is the domain of Christian theological systems which exclude non-Christians from salvation. Under this heading falls Christian insistence that "God only revealed himself through one means (Jesus) and through one tradition (Christianity)." *Inclusivism* is the domain of systems which allow that adherents of other religions are somehow included in (or, will benefit from) the economy of salvation through Christ. *Pluralism* is the domain of Christian theological systems premised on the notion that no single religion has the monopoly on salvation, nor is there any way to judge between the claims.

Alan Race's paradigm emerged from, and continues to be prominent in, Christian theological discussions. However, as numerous articles and books attest, it has also been used by scholars to sort out attitudes toward religious manyness in various other worldviews. While the exclusivist-inclusivist-pluralist paradigm remains in broad use, criticism of it has been constant and far-ranging. Perry Schmidt-Leukel details eight frequently-voiced objections to it:

1. The paradigm "has an inconsistent structure," because the exclusivist, inclusivist, and pluralist positions "are not of the same genre and do not address the same questions."

2. The paradigm is "misleading, because it obscures or misses the real issues of a theology of religions."

3. The paradigm is too narrow; more than three options exist.

4. The paradigm is too broad. Some say the only real option is exclusivism; pluralism and inclusivism are actually subtypes of it; or, that the only real option is inclusivism (pluralism and exclusivism being subtypes of it).

5. The paradigm is too coarse or too abstract. Real theologies are more complex and nuanced than it acknowledges.

6. The paradigm is misleading, because religions are just too diverse (and Race's paradigm does not account for this diversity).

7. The paradigm is offensive; the terms are too often used polemically.

8. The paradigm is pointless; none of us gets to choose these options, really.

In spite of these objections, Schmidt-Leukel insists that the paradigm still works just fine—as long as the terms are used only as he defines them—and he offers *very* explicit definitions![13] Terrence Tilley (whose ideas figured in this volume's Introduction) remarks that the Schmidt-Leukel defense of Alan Race's three-term paradigm saves it "only by making it so abstract as to be useless."[14] Paul Hedges complains that it "responds to criticisms [of the Race paradigm] by transforming a descriptive, phenomenological typology into a 'logically precise and comprehensive classification.'" The result may be logically consistent, but creates its own problems.[15]

For me, the obvious problem with the Schmidt-Leukel solution is that it relies on rigidity of definition of terms. However, language is flexible; it leaks, warps, morphs. Even when working definitions of terms are stipulated, it is nearly impossible to nail down their meanings firmly in the manner he proposes. My students will continue to hear definitions of their own choosing when I speak certain problematic terms. Moreover, I am as likely to be teaching alongside a sociologist or anthropologist as another theologian, so I prefer to use terms whose meanings hold up across disciplines. *Pluralism* is not such a term.

In response to discomfort with Alan Race's categories for sorting out Christian theologies of religious manyness, a number of alternate typologies have been proposed. Among the more interesting is Paul Knitter's four-category framework: *Replacement Model* (Only One True Religion); *Fulfillment Model* (One Fulfills the Many); *Mutuality Model* (Many True Religions Called to Dialogue); *Acceptance Model* (Many True Religions: So Be It).[16] Knitter wants us to feel attracted to insights and power of *each* of his four theological models. The label he has chosen for each is meant, he insists to be a "neutral, or nonjudgmental" reflection of what that model is about.

While Knitter admits that each of his models has its drawbacks, the *Acceptance Model* embraces "the real diversity" among religions, he says. It asserts that "the religious traditions of the world are really different, and we have to accept those differences." It does not try to uphold the superiority of any one religion, nor does it search for a simple, essential commonality. Rather, it often expresses itself in advocacy of dialogue as "a good neighbor policy". *Acceptance-Model* theologians recognize dialogue's benefits, Knitter explains, but also recognize its limitations and dangers. In order to be good neighbors to each other, each religion "needs to recognize that 'good fences make good neighbors.'" Religions by definition are boundary-setters—a point Catherine Albanese also makes in her *America: Religions & Religion*. There is no "common yard" that religions share, Knitter admits; every religion has its own backyard, and each should be left to tend its own.[17]

Knitter's *Fulfillment Model* is similar to what is called *Inclusivism* in some other systems. In fact, one insight he claims to have discerned by means of his own *Acceptance* category is that we are all Inclusivists. We can't help but view, hear, and understand the religious other from our own religious perspective. We always stand somewhere when we meet; we always start at a location when we move. No matter how open-minded we are, we assess the truth/beauty of another religion according to our (rather than their) criteria, and "include" them in the fruition we offer. We're always including the other in what we hold dear and in what we already are; there is no neutral place. By not letting the other be "other" we are being imperialist. Any common ground might actually have to be created (rather than discovered) via dialogue.[18]

For Knitter, the *Acceptance Model* contrasts with the other models in the way it regards differences. In the other categories, differences are something to be *gotten beyond*. But here, differences are just as valuable as similarities, maybe more valuable. He warns that the drive toward unity (oneness over manyness) can be dangerous. On the basis of God's otherness, the *Acceptance Model* challenges Christians to accept religious otherness and manyness.[19] This is in line with the notion that delighting in the differences, even the deepest ones, can be the basis for fruitful dialogue and collaboration.

Having heard all of this and more, Paul Hedges attempts to rehabilitate Alan Race's typology with the sharp reminder that it was designed to be *descriptive* (not *prescriptive*). It is meant to indicate the positions theologians have taken, not to specify what positions should be taken. To those who complain that the Race paradigm puts too much emphasis on salvation, Hedges counters that *salvation* is the question at the center of most theologies of religions, historically. Thus it only makes sense to sort them according to soteriological positions. And that is this typology's main purpose: to offer guidelines for sorting ideas. Further, each of its three categories always were meant as umbrella-terms, meant to name "a spectrum of approaches." So, moving forward, Hedges recommends *exclusivisms, inclusivisms, pluralisms*. Finally, he insists, the typology's categories are permeable, rather than rigid: a thinker's ideas may well straddle two or more categories. (Once again, we see something analogous to a Venn diagram.) As someone who once had the experience of being "accused" of exclusivism, then inclusivism, then pluralism in rather short order during a single one-hour interfaith roundtable discussion, I understand this last point; but it makes me all the more reluctant to use the paradigm in my teaching. Thus my preference for using *pluralism* to name a positive attitude toward the phenomenon of religious manyness rather than a soteriological position; and, my desire for other vocabulary to speak of the attitudes and projects which properly belong in the third category (*pluralism*) of Alan Race's typology—a paradigm which, I recognize, will always be hovering in the background of discussions of theologies of religious manyness.

Distinctly Episcopal

If Anglicanism (of which The Episcopal Church is an expression) brings a unique charism to the arena of interreligious relations, it is its very nature as *communio oppositorum*. That is, at its core, Anglicanism—as a Christian *via media*, at once catholic and reformed—is an ongoing attempt to hold "difference" together. There will always be a range of Anglican responses to religious manyness; what will be decidedly *Anglican* will be the effort to hold together these diverse answers. Yet the Anglican approach does have its own character. This given, what might we say is *distinctly Episcopal* in the interreligious activity of The Episcopal Church since the World's Parliament of Religions (Chicago 1893)? What can be discerned from our close readings of the interreligious-relations documents emerged from or have been embraced by The Episcopal Church since the release of *Guidelines for Christian-Jewish Relations* (1988)?

We might begin by noting that Anglicanism takes a high, but measured, view of the Bible. Like all Anglicans, Episcopalians hear vast quantities of Scripture during public worship. Episcopal teaching embraces the Anglican notion that the Bible contains all things necessary to salvation—but that not everything contained in the Bible is necessary to salvation. Scripture is the human record of God's revelation, and its authority is moderated by tradition and reason. It is interesting, therefore, to evaluate the incorporation of scripture into the Church's interfaith documents. We see that its *Theological Statement* (2009) makes significantly more use of biblical texts to underscore its argument than its direct predecessors, the 1988 *Guidelines* and the 1994 *Principles*. Neither of these earlier documents contains direct biblical citations. The decision to use more scripture in *Theological Statement* (2009) was influenced by the NCCC Policy Statement (1999), which was laden with biblical material;[20] even more so, a cue was taken from the NIFCON report, *Generous Love*. The 1988 and 1994 documents are rather short; perhaps that is a factor in their lack of quotations of scripture. However, *On Waging Reconciliation* (2001) is also quite short; yet it quotes Colossians, Deuteronomy, and Romans. Because it responds to a Muslim document laden with references to and quotations of Qur'ān and Bible, *Renewing Our Pledge* (2008) is enthusiastically biblical, incorporating at least nineteen direct quotations into its text.[21] It would seem that, in the 21st century, The Episcopal Church is learning to be more explicitly biblical when mounting a theological argument.

In the interfaith documents of The Episcopal Church, some characteristically Anglican attitudes toward certain theological themes are discernible with varying degrees of emphasis, depending on a document's character and purpose. I shall comment on six.

1. For Episcopalians, striving toward positive interreligious relations is a direct consequence of the Baptismal Covenant. The major documents presented in the preceding five chapters all were crafted after a major revision of the Book of Common Prayer became canonical in 1979. With this revision came the addition of a Baptismal Covenant to the rite of initiation. This item has become central to Episcopal theological reflection. *Companions in Transformation* (2003),

Renewing Our Pledge (2008), and the *Theological Statement on Interreligious Relations* (2009) make direct mention of it.

Episcopalians are heir to the notion that praying shapes believing, as we have said. The corollary to this is that what is said in liturgy should be observable in a worshiping community's behavior beyond it. As explained in this volume's Introduction, Episcopalians reaffirm the Baptismal Covenant[22] at various points throughout the liturgical year. Catechetical in form, the Covenant begins with affirmation of belief in the classical Christian doctrines enshrined in the Apostles' Creed. The congregation then is asked a series of questions about faith-in-action, and answers each question by saying, "I will, with God's help." This is the vehicle by which Episcopalians promise, among other things, to seek and serve the face of Christ in all persons, loving their neighbor as themselves; they promise to "strive for justice and peace among all people, and respect the dignity of every human being." Several Episcopal documents, therefore, rest on a notion that conduct of positive interfaith relations is an action stemming from core Episcopal-Christian identity. Given the promises made and reaffirmed through the Baptismal Covenant, witness is an interfaith concern and practice—but so is the practice of hospitality and mutuality. Since, in their several ways, all six documents cast dialogue in terms of authentic mutual witness, it should be clear that The Episcopal Church sees in interreligious dialogue the potential for (even the likelihood of) deepening one's own faith.

Directly related to the Baptismal Covenant is the prominence of neighbor-love as a theme of interreligious relations; a corollary is the Ninth Commandment's mandate not to bear false witness against one's neighbor. See, for example, the *Preface to Guidelines for Christian-Jewish Relations* (1988), which mentions this directly; see also, *Renewing Our Pledge* (2008). The Ninth Commandment's relation to interfaith matters is prominent in The Episcopal Church's efforts to address anti-Judaism. It is latent in the fact that, in the statements most directly related to Islam and Muslims, there is no hint of the Islamophobic rhetoric so prominent in certain streams of US culture during the past decade.

Mentioned in the NCCC Policy Statement, the biblical theme of neighbor-love is foundational to Section III of *Guidelines for Christian-Jewish Relations* (1988), which addresses hatred and persecution of Jews as "a continuing concern." In *Principles for Interfaith Dialogue* (1994) this theme informs the directive to "approach others with the same kind of respect we would wish to be accorded." It is developed to the greatest degree in *Renewing Our Pledge* and in the 2009 *Theological Statement.* Closely related to love of neighbor is the inclusion in several of the documents of advice against (if not outright condemnation of) proselytism.

As a close reading of the documents assembled for this study will reveal, a connection to baptism is made in the development of each of the remaining themes on which I am focusing here.

2. **Anglican radical incarnationalism—characteristic of Anglican theology, and prominent in Episcopal thinking—has direct consequences for interfaith relations.** Since at least the nineteenth century, Anglican theologians have labored to foreground from earlier Christian thought the notion of the centrality of the Incarnation. *Anglican radical incarnationalism* embraces the notion that, as Urban Holmes puts it, "even if humanity had never sinned, God [still] would have become flesh."[23] Radical incarnationalism implies, among other things, that, since God created everything that is, the material world is good. It means that the Incarnation encompasses all aspects of life—including life's pain, ambiguity, evil, the entirety of human experience. It reminds us that Christ is the transformer, not the projection, of culture.[24] A close reading of The Episcopal Church's legacy of interreligious relations documents indicates that, as this Church's theology of religious manyness has taken shape over the past half-century, it has always been radically incarnational and has become increasingly clearly so. For example, the pastoral letter *On Waging Reconciliation* asserts that, through Christ, God's "radical act of peace-making is nothing less than the right ordering of all things according to God's passionate desire for justness, *for the full flourishing of humankind and all creation.*"[25]

3. **In Episcopal thought, the doctrine of Creation is about God's will for what is, rather than an explanation of how all things came to be.** Thus Episcopalians take seriously the notion that all human beings are made in God's image and after God's likeness. This is embedded in the Baptismal Covenant, as explained above. The consequence for interfaith relations is the discernment that diversity is a good. We saw in Chapter Three how Thomas Breidenthal's Neighbor-Christology offers a way forward in the celebration of difference.

4. **Closely related, then, to themes of Creation, is pneumatology.** In this regard, we have heard the Episcopal documents speak of God-on-the-move, or pondering "what God is up to" in the world. This is especially in the foreground of the missiological statement *Companions in Transformation* (2003). The pneumatological language in both *Renewing Our Pledge* (2008) and the *Theological Statement* (2009) make use of the poetic language regarding the activity of the Holy Spirit found in Lambeth 1988's *Christ and People of Other Faiths*, and this move us directly into themes of soteriology and eschatology.

5. Reconciliation—a much-used term and notion in the interfaith documents of The Episcopal Church—is the rubric under which come Episcopal soteriological and eschatological teachings. Reconciliation is a notion foundational to the *Guidelines for Christian-Jewish Relations* (1988). The NCCC Policy Statement (1999) devotes paragraphs 31–35 to the theme of reconciliation, saying, "Through Jesus Christ, Christians believe God offers reconciliation to all." Presiding Bishop Griswold's September 2001 sermon declares: "God's compassion, God's mercy, God's loving kindness, God's fierce bonding love is the active principle that effects reconciliation: the gathering up of all things into a unity in which difference is both honored and reconciled in the fullness of God's ever creative imagination."[26]

Christian understandings of salvation are given special attention in the 2009 *Theological Statement*, but are also particularly clear in the NCCC Policy Statement (1999) and in *On Waging Reconciliation* (2001). A related theme, that God is at work in all of creation (thus that God's gracious love is not limited to the Christian community) can be found in all of these documents—vigorously so in most of them. While individual Episcopalians can be found at every node on the gamut from particularism to universalism, the official documents lean toward universalism. "In any event, it is God who converts people," says *Principles for Interfaith Dialogue* (1994).

Salvation happens through Christ—Episcopal documents are clear about this, but *exactly how this happens* is not spelled out. There are parallels in Anglican attitudes toward the Eucharist which acknowledge the mystery, but prefer not to get caught up in arguments over whether transubstantiation is involved: "Thou art here, we ask not how," asserts one Eucharistic hymn.[27] Similarly, we see a leaning toward the notion that God is at least as generous in salvation as in creation. Eschatologically, we live in the "already but not yet." Our efforts at reconciliation can be seen as attempts to make real in the here-and-now the future perfection God has accomplished already through Christ. We dare to hope that God is drawing all of creation back to Godself through Christ. It should be clear that The Episcopal Church's teaching on interreligious relations encourages Episcopalians to "offer our gifts for the carrying out of God's ongoing work of reconciliation" toward our mutual flourishing.[28]

6. **Episcopal teaching is unabashedly Trinitarian.** Without doubt, the Trinitarian underlay can be discerned in each public statement examined here. The NCCC Policy Statement (1999) and *Renewing Our Pledge* (2008) are quite overt in this regard. While Trinitarian imagery may not be most helpful when in direct conversation with someone of another religion, I am convinced that Trinitarian theology offers abundant resources for understanding and celebrating religious diversity as a good.

An article by Dwight Zscheile, published near the time of the approval of The Episcopal Church's *Theological Statement on Interreligious Relations* (2009), provides some thinking on the intersection of ecclesiology and the doctrine of the Trinity which, it seems to me, has implications for interreligious relations. Zscheile argues that Episcopal mission should be reframed "in a more theological and Trinitarian direction using themes of communion, companionship, creativity, and cultivation."[29] It seems to me that something similar could be encouraged regarding interreligious relations.

Zscheile draws directly on Orthodox discussions of the doctrine of the Trinity in social terms—in which otherness and diversity are to be celebrated as integral to creation, rather than looked on as cause for concern and division.[30] The interfaith implications of this conclusion seem obvious. Zscheile calls on The Episcopal Church to move "toward a more apostolic, Trinitarian community in which otherness flourishes within God's outward-reaching (*ekstasis*) movement toward all creation."[31] I wonder: Might an interfaith ecclesiology also do this? Zscheile says that if The Episcopal Church were to imagine its mission in more thoroughly Trinitarian terms, it would place more emphasis on mutuality, interdependence, and reciprocity. That is very much what is meant when the great Buddhist teacher-activist Thích Nhất Hạnh says "we inter-are."[32] We might swap *interreligious bridge-building* for mission here. Church conduct of interreligious relations with "stress on mutuality, interdependence, and reciprocity" would be welcomed by many leaders of other religion-communities.

Zscheile calls for fresh attention to the theological principle of participation in the Triune God's life. Taking this into the realm of interreligious relations (and paraphrasing Zscheile somewhat, as I do), I suggest that manifesting the reality of having been made in the Triune God's image and after the Triune God's likeness requires that we strive "to live in deep, right-ordered relationship with God and all of creation;" and that "all of creation" includes our neighbors whose religious convictions and communities differ from ours.[33]

Marjorie Suchocki is helpful here. She argues that the Christian doctrine of the Trinity implies that God's very essence encompasses irreducible difference. Therefore, diversity is eternal. This being the case, she asserts: "then surely religions themselves are irreducibly different." Since, in Christian understanding, all of humanity is made in the image and likeness of God, all of humanity models the Trinity! If this be so, then the implication is that each religious tradition "must remain true to itself, essentially unlike the others, even as it continues its living development." Human beings "are called to become community together not by negotiating our differences, suppressing our differences, or by converting from our differences, but in and through our differences."[34]

In sum, we can say that, for at least the past two decades, Episcopal Church interreligious-relations theology has been quite clearly radically incarnational. It affirms that God is no less generous in salvation than in creation, that God is somehow drawing all of creation back to Godself through Christ. Trinitarian emphasis on mutuality, interdependence, and reciprocity has implications for love of neighbor, for embassy, for hospitality. As interfaith leader Samir Selmanovic puts it: "On our intercommunicating and interdependent planet...Our lives are intertwined, and our future hangs on our ability to set our eyes higher than peaceful coexistence." We need, he says, to "learn to *thrive* interdependently."[35]

We have considered several paradigms for sorting out Christian theologies of religious manyness. Where in these schemes might The Episcopal Church's theology of interreligious relations be located? With regard to the Owen Thomas model, we might say that the Church's official statements express elements of what he calls the *Christian-presence* approach, in that they often express "a way of meeting persons of other religions" without offering an interpretation of the fact of religious manyness. They also express characteristics of his Essence position, in that an underlying assumption for all of these documents is that Judaism, Islam, Hinduism, Buddhism, and so on do share a common "something;" or, conversely, that Christianity shares the category *religion* with them. There is no quibbling over the rightness or the sharing of that category. Further, they express elements of his Revelation/Sin position—in their affirmation that God reveals Godself universally in creation.

With regard to the Alan Race paradigm, The Episcopal Church's official thinking is most definitely some form of *inclusivism*. As for Paul Knitter's framework, his *Acceptance Model* offers a good description of what is at play in The Episcopal Church's public statements. Under the *Acceptance Model's* banner fall theologies of religious manyness which attempt to achieve balance between universality and particularity. Theologies under this rubric try to avoid putting so much stress on "the particularity of one religion that the validity of all the others is jeopardized." At the same time, they try to avoid placing so much emphasis on the validity of all religions that "real particular difference" is obscured. Rather, *Acceptance Model* theologies assert "the real diversity of all faiths"—those which acknowledge that "the religious traditions of the world are really different, and we have to accept those differences."[36] For the most part, this is an apt description of The Episcopal Church's interreligious relations attitudes of the past half-century.

Interfaith Relations as Social Teaching

Writing in 1990, Robert Hood strove to demonstrate that, indeed, The Episcopal Church does have *social teachings*—defined as "theological ideas and models formulated by the church's hierarchy intended to govern and influence the shaping of public policy, private conduct, and private thinking in the social arena."[37] Hood investigated what authoritative Episcopal Church sources had to offer on four topics: peace and war; race; marriage and family life; and, the economy. Intrigued by his framing of the topic, I ask: Should not "interreligious relations" be listed among the categories of church social teachings? I insist that it should.

If interreligious relations be a category of Episcopal social teachings, then what theological ideas and models has The Episcopal Church formulated in the hope of governing and influencing public policy, private conduct, and private thinking with regard to individuals and groups who embrace some other religion? We have seen such ideas and models in each chapter of this book. To an extent, social teachings are the Church's "public relations voice," but also an articulation of the Church's vision.[38] *On Waging Reconciliation* exemplifies Episcopal Church social teaching in that sense. Christian social teachings, Hood observes, are an effort "to portray a theological vision and to establish boundaries and limits from a Christian perspective as to what can be called legitimate public and private conduct for [this branch of] Christians." Following Hood, I have asked whether there is a particularly Episcopal way of setting guidelines and boundaries in forming criteria for interreligious interaction.[39] *Guidelines for Christian-Jewish Relations* (1988) and the *Theological Statement* (2009) show us that way.

Practicality

For both the NCCC and The Episcopal Church little money for interfaith programming has been available during the past several decades; neither institution has been able to mount very many large-scale conferences or consultations, let alone ongoing upper-level interreligious dialogues. However, the crafting of formal guidelines and rationales actually may be more useful and longer lasting. *Theological Statement on Interreligious Relations*, like its predecessors *Guidelines* (1988) and *Principles* (1994), includes practical strategies; they can be useful years after their delivery. However, they are useful only to the extent action is informed by them. These documents beg to be used. They can provide a basis for action that is purposeful, directive, not haphazard. They also warn that interfaith work requires preparation; and that includes our own self-preparation.

A criticism which may be leveled at all of the documents surveyed in this book is that they result from a process in which they are vetted only by people who already share the assumptions of their authors. The Christian-Muslim relations documents in particular raise an important question: Is it possible for a single document to do three things at once:

- Empower those Christians who are ready to try positive relationship building,

- Placate or comfort those who come to the table filled with hurt and anger,

- Assure those on the other side of the table that Episcopalians are ready and willing to work together with them for the common good because we are Christians (not in spite of that fact)?

In critiquing these documents, we might by now have noticed their range in style. The process by which documents are formulated, written, and approved is very different in The Episcopal Church from that of NIFCON or Lambeth Palace, on the one hand, or the NCCC Commission on Interfaith Relations on the other. The process of getting a resolution through General Convention is not as conducive to the crafting of elegant prose as is the case with NIFCON, Lambeth Palace, and the NCCC. Eloquent prose is memorable and convincing; it can "preach." So I yearn for Episcopal interfaith documents to be more poetic even as I realize that such rhetoric draws criticism for being obscure, as we saw in Chapter Four.

A final practical point is this: throughout the past half-century, The Episcopal Church's public statements testify to a preference for what Kusumita Pedersen has called "Abrahamic exclusivism." In official interfaith work by Christian bodies, she notes, "Christian ecumenism comes first, followed by relations with the Jews and then with Islam. After that comes 'everyone else.'" In fact, the documents we have studied notwithstanding, the practical and programmatic attention of the The Episcopal Church to interfaith concerns has been rather limited. Attention to Judaism has outpaced attention to any other bilateral interreligious dialogue. "Dialogue and cooperation among the Abrahamic faiths are not only of great intrinsic importance but are also essential to interfaith work's ultimate goals of global peace and understanding," Pedersen admits. "They should be pursued, however," she stresses, "without regarding the non-Abrahamic religious traditions as inferior or their issues as of little consequence."[40] The most recent teaching of The Episcopal Church would seem to be in agreement with her assessment. If the Church were to move officially beyond Abrahamic engagement, what forms might that take?

During the 1990s and the first half-decade of the 21ˢᵗ century, David Eckel, an authority on Buddhism and Christian-Buddhist dialogue,[41] represented The Episcopal Church on the NCCC Interfaith Commission and served on the Church's own various interfaith task forces as well. In both venues, Eckel called repeatedly for more attention to the dharmic religions. To date, only minimal action has been taken. Tarunjit Singh Butalia of the World Sikh Council–America Region was included among the inter-religious guests of the 2006 General Convention, for example. By contrast, beginning in 2006, the US Conference of Catholic Bishops held several Sikh-Catholic National Retreats, with interesting results. The Episcopal Church has ample expertise in its midst for the conduct of fruitful dialogue with America's dharmic religion-communities.

In the essay, from which I derive the term *religious manyness,* Catherine Albanese reminds us that America's "original manyness" comprises some 550 indigenous societies with diverse languages, customs, concepts of the divine, and so on.[42] Some of these religion-communities persist, and are part of the complexity of multireligious America. Some members of these communities are devout Episcopalians. Adding to America's religious manyness are the adherents of various earth-based religions with roots in Europe. Grassroots interreligious councils and projects often include these communities. They are willing partners in the service of caring for creation—which has been a major concern of a Church which claims Celtic spirituality as part of its heritage. To what extent have Native and other earth-based communities been included in, or addressed by, official Episcopal Church interreligious efforts? The Episcopal Church has an Office of Native American/Indigenous Ministries which works on full inclusion of Native and Indigenous peoples in the life and leadership of the Church. What intersections have occurred between its efforts and the efforts of the other offices and Standing Commissions we have met in the foregoing discussion? The official documents analyzed herein do not tell us; but this is a topic deserving study.

Ecclesiology

In blogging about the proper name for the church he serves, Mark Harris, of the Diocese of Delaware, notes that "we may have been 'formerly' known as ECUSA…but that was never what we were 'formally' known as." The preferred title is "The Episcopal Church"—as we have called it throughout this book. As we made clear in the Introduction, this is a multinational church, with an institutional presence in some sixteen countries. Its headquarters is in the US; so, we may say that this church is in the USA, but not of it. Harris asks, "If we are an international church then to what extent are we willing to look again at what it means to be 'in' and not 'of the United States of America?"[43] I join him in asking that question as it bears upon interreligious relations.

In other words, for The Episcopal Church, next steps in theology of religious manyness ought to be tied closely to questions of ecclesiology. "It is certainly true that The Episcopal Church comes across as precisely an American church institution even while claiming to be international in scope," Harris notes. "Our claim to be an international church is quite appropriate, but only to the extent that we take seriously the breadth of engagement possible in such a church." I agree. It would, for example, be interesting to research how well the *Theological Statement on Interreligious Relations* speaks to and for the interfaith concerns of Episcopalians in the fifteen nations beyond the US in which The Episcopal Church is present institutionally. In doing so, it would be important to ask where the document speaks helpfully to Episcopalians in this place and where it falls short. We know from NIFCON meetings and consultations that the twin themes of embassy and hospitality as a strategy for interreligious relations are heard quite differently in Pakistan and Nigeria than they are in the US and the UK. What themes or turns of phrase in *Theological Statement* (2009) work well in Taiwan or Italy? Which are dissonant? When it comes to interreligious relations, our claim to be international will have more credibility if our next interreligious relations documents reflect on our multinational-ness boldly. If they can succeed in doing so, they will contribute vitally toward our mutual flourishing.

Notes

1. Veli-Matti Kärkkäinen, *An Introduction to the Theology of Religions: Biblical, Historical & Contemporary Perspectives* (Downers Grove, Illinois: InterVarsity Press Academic, 2003), 55ff.
2. Jacques Dupuis, *Toward a Christian Theology* (Maryknoll, New York: Orbis, 2002), 68.
3. See Lucinda Mosher, *Belonging* (New York: Seabury Books, 2005).
4. Kärkkäinen, 19.
5. Such WCC publications include *Living Faiths and Ultimate Goals* (1974); *Towards World Community: Resources and Responsibilities for Living Together* (1975)–both edited by Stanley J. Samartha.
6. Paul Knitter, *Introducing Theologies of Religions* (Maryknoll, New York: Orbis, 2002).
7. Paul Hedges suggests this in his "A Reflection on Typologies: Negotiating a Fast-Moving Discussion," Chapter Two in Alan Race & Paul M. Hedges, *Christian Approaches to Other Faiths* (London: SCM Press, 2008), 25.
8. Owen C. Thomas, *Attitudes Toward Other Religions* (SCM, 1969). An Episcopal priest, Thomas taught at Episcopal Divinity School 1952–1993. In an email exchange during the spring of 2012, Thomas recalled that his interest in general questions concerning religious diversity was informed by the fact that his mother was the Director of the League of Nations Association (forerunner of the United Nations Association), and she had often spoken or written on these issues.
9. Thomas explains further that relativism may be cultural (i.e. each religion is an appropriate expression of its culture); or epistemological (i.e. having to do with viewpoints about the origin, nature, limits, and methods of human knowledge—thus one cannot know absolute truth, only truth for oneself); or teleological (i.e. having to do with ultimate purpose, thus seeing all religions as different paths to the same goal).
10. Paul Hedges, "A Reflection on Typologies," 17.
11. Terry Muck, "Instrumentality, Complexity, and Reason: A Christian Approach to Religions," *Buddhist-Christian Studies* 22 (2002): 115–21.
12. Alan Race, *Christians in Religious Pluralism: Patterns in the Christian Theology of Religions* (London: SCM Press, 1983). Thomas would return to the topic of theologies of religious manyness in 1991, while in residence at the Rockefeller Foundation Conference and Study Center at Bellagio, Italy. The result would be an essay in which he argues that all Pluralist views reduce to a form of Inclusivism. See his "Religious Plurality and Contemporary Philosophy: A Critical Survey," in *Harvard Theological Review* 87, no. 2 (1994): 197–213.
13. Perry Schmidt-Leukel, "Exclusivism, Inclusivism, Pluralism: The Tripolar Typology—Clarified and Reaffirmed," in *The Myth of Religious Superiority: Multifaith Explorations of Religious Pluralism*, ed. Paul F. Knitter (Maryknoll, New York: Orbis, 2005), 18–22.
14. Terrence W. Tilley, *Religious Diversity and the American Experience: A Theological Approach* (New York: Continuum, 2007), xii.
15. Paul Hedges, "A Reflection on Typologies," 23, 24.
16. Paul Knitter, *Introducing Theologies of Religions.*
17. Catherine Albanese, *America: Religions & Religion*, 4th ed. (Belmont, California: Thomson Wadsworth, 2007), 4ff. Paul Knitter, *Introducing Theologies of Religions*, 183.
18. Knitter, 218.

19. Knitter, 219–21.

20. Some 23 Bible passages are cited in the NCCCUSA Policy Statement, which draws from Genesis, Psalms, Amos; Matthew, Luke, John, Acts, Romans, 1 & 2 Corinthians, Colossians, James. It also quotes Hebrews 13:2, but without attribution; there is also allusion to Exodus, Joshua, and Ruth specifically, and to the entirety of the Hebrew Scriptures generally.

21. Passages are quoted from Genesis, Exodus, Isaiah, Micah, Matthew, Luke, Acts, Romans, Galatians, and Philippians. The document also excerpts the canticle *Dignus es*, the text for which is derived from Revelation, and can be found in the 1979 Book of Common Prayer, 93–94.

22. Again, for the Baptismal Covenant text, see the 1979 Book of Common Prayer, 304f.

23. Urban T. Holmes, *What Is Anglicanism?* (Wilton, Connecticut: Morehouse-Barlow, 1982), 28. Throughout chapter four, "The Incarnation," Holmes draws attention to what others, particularly William Porcher DuBose, have said in this regard.

24. In addition to Holmes, see Carl P. Daw, Jr., "The Spirituality of Anglican Hymnody: A Twentieth-Century American Perspective," in *The Hymnal 1982 Companion*, Volume One, ed., Raymond F. Glover (New York: The Church Hymnal Corporation, 1994), 11.

25. *On Waging Reconciliation* (2001). (Emphasis mine.) See Appendix for full text.

26. For Griswold's sermon text, see Appendix.

27. See "Lord, enthroned in heavenly splendor," Stanza 2: No. 307 in *Hymnal 1982*.

28. *On Waging Reconciliation.*

29. Dwight J. Zscheile, "Beyond Benevolence: Toward a Reframing of Mission in the Episcopal Church," *Journal of Anglican Studies* 8, no. 1 (2009): 83.

30. Zscheile, 96. See, for example, John Zizioulas, *Communion and Otherness* (London: T&T Clark, 2006).

31. Zscheile, 96.

32. Thích Nhất Hạnh, Being Peace (Berkeley, California: Parallax Press, 1987), 87.

33. Zscheile, 100.

34. Marjorie Hewitt Suchocki, *Divinity & Diversity: A Christian Affirmation of Religious Pluralism* (Nashville, Tennessee: Abingdon Press, 2003), 16.

35. Samir Selmanovic, *It's Really All About God: How Islam, Atheism, and Judaism Made Me a Better Christian* (New York: Jossey-Bass, 2011), 18–19.

36. Knitter, 173.

37. Robert E. Hood, *Social Teachings in the Episcopal Church* (Morehouse, 1990), ix.

38. Hood, 1–2.

39. Hood, 3.

40. Kusumita P. Pedersen, "The Interfaith Movement: An Incomplete Assessment," *Journal of Ecumenical Studies* 41, no. 1 (Winter 2004): 91.

41. Malcolm David Eckel is Professor of Religion at Boston University. His publications include *Buddhism: Origins, Beliefs, Practices, Holy Texts, Sacred Places* (New York: Oxford University Press, 2002).

42. Albanese, *America: Religions & Religion*, 24ff.

43. Mark Harris, "What's in a Name?" *Preludium*, 4/17/2007. http://anglicanfuture.blogspot.com/2007/04/whats-in-name.html. Last accessed: 26 July 2012.

APPENDIX

Guidelines for Christian-Jewish Relations
For use in The Episcopal Church
General Convention of The Episcopal Church
July, 1988[‡]

Preface to the Guidelines

One of the functions of the Christian-Jewish dialogue is to allow participants to describe and witness to their faith in their own terms. This is of primary importance since self-serving descriptions of other people's faiths are among the roots of prejudice, stereotyping and condescension. Careful listening to each other's expression of faith enables Christians to obey better the commandment not to bear false witness against their neighbors. Partners in dialogue must recognize that any religion or ideology which claims universality will have its own interpretations of other religions and ideologies as part of its own self-understanding. Dialogue gives the opportunity for mutual questioning of those understandings. A reciprocal willingness to listen, learn and understand enables significant dialogue to grow.

I. Principles of Dialogue
The following principles are offered to aid and encourage the Episcopal Church to make an increasingly vital and substantive impact on the dialogue.

1. In all dialogue, recognition of marked cultural differences is important. The words employed in religious discussion are not innocent or neutral. Partners in dialogue may rightly question both the language and the definitions each uses in articulating religious matters.

2. In the case of Christian-Jewish dialogue, an historical and theological imbalance is obvious. While an understanding of Judaism in New Testament times is an indispensable part of any Christian theology, for Jews a "theological" understanding of Christianity is not of the same significance. Yet neither Judaism nor Christianity, at least in the Western world, has developed without interaction with the other.

3. The relations between Jews and Christians have unique characteristics, since Christianity historically emerged out of early Judaism. Christian understanding of that process constitutes a necessary part of the dialogue and gives urgency to the enterprise. As Christianity came to define its own identity in relation to Judaism, the Church developed interpretations, definitions and terms for those things it had inherited from Jewish traditions. It also developed its own understanding of the Scriptures common to Jews and Christians. In the process of defining itself, the Church produced its own definition of God's acts of salvation. It should not be surprising that Jews resent those scriptural and theological interpretations in which they are assigned negative roles. Tragically, such patterns of thought have led Christians to overt acts of condescension,

---

[‡]   Used with permission from The Archives of The Episcopal Church.

prejudice and even violent acts of persecution. In the face of those acts, a profound sense of penitence is the necessary response.

4. Many Christians are convinced that they understand Judaism since they have the Hebrew Scriptures as part of their Bible. This attitude is often reinforced by a lack of knowledge about the history of Jewish life and thought through the 1900 years since Christianity and Judaism parted ways.

5. There is, therefore, a special urgency for Christians to listen, through study and dialogue, to ways in which Jews understand their own history, their Scriptures, their traditions, their faith and their practice. Furthermore, a mutual listening to the way each is perceived by the other can be a step toward understanding the hurts, overcoming the fears, and correcting the misunderstandings that have separated us throughout the centuries.

6. Both Judaism and Christianity contain a wide spectrum of opinions, theologies, and styles of life and service. Since generalizations often produce stereotyping, Jewish-Christian dialogue must try to be as inclusive of the variety of views within the two communities as possible.

II. The Necessity for Christians to Understand Jews and Judaism

1. Through dialogue with Jews, many, though yet too few, Christians have come to appreciate the richness and vitality of Jewish faith and life in the Covenant and have been enriched in their own understandings of Jesus and the divine will for all creatures.

2. In dialogue with Jews, Christians have learned that the actual history of Jewish faith and experience does not match the images of Judaism that have dominated a long history of Christian teaching and writing, images that have been spread by Western culture and literature into other parts of the world.

3. Jesus was a Jew, born into the Jewish tradition. He was nurtured by the Hebrew Scriptures of his day, which he accepted as authoritative and interpreted both in terms of the Judaism of his time and in fresh and powerful ways in his life and teaching, announcing that the Kingdom of God was at hand. In their experience of his resurrection, his followers confessed him as both Lord and Messiah.

4. Christians should remember that some of the controversies reported in the New Testament between Jesus and the "scribes and Pharisees" found parallels within Pharisaism itself and its heir, Rabbinic Judaism. The controversies generally arose in a Jewish context, but when the words of Jesus came to be used by Christians who did not identify with the Jewish people as Jesus did, such sayings often became weapons in anti-Jewish polemics and thereby their original intention was tragically distorted. An internal Christian debate has been taking place for some years now about how to understand and explain passages in the New Testament that contain anti-Jewish references.

5. From the early days of the Church, many Christian interpreters saw the Church replacing Israel as God's people. The destruction of the Second Temple of Jerusalem was understood as a warrant for this claim. The Covenant of God with the people of Israel was seen only as a preparation for the coming of Jesus. As a consequence, the Covenant with Israel was considered to be abrogated.

6. This theological perspective has had fateful consequences. As Christians understood themselves to replace the Jews as God's people, they often denigrated the Judaism that survived as a fossilized religion of legalism. The Pharisees were thought to represent the height of that legalism; Jews and Jewish groups were portrayed as negative models; and the truth and beauty of Christianity were thought to be enhanced by setting up Judaism as false and ugly. Unfortunately, many of the early Church fathers defamed the Jewish people.

7. Through a renewed study of Judaism and in dialogue with Jews, Christians have become aware that Judaism in the time of Jesus was in but an early stage of its long life. Under the leadership of the Pharisees, the Jewish people began a spiritual revival of remarkable power, which gave them the vitality capable of surviving the catastrophe of the loss of the Temple. It gave birth to Rabbinic Judaism, which produced the Talmud, and built the structures for a strong and creative life through the centuries.

8. Judaism is more than the religion of the Scriptures of Israel (called by Christians the Old Testament and by Jews the Hebrew Scriptures or the Hebrew Bible). The Talmud and other later writings provide interpretations that for much of Judaism are central and authoritative with the Torah.

9. For Christians, the Bible (that is, the two Testaments) is also followed by traditions for interpretation, from the Church Fathers to the present time. Thus, both Judaism and Christianity are nurtured by their Scriptures, scriptural commentaries and living and developing traditions.

10. Christians as well as Jews look to the Hebrew Bible as the record of God's election of and covenant with God's people. For Jews, it is their own story in historical continuity with the present. Christians, mostly of gentile background since early in the life of the Church, believe themselves to have entered this Covenant by grace through Jesus Christ. The relationship between the two communities, both worshipping the God of ancient Israel, is a given historical fact, but how it is to be understood and explained theologically is a matter of internal discussion among Christians and Jews in dialogue.

11. What Jews and Christians have in common needs to be examined as carefully as their differences. Finding in the Scriptures the faith sufficient for salvation, the Christian Church shares Israel's trust in the One God, whom the Church knows in the Spirit as the God and Father of the Lord Jesus Christ. For Christians, Jesus Christ is acknowledged as the only begotten of the Father, through whom millions have come to share in the love of, and to adore, the God who first made covenant with the people of Israel. Knowing the One God in Jesus Christ through the Spirit, therefore, Christians worship One God with a trinitarian confession involving creation, incarnation, and pentecost. In so doing, the Church worships in a language that is strange to Jewish worship and sensitivities, yet full of meaning to Christians. Dialogue is a means to help clarify language and to lead to the grasp of what the participants are really saying.

12. Christians and Jews both believe that God has created men and women and has called them to be holy and to exercise stewardship over the creation in accountability to God. Jews and Christians are taught by their Scriptures and traditions to recognize their responsibility to their neighbors, especially the weak, the poor, and the oppressed. In various and distinct ways they look for the coming of the Kingdom of God. In dialogue with Jews, many Christians have come

to a more profound appreciation of the Exodus hope of liberation, praying and working for the coming of justice and peace on earth.

13. Jews found ways of living in obedience to Torah both before and after the emergence of Christianity. They maintained and deepened their call to be a distinctive people in the midst of the nations. Jews historically were allowed to live with respect and acceptance in some of the cultures in which they resided. Here their life and values thrived and made a distinct contribution to their Christian and Muslim neighbors. It is a sad fact, however, that Jews living in Christian countries have not fared better than those in non-Christian countries.

14. The land of Israel and the city of Jerusalem have always been central to the Jewish people. "Next year in Jerusalem" is a constant theme of Jewish worship in the diaspora. The continued presence of Jews in that land and in Jerusalem is a focal point for Judaism and must be taken into account in dialogue.

15. Many Jews differ in their interpretations of the religious and secular meaning of the State of Israel. For almost all Jewish people, however, Israel is an integral part of their identity.

16. Jews, Christians and Muslims have all maintained a presence in that land for centuries. The land is holy to all three, though each may understand holiness in different ways.

17. The existence of the State of Israel is a fact of history (see General Convention Resolution affirming "the right of Israel to exist as a free state within secure borders," *Convention Journal* 1979, p. C-104. However, the quest for homeland status by Palestinians—Christian and Muslim—is a part of their search for identity also, and must be addressed together with the need for a just and lasting solution to the conflict in the Middle East.

III. Hatred and Persecution of Jews—A Continuing Concern

1. Christians need to be aware that hatred and persecution of Jews have a long, persistent history. This is particularly true in countries where Jews have been a minority presence among Christians. The tragic history of the persecution of Jews includes massacres by the Crusaders, the Inquisition, pogroms and the Holocaust. The World Council of Churches Assembly at its first meeting in Amsterdam in 1948 declared: "We call upon the churches we represent to denounce anti-semitism, no matter what its origin, as absolutely irreconcilable with the profession and practice of the Christian faith. Antisemitism is sin against God and human life." This appeal has been reiterated many times. Those who live where there is a history of prejudice and persecution of the Jews can serve the whole Church by revealing that danger whenever it is recognized.

2. Teachings of contempt for Jews and Judaism in certain traditions have proved a spawning ground for such evils as the Nazi Holocaust. It has, in this country, helped to spawn the extremist activities of the Ku Klux Klan and the defacement of synagogues, and stimulates the more socially acceptable but often more pernicious discriminatory practices seen in housing patterns and in private clubs. The Church must learn to proclaim the Gospel without generating contempt for Judaism or the Jewish people. A Christian response to the Holocaust is a resolve that it will never happen again.

3. Discrimination and persecution of the Jewish people have not only deep-rooted theological but also social, economic, and political aspects. Religious differences are magnified to justify ethnic hatred in support of vested interests. Similar manifestations are also evident in many interracial conflicts. Christians are called to oppose all religious prejudices through which Jews or any people are made scapegoats for the failures and problems of societies and political regimes.

IV. Authentic Christian Witness

1. Christians believe that God's self-revelation is given in history. In the Covenant with the Jewish people at Mt. Sinai, the sacred law became part of our religious heritage. Christians see that same God embodied in the person of Jesus Christ, to whom The Church must bear witness by word and deed among all peoples. It would be false to its deepest commitment if the Church were to deny this mission. The Christian witness toward Jews, however, has been distorted by coercive proselytism, conscious and unconscious, overt and subtle. The Joint Working Group of the Roman Catholic Church and the World Council of Churches has stated: "Proselytism embraces whatever violates the right of the human person, Christian or non-Christian, to be free from external coercion in religious matters" (*Ecumenical Review*, 1/1971, p. 11).

2. Dialogue can rightly be described as a mutual witness, for witness is a sharing of one's faith conviction without the intention of proselytizing. Participants are invited to hear each other in order to understand their faiths, hopes, insights and concerns. The goal of dialogue is to communicate truth as the participants perceive it within their own traditions. The spirit of dialogue is to be present to each other in full openness and human vulnerability.

V. Practical Recommendations

1. It is recommended that the relationship between Christians and Jews be observed liturgically each year. A fitting occasion would be on or near the observance of Yom HaShoah, the Holocaust remembrance, since Jews and Christians would then have a common, or approximately common, day of observance. Another such occasion for an annual observance might be the Feast of St. James of Jerusalem on October 23, or a Sunday before or after that date.

2. It is recommended that in the services of the Church and in church school teaching, careful explanations be made of the New Testament texts which appear to place all Jews in an unfavorable light, particularly the expression "the Jews" in the English translations of the Gospel of John and in other references (see General Convention Resolution on "Deicide and the Jews," *Journal* 1964, pp. 279-80).

3. It is recommended that each diocese of the Church not already having a Committee on Christian-Jewish Relations establish one at the first opportunity in order to coordinate efforts and help to avoid haphazard and unrelated activities.

4. It is recommended that each parish situated in an area with a significant Jewish population organize with proper care and oversight an ongoing dialogue with Jews. If the dialogue is to be thorough and productive, it must include basic local exchanges between Episcopal and Jewish congregations.

5. It is recommended that seminaries of the Church undertake programs for their students which promote a greater understanding and appreciation for our common heritage with the

Jews as well as for living Judaism today, addressing in particular those matters which eliminate prejudice and the presuppositions that feed it.

6. It is recommended that cooperation with Jewish and interreligious organizations concerned with service and the common good, interreligious programs, cultural enrichment and social responsibility be continued and intensified.

Principles for Interfaith Dialogue

The Presiding Bishop's Advisory Committee on Interfaith Relations

General Convention of The Episcopal Church, 1994 [‡]

Episcopal Churches across the country are finding themselves increasingly aware of religious diversity in their own communities. We now live side by side with organized groups representing many of the great religious traditions of the world who share our concern for peace, justice and the common good.

> With them we have the need to affirm spiritual values in a materialistic society and we also have the duty to remove any supposed religious justification for discrimination based on prejudice and ignorance.[*]

Dialogue as Mutual Understanding

1. Meet the people themselves and get to know their religious traditions. In many communities there are places of worship of the world's great religions. Several of these religious communities have national and regional organizations, frequently with people who have responsibility for interfaith dialogue and cooperation. There are also bodies that have as their purpose the fostering of better relationships among people of different faith communities.

2. Whenever possible, engage in dialogue ecumenically. Generally dialogue is best done with representatives of several Christian traditions at the same time. When we seek to explain ourselves to others, the differences between Christians are seen in a different light. An ecumenical approach to dialogue allows us to focus on those things which are essential in Christian teaching. While individual approaches need not be discouraged, a ministerial association or local council of churches might well be the more appropriate body to initiate dialogue.

3. Allow others to speak for themselves. Too often stereotypes keep us apart from people of other faiths. One obvious way of avoiding this is to let the dialogue partners describe themselves, as we would expect to speak for ourselves. This is not to say that our listening must always be uncritical. Our questions will only be accepted as we show that we want to learn and understand. One way of ensuring this kind of balance is to plan the dialogue together.

4. Be aware of other loyalties. We always bring into relationships a cluster of theological commitments and cultural loyalties. An awareness of this can help us avoid unrealistic expectations

[‡]   Used with permission from The Archives of The Episcopal Church.

and help focus on central, rather than peripheral, issues. Acknowledgment of our own and others' loyalties can pave the way to deeper sharing.

5. Prepare carefully for dialogue. Dialogue ventures will be most successful with mutual planning and preparation.

a. It is important to approach others with the same kind of respect we would wish to be accorded. They cherish their beliefs and practices as deeply as we do our own, however different they may appear to us.

b. Every religious tradition, including our own, has unworthy adherents and unpleasant episodes in its history. True dialogue is not possible if only the best of one tradition is contrasted with the worst of others.

c. Issues of separation must be addressed as well as those of unity. Dialogue is not furthered when painful or difficult issues are glossed over. However, this should not be done with an attitude of superiority, or solely in an effort to air grievances. Dialogue should include an awareness of our own contribution to division and misunderstanding.

d. By engaging in dialogue we Christians are not being asked to compromise our faith that God was revealed in the person of Jesus Christ. Our understanding of our own faith should be clear, so that the Christian perspective can be fairly presented to dialogue partners. Dialogue, however, should not be a subtle form of proselytizing, but an occasion for mutual sharing.

Dialogue as Common Action

1. *Deal with issues related to living together as part of the human community.* This may well be the basis upon which dialogue begins. Our planet is too small and the problems confronting it too great for people of faith to attempt to work in isolation or from a position of conflict. Some matters on which an interfaith approach is possible include:

a. Joint approaches to government on matters of economic, social, political, and cultural concern.

b. Urging respect for human rights and religious freedom, not only for ourselves, but for others also.

c. Coordinated efforts to deal with global issues such as world peace, the environment, or hunger.

2. *Foster efforts at education and communication among people of different faiths.* Education is both a consequence of and a way into interfaith dialogue. The effort to learn and understand will bring us into closer contact, while that contact will lead us to want to share our learning with others.

a. In our pluralistic society it is important that people have an appreciation of the rich religious heritage of those who make up our community. People are pleased, for example, when their major religious festivals are acknowledged. These can provide the occasion for learning more about the faith concerned.

b. Sustained contact with people of other faiths can begin to break down false images with which many of us have grown up, and to which we are still often exposed. Efforts should be made to challenge such stereotypes wherever they may be encountered, including those in our own educational and liturgical material.

c. Among the places where such educational efforts can be focused are schools, universities, seminaries, church schools, and other institutions for adult education.

d. Inaccurate media coverage of minority religious groups can be detrimental. Positive relations should be developed with the media so that their potential for increasing public awareness about people of different faiths can be fully utilized.

e. Efforts should also be made to educate travelers about the religious traditions and sensibilities of the people in the countries they visit, and to encourage them to share their experiences on their return.

f. Representatives of other faith groups should be consulted and, were possible, involved in the preparation of educational materials that portray their history, beliefs, and practices.

3. *Share spiritual insights and approaches to worship that respect the integrity of each tradition.* There is much that religious people can share in an atmosphere of learning and openness. However, people of other traditions are no more anxious than we are to engage in acts of worship which blur very real differences of theology or world view. Neither do they relish the appropriation by others of their religious symbols or sacred texts.

a. Attendance at another community's acts of worship should always be accompanied by careful preparation and an opportunity to ask questions afterward, preferably answered by members of that tradition.

b. Christians who are present during the worship of another faith community may be unable to participate fully in everything that is said and done. Nonetheless they should attend with the attitude that the event is an important part of the spiritual life of the participants.

Prayer for people of other religious traditions is valuable, especially during times of particular need or when it is for better relationships with them. Some Christians feel that they should pray for the conversion of others to Christ, while others would argue that this should not be done. In any event, it is God who converts people. Christians themselves are far from fully understanding or obeying God's will. It is inappropriate to single out any one religious group as being in particular need of conversion in a way that fosters prejudice.

* We are grateful for permission to quote extensively in this document from *Guidelines for Interfaith Dialogue* produced by the Ecumenical Office of the Anglican Church of Canada, Toronto, 1986.

Interfaith Relations and the Churches
A Policy Statement of the
National Council of the Churches of Christ in the U.S.A. [‡]

Developed by the Interfaith Relations Commission of the National Council of the Churches of Christ in the USA, and adopted by the NCC General Assembly on November 10, 1999, this statement is the result of a four-year process of consultation with member communions and with NCCCUSA program units, in particular the Faith and Order Commission and the Ecumenical Networks Commission, and the Black Church Liaison Committee. At a number of stages, representatives of other religious traditions also shared responses to the document, which have been helpful in its creation.

This Statement provides policy guidelines for the National Council of Churches, and is offered for the consideration of its member communions as a source for guidance, reflection, and action. It is our hope as well that it will contribute to the wider discourse on religious diversity and community in our national life.

1. Preamble [‡‡]

2. "As you have sent me into the world, so I have sent them into the world" (John 17:18). As disciples, we seek to testify to the love of God in Jesus Christ our Lord, to embody that love in the world, and to respond to the leading of God's Holy Spirit. We seek God's grace in our common effort to understand ever more fully how to live as the body of Christ in this religiously plural and culturally diverse time and place.

3. We speak out of a changing experience of religious diversity in our country. Events in the United States and across the world have made us more aware of the significance of the world's religions and their influence on politics, economics, and cultures. We speak out of what we have been learning in our shared ecumenical life. At home and abroad, the work of building Christian unity and our efforts for peace and human development are increasingly intertwined with questions regarding our relationships with those of religious traditions outside the historic Christian church.

4. Historical, Political and Social Context

5. The Americas have always been religiously plural. For millennia, their indigenous peoples have practiced their religions, diverse yet all based on respect for and connectedness with the earth and all of creation. Christians of various backgrounds made up the bulk of the settlers from Europe. But Jews were also among the original colonists and participated in the American Revolution. Muslims and practitioners of African religions arrived with those brought from Africa, most as slaves. Immigrants who came from Asia in the 19th century to work in American industry and agriculture brought with them a variety of Asian religious traditions.

---

‡   Reprinted with permission from the NCCC.
‡‡   Paragraphs 1, 16, and 45 are section headings.

6. The USA's history has not always been marked by tolerance or inclusivity. Religious liberty and freedom developed here only slowly, despite the protections of the First Amendment to the Constitution. Early visions of that freedom were (and unfortunately still are) often infected with triumphalism and racism. We must confess that Christians participated in attempts to eradicate indigenous peoples and their traditional religions. We must acknowledge the complicity of many of our churches in slavery, a system in which most African Americans were prohibited from practicing Islam or African traditional religions.

7. Today the spectrum of religious tradition and practice in the United States is wider and more complex than ever before. Islam, Buddhism, Judaism, Hinduism, Sikhism, Native American traditions, Baha'i, and other faiths are now part of the American landscape. Many factors have contributed to this increased diversity. These include changes such as the U.S. Immigration Act of 1965 and subsequent immigration policy, increasing global inter-connections, the growth of American-born religious movements, and the increasing willingness of Americans to make religious commitments outside their tradition of birth.

8. This increased religious diversity is a result of the changed cultural and ethnic makeup of our communities and our churches. For many of our congregations, interreligious and intercultural relations are an integral part of community and family life. Many church members have children, parents, sisters and brothers, spouses or other relatives who belong to another religious tradition. People of other faiths confront, as do many Christians, discrimination in access to housing, job opportunities, or political and social position. In their efforts to address community problems, provide hope for a better society, and work for justice, Christians find themselves working side-by-side with men and women who practice religions other than their own.

9. Interfaith relations also play a prominent role in our international concerns. In many parts of the world, religion plays an important role in politics, in economic and social development or the lack of it, in communal strife or reconciliation. We see the growth of fundamentalism among Christians, Muslims, Jews, Buddhists, Sikhs, and Hindus. We note the central role religion often plays in a community's understanding of justice, moral good, and its own identity, and we see the involvement of religion for good and for ill in the struggles in many places in the world. News reports often reinforce our stereotypes and provide an erroneous base of information from which many form lasting impressions of other religious traditions and those who practice them.

10. In our community institutions and in the public sphere, we increasingly face issues involving interreligious understanding and cooperation. Too often, people of other faiths experience stereotyping based on both religious difference and ethnicity. The interpretation and implementation of religious freedom is a matter of lively debate. The National Council of Churches relates to other religious communities on a broad range of public policy issues and questions of fundamental social dignity. New voices and new issues are challenging traditional understandings of who and what we are as a people in the United States. The churches struggle to understand their relation to this diversity of views and people, taking their part in our society's current efforts to discern a new and more inclusive civic identity.

11. A Continuing Dimension of the Church's Life

12. Although this situation in which we live may seem to be new, it has many parallels throughout biblical history. In the stories of the Hebrew Scriptures, God relates to the Jewish people against a backdrop of religious diversity. In early Christian writings, we see that Christianity originated as a Jewish movement often in tension with other Jewish movements of the time. These tensions are often reflected in the Christian Scriptures. The life, death, and resurrection of Jesus took place in one of the most religiously complex environments of the ancient world.

13. The Church of Christ has always lived among peoples of many different cultures and religions. Thus we join Christians of many times and places when we ask, How do we live in faithfulness to the Gospel when our friends and neighbors, colleagues and associates, parents and children are members of other religious traditions or no religion at all?

14. Interfaith relations and the challenge of ministry in a religiously plural world raise a number of ecumenical questions. Some questions divide the churches in terms of theology, or practice, or a mixture of the two. These include the relationship between evangelism and dialogue, concerns about intermarriage, and issues regarding interfaith worship or common prayer. These issues warrant further consultation among the churches. As we become increasingly aware that the whole Church of Christ stands together in a common ministry in relation to men and women of other religions, these questions become more urgent.

15. There are two aspects to this challenge. Theologically, as a fellowship of Christian communions, we ask new questions about our religious identity: How do we understand our relationship to God, to other Christians, and to those of other religious traditions? How do we understand the relationship between these men and women and God? Practically, we ask about Christian discipleship: How can we best live a life of faithful witness and service in a multi-faith context?

16. Reflections on Theology and Practice

17. We are indebted to the efforts of Christians from many different confessional traditions and ecumenical bodies who have struggled with these questions. We are instructed by the thinking of the Second Vatican Council, in particular its document *Nostra Aetate* (1965) and subsequent reflections, and the attention given to this issue by bodies such as the Lambeth Conference of the Anglican Communion, the Lutheran World Federation and the World Alliance of Reformed Churches. Our efforts to think and work together in this area of interfaith relations as the National Council of Churches owe much also to the pioneering work of the World Council of Churches. In its *Guidelines on Dialogue* (1979, #12) that body noted that its member churches "will need to work out for themselves and with their specific partners in dialogue statements and guidelines for their own use in particular situations."

18. Some member churches of the NCCC have developed policies or study documents on interfaith relations or on specific bilateral interreligious relationships. The Faith and Order Commission of the NCCC has studied those elements within particular confessional traditions which might inform their theological understanding of our relations with other religious traditions. In addition, the Ecumenical Networks Commission and many of the member churches maintain ties with local and regional ecumenical and inter-religious councils. Some member communions also have ties to national and international multi-religious efforts. Christians take part in many inter-religious efforts of social ministry and advocacy. We are grateful for, and indebted to all of this work.

19. God and Human Community

20. Understanding the churches' relationship to people of other religious traditions begins in the recognition of God's many gifts to us, including that of relationship. All are made in the image of God (Genesis 1:27.

When we meet a human being, no matter what her or his religion, we are meeting a unique creation of the living God. "One is the community of all peoples, one their origin, for God made the whole human race to live on all the face of the earth." All are equal in God's sight; each is equally the object of God's love and potentially open to receive "a ray of that truth which enlightens all [humanity]." Because we are all children of the one God we are all related to one another. It is in this sense that we may call all men and women our brothers and sisters. (We also recognize a specific use of this familial language to refer to those within the household of Christian faith.) Community is itself a divine gift which we are called to make real in our lives.

21. In our Christian understanding, relationship is part of the nature of God. In God's own essence, Father, Son and Holy Spirit are in dynamic interrelationship, a unity of three in one. Similarly, humanity is created in diversity. In the scriptural account of creation, it is the first humans in community who together constitute the image of God. Being made in God's image we are created to live a life of relationship, and called to claim the unity in our human diversity.

22. We recognize, however, that though we are given this gift of community, we act in ways that break or undermine it. Too often we set ourselves against each other. We become separated from God, and alienated from God's creation. We find ourselves in seemingly irreconcilable conflict with other people. We confess that as human beings we have a propensity for taking the gift of diversity and turning it into a cause of disunity, antagonism and hatred—often because we see ourselves as part of a unique, special community. We sin against God and each other.

23. This is part of the reality of our human condition. We see it in the ease with which our father Adam accuses our mother Eve: "The woman you gave me for a companion, she gave me the fruit" (Genesis 3:12). Within a generation, the vision of the community for which we are created had become so distorted that Cain can challenge God with the question, "Am I my brother's keeper?" (Gen. 4:9).

24. Scripture suggests that our responsibility extends not only to a brother or sister, but also to the stranger. Hebrew Scripture celebrates the wider community to which humanity is called in the stories of Melchizedek, Jethro, Rahab and Ruth, and the Hittites who offered hospitality to Abraham. In the Torah God enjoins the Jewish people to treat the sojourner as part of their own community. Throughout the Bible, hospitality to the stranger is an essential virtue. We recall both the words of the Epistle to the Hebrews, "Do not neglect to show hospitality to strangers, for by doing that some have entertained angels without knowing it," and the example Jesus gives in the parable of the Good Samaritan (Luke 10: 25-37).

25. In the churches' long history with people of other religions, as we have struggled to make actual God's gift of community, we have acted both faithfully and unfaithfully. While Christians have suffered persecution at the hands of those of other faiths and from each other, we have much to repent. Christians have persecuted Jews, and crusaded against Muslims. Christians have enslaved Africans and other peoples, and have participated in subordinating indigenous peoples

and erasing their religious traditions. Many Christians have accepted or perpetuated the use of their religion to bless the imposition of Western culture and economic domination. Anti-Semitic and anti-Muslim biases, together with racism and ethnic biases have flourished among us.

26. We can rejoice that Christians were leaders in the anti-slavery movement, and have worked for the human and communal rights of many peoples. Christians have fought oppressive economic and social systems of many societies including our own, and have resisted injustice without regard to cost. Christians also have invited transformation of those ways of living that damage others and undermine the one human community. In many of these efforts Christians have worked closely with people of other faiths.

27. Our experience, therefore, is a mixture of successes and failures in building loving community and in exercising our stewardship of God's creation in justice and peace. We must struggle to reject or reform all those human actions and systems that destroy or deny the image of God in human beings or that tear down the structures of human community. On the other hand, we must seek to affirm all human impulses which build up true community.

28. Because God is at work in all creation, we can expect to find new understanding of our faith through dialogue with people of other religions. Such interaction can be an opportunity for mutual witness. However, mutual witness does not always take place in a context of mutual respect. We may fail in our efforts to reflect God's love for all; and even on those occasions when we succeed in the practice of a respectful presence, we do not always find our success mirrored by our conversation partners.

29. We find ourselves in need of repentance and reconciliation. Again and again we are reminded "of the Christian Church as a sign at once of people's need for fuller and deeper community, and of God's promise of a restored human community in Christ." As we wait for the fulfillment of God's promise, we commit ourselves to work for fuller and deeper community in our own time and place.

30. Jesus Christ and Reconciliation

31. The revelation of God's love in Jesus Christ is the center of our faith. Incarnating both the fullness of God and the fullness of humanity, Jesus Christ initiates a new creation, a world unified in relationship as God originally intended. We believe that Jesus Christ makes real God's will for a life of loving community with God, with the whole human family and with all creation. Through Jesus Christ, Christians believe God offers reconciliation to all. "In Christ God was reconciling the world to [God]self" (2 Corinthians 5:19).

32. It is our Christian conviction that reconciliation among people and with the world cannot be separated from the reconciliation offered in Jesus Christ. Jesus, addressing the crowds and the disciples on the mountain (Matthew 5:1 and 7:28), teaches that any who would offer their gift at God's altar, must first be reconciled to their brothers and sisters in the human family (Matthew 5:24. The hope of a cosmic reconciliation in Christ is also central to Christian scripture: "The creation itself will be set free from its bondage to decay and will obtain the freedom of the glory of the Children of God" (Romans 8:21).

33. Jesus Christ is also the focus of the most vexing questions regarding how Christians understand their relationship with men and women of other religions. Christians agree that Jesus Christ incarnated—and incarnates still—the inexhaustible love and salvation that reconcile us all. We agree that it is not by any merit of our own, but by God's grace that we are reconciled. Likewise, Christians also agree that our discipleship impels us to become reconciled to the whole human family and to live in proper relationship to all of God's creation. We disagree, however, on whether non-Christians may be reconciled to God, and if so, how. Many Christians see no possibility of reconciliation with God apart from a conscious acceptance of Jesus Christ as incarnate Son of God and personal savior. For others, the reconciling work of Jesus is salvific in its own right, independent of any particular human response. For many, the saving power of God is understood as a mystery and an expression of God's sovereignty that cannot be confined within our limited conceptions. One question with which we must still struggle is how to define the uniqueness of God's self-revelation in Jesus Christ in the light of such passages as "I am the way, and the truth, and the life. No one comes to the Father except through me" (John 14:6); "There is salvation in no one else, for there is no other name under heaven given among mortals by which we must be saved" (Acts 4:12); "In him all the fullness of God was pleased to dwell, and through him God was pleased to reconcile to himself all things" (Colossians 1:19-20); and "as all die in Adam, so all will be made alive in Christ" (1 Corinthians 15:22).

34. As Christians we recognize that Jesus is not central to other religious traditions. For men and women in other communities, the mystery of God takes many forms. Observing this, we are not led to deny the centrality of Christ for our faith, but to contemplate more deeply the meaning of St. Paul's affirmation: "Ever since the creation of the world, (God's) eternal power and divine nature, invisible though they are, have been understood and seen through the things [God] has made" (Romans 1:20). Christians disagree on the nature and extent of such "natural revelation" and its relation to salvation. No matter what our view on this may be, we can be open to the insights of others.

35. We recognize that scripture speaks with many voices about relationship with men and women of other religious traditions. We need to devote further attention to issues of interpreting scriptural teaching. But as to our Christian discipleship, we can only live by the clear obligation of the Gospel. When Jesus was asked, "What must I do to inherit eternal life?" he, referring to his Jewish tradition, answered, "You shall love the Lord your God with all your heart and with all your soul and with all your strength, and with all your mind; and your neighbor as yourself" (Luke 10:25-27). Love of God and love of neighbors cannot be separated. We rejoice in our common conviction that Jesus calls us to ministries of reconciliation.

36. The Spirit of God and Human Hope

37. The presence and power of the Holy Spirit fill us with hope. The realities of religious fragmentation and conflict could become a cause of despair, especially in a world of broken community, racked by division and hate based on color, language, ethnicity, and class. We are pained when our religious traditions do not empower us to build community. Yet we have hope because of the Holy Spirit, who hovered over the waters when the earth was void and without form (Genesis 1:2), who brings order out of chaos, and can reshape our warped societies.

38. We believe that our relationships with people of other religious traditions are being shaped by the Spirit who, like the wind, "blows where it chooses" (John 3:8). Though we do not always understand the Spirit's purposes, we need never be without hope, for neither we nor the rest of creation are ever without the Spirit of God.

39. In this time of constant change, a sometimes bewildering variety of technologies, cultures, religions and languages impinges upon our lives. The ways in which we should witness and act to bring about reconciliation in our torn world are not always clear. But the Spirit enables us to discern how to nurture the loving community of persons which is God's intention for creation, and gives us the strength to keep working toward it.

40. Our experience of the transforming power of God's love overflows in joyous anticipation of a renewed and reconciled humanity. As the Body of Christ, we are called to live out this new reality and to be a sign of the restored community to which all people are called. Through the power of the Holy Spirit, we witness in word and deed to this hope.

41. This witness will be as varied as the many circumstances in which we meet men and women of other faiths. We meet them in our families and among our friends and colleagues; at the corner store and the doctor's office, in community action groups, and at work. We meet in boardrooms and schoolrooms, facing common agendas and concerns. Since God is the Lord of history, we can be open to the presence of God's Spirit in these encounters. They invite us to faithful service and witness.

42. We are aware that our churches are part of the body of Christ throughout the world. Our encounters with people of other faiths here in the U.S. are informed by the experience and reflection of our sisters and brothers living among men and women of many religious traditions in many nations. We stand in solidarity with each other, taking a role in international dialogue and seeking in our own circumstances to be faithful to the gospel.

43. We do not always agree, however, on how best to love our neighbors. Commitment to justice and mutual respect is the paramount consideration for some. For them the practice of Christian love is the most powerful witness to the truth of the Gospel. Others, while not denying the witness of faithful lives, believe that love demands the verbal proclamation of the Gospel and an open invitation to all people to be reconciled to God in Christ. Still others understand evangelization as our participation in God's transformation of human society. As we seek to respond to God's call to love our neighbor, we all must seek to avoid ways of interaction which do violence to the integrity of human persons and communities, such as coercive proselytism, which "violates the right of the human person, Christian or non-Christian, to be free from external coercion in religious matters." We pray for the inspiration of the Holy Spirit that through our life with all men and women, of every religion, color, language, and class, we will be instruments of God to build that time in which "steadfast love and faithfulness will meet; righteousness and peace will kiss each other" (Psalm 85:10).

44. Clearly, a basic aspect of our relationship to people of religious traditions other than our own must be to engage in the struggle for justice, as the prophet Amos challenges us: "Let justice roll down like waters, and righteousness like an everflowing stream" (Amos 5:23-24). Our actions must be based on genuine respect for all men and women. "The wisdom from above is first pure, then peaceable, gentle, willing to yield, full of mercy and good fruits, without a trace of partiality or hypocrisy" (James 3:16-17). And beyond respect, we are called to love all people so that, by the working of the Holy Spirit, we may "above all, clothe [our]selves with love, which binds everything together in perfect harmony" (Colossians 3:14).

45. Marks of Faithfulness

46. In the light of our reflections on Christian discipleship, we can discern ways to approach the challenges of our multi-religious society. We will serve faithfully, meeting others with open hearts and minds.

47. ***All relationship begins with meeting.*** The model for our meeting others is always the depth of presence and engagement which marked Jesus' meeting with those around him. In our every-day lives, we will meet and form relationships with men and women of other religious traditions. At times these may be difficult relationships, based on bitter memories. However, we have been created for loving community and will not disengage from trying to build bridges of understanding and cooperation throughout the human family.

48. ***True relationship involves risk.*** When we approach others with an open heart, it is possible that we may be hurt. When we encounter others with an open mind, we may have to change our positions or give up certainty, but we may gain new insights. Prompted to ask new questions, we will search the Scriptures and be attentive to the Spirit in new ways to mature in Christ and in love and service to others. Because those we meet are also God's beloved creatures, this risk is also opportunity. Our knowledge and love of God can be enriched as we hear others proclaim to us how God has worked and empowered their lives.

49. ***True relationship respects the other's identity.*** We will meet others as they are, in their particular hopes, ideas, struggles and joys. These are articulated through their own traditions, practices and world-views. We encounter the image of God in the particularity of another person's life.

50. ***True relationship is based on integrity.*** If we meet others as they are, then we must accept their right to determine and define their own identity. We also must remain faithful to who we are; only as Christians can we be present with integrity. We will not ask others to betray their religious commitments, nor will we betray our commitment to the gospel of Jesus Christ.

51. ***True relationship is rooted in accountability and respect.*** We approach others in humility, not arrogance. In our relationships we will call ourselves and our partners to a mutual accountability. We will invite each other to join in building a world of love and justice, but we will also challenge each other's unjust behavior. We can do both only from an attitude of mutual respect.

52. ***True relationship offers an opportunity to serve.*** Jesus comes among us as a servant. We too are given the opportunity to serve others, in response to God's love for us. In so doing, we will join with those of other religious traditions to serve the whole of God's creation. Through advocacy, education, direct services and community development, we respond to the realities of a world in need. Our joining with others in such service can be an eloquent proclamation of what it means to be in Christ.

Recommendations

In response to the situation of religious plurality in which our churches minister, in light of the convictions expressed above, and in order to live out our faith commitment more fully, we, the

General Assembly of the National Council of the Churches of Christ in the United States, affirm
the following guidelines and recommendations.

I.   In regard to the life and programs of the Council:

We commit the Council to continue its relationships with people of other religious traditions. In
particular the Council should:

1. Maintain relations with national bodies of other religious communities in the United
   States, in order to foster mutual understanding and regard, examine issues affecting our
   communities in the course of our national life, and identify common concerns and appropriate coordinated responses to them;

2. Initiate conversations with people and organizations of other religious traditions in the
   United States, for example, the Hindu and Sikh communities, and others;

3. Continue to encourage dialogue with Americans of other religions to promote peace
   and justice around the globe, and in particular with American Jews and Muslims as
   integral to the churches' efforts for peace in the Middle East (Policy Statement on the
   Middle East, Nov. 6, 1980); and to encourage interreligious dialogue in other situations
   in which religion is identified as a factor in conflict situations;

4. Reinvigorate ongoing work with institutions and people of other religions and cultures
   in public policy advocacy; refugee resettlement and overseas programs; the prevention
   of family violence and abuse (Policy Statement on Family Violence and Abuse, November 14, 1990); and to initiate work in other program areas as appropriate;

5. Encourage the efforts of existing interreligious entities within the life of the Council,
   such as the Interfaith Center on Corporate Responsibility, the Interfaith Broadcasting
   Committee, and the Task Force on Religious Liberty;

6. Continue to work through collaborative bodies, including the Washington Interfaith
   Staff Committee, the U.S. Chapter of the World Conference on Religion and Peace, and
   the North American Interfaith Network;

7. Participate in international efforts to further interreligious relations, especially through
   the World Council of Churches, and organizations such as the World Conference on
   Religion and Peace;

8. Affirm that the integrity of our Christian faith and commitment is to be preserved in all
   our interfaith relationships, and recognize that religious commitments of many traditions, like the Christian, have political implications of which we should be aware. We
   should recognize and consider the political aspects of the others' religious claims, and
   be ready to explain the religious roots of our own behavior and policies;

9. Recommit ourselves to pursue religious liberty and religious freedom for all, and to defend "the rights and liberties of cultural, racial and religious minorities" (Religion and
   Civil Liberties in the U.S.A., October 5, 1955); and call again for "interfaith dialogue on
   the nature and meaning of human rights" and on "the patterns of inter-religious intolerance and practices that lead to inter-faith conflict" (Human Rights, Nov. 12, 1994),
   including both intolerance toward Christians and Christian intolerance of others;

10. Condemn all forms of religious, ethnic and racial bias, especially anti-Semitic, anti-Muslim, anti-Asian and anti-Native American bias, and other forms of sinful bigotry which turn religious differences into excuses for defamation, stereotyping and violence; and defend their victims (cf. Resolution on Prejudice Against Islam and Muslims, November 6, 1986); and commit the Council and our churches to uproot all that might contribute to such prejudice in our teaching, life and ministries;

11. Continue our efforts to achieve mutuality of understanding and growth toward maturity in relation to Native American people, so that the spiritual heritage, political reality and cultural uniqueness of each group or nation may be respected (Indian Affairs, November 4, 1978); and promote the protection of sacred sites and rituals;

12. Recommit ourselves to the development in public schools of "an intelligent understanding and appreciation of the role of religion in the life of the people of this nation," while also defending the principle that "neither the church nor the state should use the public school to compel acceptance of any creed or conformity to any specific religious practice" (The Churches and the Public Schools, June 7, 1963);

II. We charge the Council, through its Executive Board, to give priority to interfaith relations in order to:

1. Work with the churches to identify or create study resources, organize and facilitate consultations and educational conferences, offer workshops, etc.;

2. Gather information on existing programs, activities, and relationships on national, regional, and local levels;

3. Promote and participate regularly in bilateral and multilateral consultations with other religious communities to explore practical and theological concerns;

4. Coordinate the Council's interfaith work, and report to the NCCC General Assembly at least biennially.

III. In service to each other as a community of communions:

We call on member communions to work together, and with the broader ecumenical community, to equip congregations and Christian leaders to understand and engage with people of other religious traditions, and in particular to:

1. Provide study resources, sponsoring consultations, and organizing conferences to further this aim;

2. Participate in the Interfaith Relations Commission, a forum in which the churches may take counsel, make plans, and undertake joint work in this field;

3. Engage in interreligious relations ecumenically whenever and wherever possible, and share these experiences with each other, the Council, and partner churches and ecumenical bodies around the world.

IV. To member communions and their congregations, to the wider ecumenical community, and to all those of good will who seek further understanding or participation in interfaith relations, we:

1. Recommend study and use of the World Council of Churches' *Guidelines on Dialogue* (1979), the declaration *Nostra Aetate* of the Second Vatican Council (1965), and other statements of the churches. These documents offer theological insights and practical suggestions that can undergird efforts to understand and properly engage with people of other religious traditions.

2. Call attention to the statements of our member communions and of the wider Christian community regarding interreligious relations.

3. Recommend ecumenical consideration and study of our divided understandings of the nature of salvation, of appropriate forms of evangelism, of the bases in scripture and tradition for relations with those of other religious traditions, and of the concerns among us regarding interfaith marriage, worship and prayer.

4. Urge member communions, their congregations, and local ecumenical and interfaith gatherings to use the "Marks of Faithfulness" in this policy statement as a statement of commitment for study and affirmation.

5. Commend this policy statement to member communions, congregations and local ecumenical and interreligious gatherings for study, and as a catalyst to reflection and action.

6. Commend this policy statement to other religious communities in the United States for their study, and invite their reactions to it in the hope and expectation of deepening friendship.

A Sermon Preached by the Most Rev. Frank T. Griswold

Presiding Bishop and Primate of The Episcopal Church,
at St. Paul's Cathedral, Burlington, Vermont
September 21, 2001
The Sixteenth Sunday after Pentecost‡

Readings from the Revised Common Lectionary
Jeremiah 8:18-9:1
1 Timothy 2:1-7
Luke 16:1-13

My joy is gone, grief is upon me, my heart is sick...

When we find ourselves personally and corporately in "thin places" as Evelyn Underhill calls them, it is often the words of scripture, charged as they are with the joys and sorrows, the burdens and yearnings of our forebears in faith that give voice to that which is deep within us and name emotions of which we may hardly be aware.

"My joy is gone, grief is upon me, my heart is sick." Jeremiah's words are words of lamentation. "I weep day and night for the slain of my poor people." Lamentation is a mode of biblical speech which is all too familiar in many parts of our world where "violence, battle and murder" are daily realities. Our brothers and sisters from the Sudan are witnesses to this terrible truth. And now lamentation has become real among us.

By virtue of the events of September 11, we now in the U.S. join that company of nations in which ideology disguised as true religion wreaks havoc and sudden death. The invincible is shown to be vulnerable and in that moment the door is opened which, if we choose to pass through it, will lead us beyond death and destruction into a new solidarity with those for whom the evil and satanic forces of terrorism are a continuing fear and reality.

Lamentation, however, is not an end in itself, but rather it opens the way to the question "why?" which leads in turn to self-scrutiny and self-examination. What might we learn from what we have suffered and are suffering—about ourselves, and about ourselves in relationship to others? How has our consciousness been altered by what has come down so suddenly and violently upon us? What invitation emerges from that terrible fire-filled day to engage us not simply as Americans but as persons of faith?

In the gospel reading we have just heard Jesus declares that no slave can serve two masters and therefore we cannot serve God and wealth. What Jesus is pointing to when he speaks about service is what we might call the ground of our personal allegiance, the desire of our heart at its most radical depth: the fundamental orientation of my life.

If our life is ordered to God, we find ourselves caught up in God's mercy and compassion. God's "fierce bonding love," a mercy and compassion and love which stretches and expands us: cracks open our hearts of stone and transforms them into hearts of flesh—hearts capable of embracing others in the strength of God's all embracing compassion.

Many centuries ago, St. Isaac of Syria, one of the great wisdom figures of the Eastern Church, raised the question: what is a merciful and compassionate heart? He answered the question in this way:

---

‡   Used with permission from The Archives of The Episcopal Church.

It is a heart which burns with love for the whole of creation: for humankind, for the birds, for the beasts, for the demons, for every creature. When persons with a heart such as this think of the creatures or look at them, their eyes are filled with tears. An overwhelming compassion makes their heart grow small and weak, and they cannot endure to hear or see any suffering, even the smallest pain, inflicted upon any creature. Therefore they never cease to pray with tears even for the irrational animals, for the enemies of truth and for those who do them evil asking that those for whom they pray may be guarded and receive God's mercy. And for the reptiles also they pray with a great compassion, which rises up endlessly in their hearts until they shine again and are glorious like God.

This all embracing compassion which can include beasts and demons, enemies and reptiles, is beyond our effort and imagination; it is a gift. It is the consequence of Christ being formed in us, our being conformed to Christ, which is what our baptism into Christ and our weekly sharing of the Eucharist is all about.

To serve God, therefore, is not about a frantic execution of self-chosen tasks that we hope will please the Almighty, but about the mind and heart of Christ being worked in us by the Spirit so that our compassion, our just-ness are revelatory of the One who, from the cross, draws the world: all people and all things to himself—in his loving embrace.

A life ordered to wealth yields a very different fruit. Whereas compassion turns us outward in relationship to the world around us, wealth on its own disconnects us and turns us in on ourselves in self-serving defensiveness. And here wealth is not simply money but it includes such things as status, ethnicity, color, education, culture, nationality, religion and more.

Wealth is both personal and corporate. We speak for example of our nation's wealth and from it follows what we call "our national interests" which are to be defended at all costs.

In the light of the traumatic events of these past days which have claimed and touched so many lives—the lives not only of our own citizens but those of other nations as well—are we not in a spirit of lamentation invited to ask questions about ourselves and, as a nation, engage in the solemn task of self-examination?

Unquestionably, the attack on September 11 was an evil and deranged act fueled by a satanic zeal in which God the Compassionate One is transmuted into a God of suicide, murder and destruction. That being clearly said, is there not, as we seek to build a coalition of nations to join us in a war on terrorism, an invitation to examine our national interests in relationship to the global community of which we are a part?

In what ways do our own interests and their uncritical pursuit affect other nations and the welfare of their people? How are we as a nation "under God," as we call ourselves, being invited to reorder our life according to God's compassion for "humankind and for every creature"?

We, who so easily quit the global table when the conditions are not to our liking or do not serve our economic interests, are called to yield our wealth in service to God's all-embracing compassion, which is the heart of God's just-ness and God's desire for the world. Just as our efforts to disarm terrorism will require discipline and sacrifice, so too will the reordering of our national interests to serve the global family of which we are now a part in a new and vulnerable way.

The way of compassion transfigures and heals not simply those to whom it is directed, but those who practice it. Those who allow God's compassion to well up in their hearts "shine and are glorious like God," or as Isaiah says of those who inhabit compassion: "Your light shall break forth like the dawn; and your healing shall spring up quickly."

God's project, and therefore the Church's mission, is one of reconciliation: "to restore all people to unity with God and each other in Christ." And God's compassion, God's mercy, God's loving kindness, God's fierce bonding love is the active principle that effects reconciliation: the gathering up of all things into a unity in which difference is both honored and reconciled in the fullness of God's ever creative imagination.

May each of us who have been baptized into Christ be given a compassionate heart in the service of reconciliation, and may we as a nation seek our healing not through revenge and retaliation, but by "sharing our bread with the hungry" across the world. Only in that way can our light truly break forth like the dawn, and our healing spring up quickly.

Amen.

On Waging Reconciliation
Statement from Bishops of The Episcopal Church
Released by the Office of the Presiding Bishop
September 26, 2001[‡]

We, your bishops, have come together in the shadow of the shattering events of September 11. We in the United States now join that company of nations in which ideology disguised as true religion wreaks havoc and sudden death. Through this suffering, we have come into a new solidarity with those in other parts of the world for whom the evil forces of terrorism are a continuing fear and reality.

We grieve with those who have lost companions and loved ones, and pray for those who have so tragically died. We pray for the President of the United States, his advisors, and for the members of Congress that they may be given wisdom and prudence for their deliberations and measured patience in their actions. We pray for our military chaplains, and for those serving in the Armed Forces along with their families in these anxious and uncertain days. We also pray "for our enemies, and those who wish us harm; and for all whom we have injured or offended." (BCP, page 391)

At the same time we give thanks for the rescue workers and volunteers, and all those persons whose courageous efforts demonstrated a generosity and selflessness that bears witness to the spirit of our nation at its best. We give thanks too for all those who are reaching out to our Muslim brothers and sisters and others who are rendered vulnerable in this time of fear and recrimination.

We come together also in the shadow of the cross: that unequivocal sign that suffering and death are never the end but the way along which we pass into a future in which all things will be healed and reconciled. Through Christ "God was pleased to reconcile to himself all things whether on earth or in heaven, by making peace through the blood of his cross." (Col. 1:20) This radical act of peace-making is nothing less than the right ordering of all things according to God's passionate desire for justness, for the full flourishing of humankind and all creation.

This peace has already been achieved in Christ, but it has yet to be realized in our relationships with one another and the world around us. As members of a global community and the worldwide Anglican Communion, we are called to bear one another's burdens across the divides of culture, religion, and differing views of the world. The affluence of nations such as our own stands in stark contrast to other parts of the world wracked by the crushing poverty which causes the death of 6,000 children in the course of a morning.

---

‡   Used with permission from The Archives of The Episcopal Church.

We are called to self-examination and repentance: the willingness to change direction, to open our hearts and give room to God's compassion as it seeks to bind up, to heal, and to make all things new and whole. God's project, in which we participate by virtue of our baptism, is the ongoing work of reordering and transforming the patterns of our common life so they may reveal God's justness—not as an abstraction but in bread for the hungry and clothing for the naked. The mission of the Church is to participate in God's work in the world. We claim that mission.

"I have set before you life and death…choose life so that you and your descendants may live," declares Moses to the children to Israel. We choose life and immediately set ourselves to the task of developing clear steps that we will take personally and as a community of faith, to give substance to our resolve and embodiment to our hope. We do so not alone but trusting in your own faithfulness and your desire to be instruments of peace.

Let us therefore wage reconciliation. Let us offer our gifts for the carrying out of God's ongoing work of reconciliation, healing and making all things new. To this we pledge ourselves and call our church.

We go forth sober in the knowledge of the magnitude of the task to which we have all been called, yet confident and grounded in hope. "And hope does not disappoint us, because God's love has been poured into our hearts through the Holy Spirit that has been given to us." (Romans 5:5)

"May the God of hope fill us with all joy and peace in believing through the power of the Holy Spirit." (Romans 15:13)

Companions In Transformation
The Episcopal Church's World Mission In A New Century
Mission Vision Statement presented by the
Standing Commission on World Mission to the 2003 General Convention[‡]
Excerpts

Introduction

The Standing Commission on World Mission offers to the people of the Episcopal Church, through the General Convention of 2003, a vision for the church's world mission in the future. Turmoil and change in the church and on the planet make it imperative that world mission, one of the church's most extensive engagements with the wider world, be guided by reflection on the past, discernment in the present, and vision for the future. The future we realistically anticipate is the next six triennia, to the year 2020.

This point in time is appropriate for such an enterprise for several reasons.

- World mission interest and activity have surged anew in our church, following widespread disillusionment with world mission in the mid-20th century.

- Major new networks in the Episcopal Church and Anglican Communion have emerged, following an earlier diminution of mission investment and structure.

‡ © Church Publishing Inc., NY, NY. Used with permission.

- Globalization of communication, culture and economics has developed as a major dynamic in international life.

- Church funds are being released as the church's covenanted commitments decrease to former Episcopal jurisdictions that are now autonomous Anglican provinces.

- The events of and following 11 September 2001 have prompted reflection about inter-religious relations and the projection of US presence abroad.

- The 20/20 Initiative, which seeks to double Episcopal Sunday church attendance by 2020, is reshaping the church's expectations of its life and profile in society.

These and other developments make it imperative to take stock now and look to the future. For this envisioning, the Commission consulted with many companions in mission: the Episcopal Partnership for Global Mission and its member organizations in the areas of sending, hosting, education, funding and networking; the Seminary Consultation on Mission; international mission companions in Africa, Asia, Europe, Latin America, and Oceania; agencies in other Anglican provinces; ecumenical companions; and missionaries of the church serving through various agencies.

The canons charge the Commission to advise the church on mission policy. We offer this document as a resource for guidance in the mission policy of the Domestic and Foreign Missionary Society and for the many other groups who share in the Episcopal Church's world mission.

I. Theological Basis: God Is On Mission In Christ

Christian mission—the activity of sending and being sent in Christ—is grounded in the missionary nature of the triune God as revealed in scripture. In creation, God reached out to create communities of life. With Israel and throughout history, God has moved to restore people to unity with God, with one another, and with all creation. In Christ, God is still on mission in the world through the Holy Spirit. The church's call is to join God in that mission.

The central act in God's mission is God's self-sending in Jesus Christ, the word made flesh and dwelling among us in love. As God's mission became incarnate in the person of Jesus, so people and communities are central in the mission in which God invites the church's participation as the body of Christ. The reign of God that Jesus announced: this we are called to proclaim and enact in mission. The love of God that Jesus expressed in presence, compassion, healing and justice: this we are called to live in mission. The reconciliation that God offers a sinful and broken world in Jesus' death and resurrection: this is the hope we offer the world in mission.

"As the Father sent me, so I send you," said the risen Christ to his disciples, including them and us in the gift of being sent by God. God's sending the Holy Spirit on Pentecost galvanized the earliest Christian community to proclaim Christ in word and deed, with power and joy. In that anointing by the Spirit, Christians from that day to our own have felt moved to cross the many boundaries among human communities to meet and share the presence and work of Christ with people different from themselves. This impulse has made Christian mission global as well as local from its inception.

Ministering in dimensions of difference, eucharistic communities of the baptized become different themselves through mission. We discover the gospel afresh and receive our identities back transfigured, closer to the likeness of Christ. This transfiguration occurred as the early community of Jesus discovered God at work beyond its own Jewish boundaries among the Gentiles, a surprising new people of God. It has continued wherever Christians have reached beyond themselves to meet and embrace others across the divides of culture, religion, race and ethnicity.

What are we sent to do? "You shall be my witnesses," said the risen Jesus. Storytelling is essential to Christian witness, telling the story of what God has done in human lives in light of the story of what God has done in Christ. In Jesus' words, "I was hungry and you fed me . . . I was naked and you clothed me," we hear our call to reach out in deed, offering Christ's whole ministry of justice and reconciliation in solidarity with a suffering world. As we meet Christ in the neighbor, God's mission transforms both the world and the community of Jesus as it rediscovers its call to discipleship. As the missionary church witnesses in word and deed, God works through it to reconcile all peoples in Christ and renew the face of the earth.

II. An Ethos For Mission: God's People Are Companions In Mission

In Christ God calls and forms the church to be a missionary people participating by the power of the Holy Spirit in God's mission in the world. The historic legacies of mission, the nature of the Episcopal Church, and the crises of the world situation highlight particular features of God's call to us today as Anglicans and Episcopalians. Missionary character is important at all levels in the church: in parishes and dioceses, in individual missionaries and their supporters, in voluntary societies, church-wide agencies and their leaders.

Companionship is the central characteristic that God's missionary people are developing in the Episcopal Church in the 21st century. God is calling our church as a whole to be a companion with other churches in the Anglican Communion and beyond. Dioceses and parishes are living out their call to be companions with dioceses and parishes in other countries. Individual missionaries are ministering as companions in their places of service.

Literally, companions share bread together. Theologically, companions share in Christ the bread of life. Today the missionary and the mission community journey with others and form community in Christ. In such companionship both missionary and supporting community are transfigured as they experience the gospel life of their companion communities. The personal and communal presence of companionship coheres with an Anglican theological emphasis on incarnation as the culmination of God's presence in the world.

Companionship in mission constitutes a shift from some modes of the colonial era, when sending churches in the Global North were sometimes confident that they had everything to teach and nothing to learn. Focus on companionship also modifies the partnership principle that has guided inter-Anglican mission relationships since the early 1970s. Mission companions in other parts of the world have felt that partnership, while helpfully moving us away from assumptions of dominance, has emphasized doing at the expense of presence, and getting tasks done rather than growing together. Solidarity with the suffering is a central expression of mission companionship. The mission church may not be able to solve the anguish, violence and injustice suffered by the companion church, but simply being present in the place of fear, loss and isolation expresses the love of Christ.

A shift from partnership to companionship has been endorsed by the Mission Commission of the Anglican Communion in its 1999 report Anglicans in Mission: A Transforming Journey.[1] It accords well with the central theme of accompaniment in the world mission work of the Evangelical Lutheran Church in America, our closest ecumenical companion.[2]

Other characteristics are integral to the ethos of mission we seek to embody. In the 21st century, God is calling Christians and the church to be a mission companion that is a:

- **Witness**—"You are witnesses of these things," said Jesus to his disciples. Witness in word means sharing the story of what God has done with us in light of the story of what God has done in Christ Jesus. Such witness is a natural and inevitable fruit of life in Christ, and it is the heart of evangelism as a mission imperative. Sharing the story with those who have never heard it is a crucial gift. This is true equally in Alabama, Austria and Azerbaijan, that is, in the public square in our own context, in the former Christendom where the gospel has been heard and widely rejected, and in places where its proclamation may be a new event. Sharing our story with others must be part of a dialogue in which we listen to the stories others share with us, whether from places of little faith or other religious paths. The religious diversity of the 21st century, like that of the early centuries of Christianity, calls us to hold together the multiple tasks of listening, learning, and bearing witness to Christ.

- **Pilgrim**—Episcopal missionaries today see themselves as pilgrims, growing in their knowledge of God through the perspectives of the people to whom they are sent, learning as much as they share, receiving as much as they give. The humility of this orientation and the missionary's eagerness to learn from companions in another culture and socioeconomic context nurtures deep and lasting relationships in mission. The cross-cultural encounter transforms us as we discover Christ afresh through another people's appropriation of the gospel. Authentic mission pilgrims neither romanticize their contexts nor focus solely on what mission is doing for themselves. Instead, the pilgrim motif opens the door to true mutuality in mission, where, as the Anglican Consultative Council said about partnership, "all are givers and all are receivers."

- **Servant**—"I came not to be served but to serve," said Jesus. Servanthood in mission means that we listen to the stated needs of our mission companions, look for signs of God's work in them, and collaborate with them in discerning how God is guiding the implementation of mission vision. It means that missionaries and the mission church put aside prior images of our companions, pre-conceived analyses of their situations, and ready-made solutions to problems. It means that missionaries seek to meet Christ in all situations, including those that arise when new circumstances supersede their stated job descriptions and postpone their cherished goals. For Episcopalians, authentic servanthood is a crucial counter to the assumptions we develop on the basis of our extraordinary access to the power of information, technology and money. Servanthood is a key mark for our church as a whole, which is sometimes perceived as a domineering church from a superpower nation.

- **Prophet**—Episcopal mission pilgrims today often find their views of political, racial and economic relationships in the world challenged and transformed. Experiences of poverty, suffering and violence alongside experiences of affluence, oppression and security often radicalize the foreigners, whether they are long-term missioners, visiting bishops, or short-term teams. These then prophesy to their sending church, prodding it to inquire more deeply into dynamics about which it may have become complacent or resigned. They often offer a similar gift in their mission site as they challenge entrenched powers of oppression. Episcopalians in the 21st century are called to prophesy both to our own church and to the world church, that the Body of Christ may be a mustard seed of God's Jubilee in the world, working justice for the whole human family.

- *Ambassador*—In addition to witnessing in word and deed as ambassadors of Christ, the missionary and mission community are ambassadors of the sending church. Individuals and teams from ECUSA must be aware always that companions are experiencing the vision, faithfulness and integrity of the Episcopal Church through their conversation, conduct and life. This calls for living out the highest ethical standards in personal honesty, respect for others, financial transparency, and faithfulness in personal and professional relationships. The role of ambassador also entails a commitment to represent fairly the life of the Episcopal Church.

- *Host*—"Let a little water be brought, and wash your feet," said Abraham to the three strangers who appeared at Mamre. "Let it be to me according to your word," said Mary to the angel Gabriel. In initiating mission, God is not forcible but invites a response of hospitality. As we receive mission companions from around the world, hospitality must be central in our response. Hospitality means that we listen to what our companions say, offer them opportunities to experience the breadth of our church, and care for their needs for food, lodging, travel and friendship. As we go abroad, we are likewise called to be generous and hospitable with those whom God brings to us.

- *Sacrament*—As the body of Christ, the church is a sacrament of Christ, an outward and visible sign of Christ's inward and spiritual grace. As members of the body, all Christians participate in the communion of the saints and so are members of the sacramental revelation of God embodied in the incarnation of Jesus Christ. A Christian on mission is a sacramental sign of God's mission to reconcile all people with one another and with God in Christ. The people and communities the missionary meets are likewise sacramental signs of God's global presence. This sacramental emphasis on persons helps both missionaries and sending groups to retain an incarnational focus on people, relationships and community, which is where God truly lives and where the most lasting impacts are made. The missionary in any place is a sign of the gospel's universality, the fact that it transcends cultural, geographical and linguistic boundaries to create local, embodied communities in Christ in all places and times.

[The text is omitted for section III. The Context For Mission: World Crisis And Mission Integrity.]

IV. Modes Of Mission: Incarnate Presence In A World Community

[The text omitted includes introductory paragraph, 1. Mission Education to Equip the Church, and 2. Missionary Sending to Offer Companionship, 3. Missionary Hosting to Offer Transfiguration, and 4. Short-Term Mission to Nourish Pilgrimage.]

5. Ecumenical and Inter-Faith Cooperation to Unify the Witness

Created in the image of the triune God, humans are by nature communal. As we worship God, proclaim the gospel, and promote justice, peace and love, we do so in community. As we are one body with many parts, we are one community with many gifts to be shared. Authentic witness respects other communities, whether in conflict or harmony, and recognizes the gifts they bring.

Dialogue and collaboration with other churches and with other faiths is a powerful witness in itself. For too long, Christian missions were denominational missions that failed to collaborate with each other. Missionaries were sometimes more effective in demonstrating the disunity of Christianity than the universal message of Christ.

All Episcopal mission activity must seek to work with our ecumenical companions, other faiths and the broader community. We must seek dialogue, at the very least, and, where possible, collaboration in ministry. Our doors should open inward to all who wish to enter, and should open outward so that those within can go out to share truly in ministry with others. The nature of our collaboration will vary considerably, but it should be based on the Lund Principle that we should not do things alone that can be done with others. With close ecumenical companions this may mean shared eucharistic feasts and joint formation programs. With other churches and with other faiths and secular groups, it might mean cooperation in reaching out to the sick, the homeless, and victims of violence.

With ecumenical and interfaith groups, initiatives to encourage contact and dialogue are imperative for reconciliation amid today's heightened tensions among religions, especially between Islam and Christianity. With all, God is calling us to join hands and speak out when religious freedom is curtailed and when the social, environmental, economic, or political welfare of communities is damaged.

It is not necessary to hold identical doctrines or practice identical liturgies in order to collaborate in the mission of Christ. Shared witness in action joins our prayer with Christ's prayer that all may be one. It allows different voices to be heard. It encourages faith's expression in the vernacular. It honors diversity in unity. It allows the Holy Spirit to move and be felt among us without the hindrance of our preconceptions. Mission becomes no longer the denomination's mission or even the church's mission, but God's mission in the world.

The Commission calls on all Episcopal mission groups to undertake intentional group reflection on the impact their work has on inter-religious relationships in the geographical areas they serve. We call on mission groups to develop links with other churches and mission agencies in the geographic areas they serve and, where possible, develop links with work done by other religious groups and by secular groups.

[*The text omitted includes sections 6. Companion Dioceses to Broaden Our Relationships, in addition to sections on Financial Grants to Catalyze Gift Exchange, 8. Episcopal and Anglican Networks to Nourish Collaboration, V. Resources For World Mission: Equipping The Church For The 21st Century, 1. A Plan to Re-Deploy the Church's World Mission Funds, 2. Specific Initiatives to Implement Companions in Transformation, and 3. A Plan to Study and Prepare to Implement the Vision in 2006*]

A Doxology

Embracing the ethos of world mission set forth in this vision and implementing its proposals will require a cultural shift in the Episcopal Church.

Where we have been paralyzed by guilt, we give ourselves to be transformed by repentance. Where we feared that cross-cultural encounters must entail cultural violence, we offer ourselves to be transfigured through walking with Christians in diverse settings. Where we trusted that our understandings are sufficient, we anticipate that international companions will energize our pilgrimage from new starting places. Where we hesitated to share Christ's gospel, we know ourselves called into religious encounters where witness and dialogue are inseparable. Where we depended on grants and programs, we feel the Holy Spirit nurturing relationships with persons and groups, and there we find Christ luminously present. Where we once suspected that the gospel is marginal to the world's real challenges, we see that Christian presence and prophecy are vital to healing in the world's crises. Where we thought that integrity calls us *out of* mission, we hear God is calling us *into* mission and realize that mission engagement is vital to Christian integrity.

With the writer to the Ephesians we exclaim: "Glory to God whose power working in us can do infinitely more than we can ask or imagine! Glory to God from generation to generation in the church, and in Christ Jesus forever and ever!"

(The remainder of the text omitted includes Standing Commission on World Misson and Further Reading on World Mission.)

1.   John Clarke and Eleanor Johnson, eds., *Anglicans in Mission: A Transforming Journey* (London and Ottawa: SPCK, 2000).

2.   Division of for Global Mission, Evangelical Lutheran Church in America, *Global Mission in the Twenty-first Century: A Vision of Evangelical Faithfulness in God's Mission* (Chicago: Evangelical Lutheran Church in America, [1999].

Renewing Our Pledge
Reflections on A Common Word Between Us and You
Prepared by Lucinda Mosher, Th.D. for
The Office of Ecumenical and Interreligious Relations
The Episcopal Church
February 10, 2008

1. On Eid al-Fitr al-Mubarak 1428 A. H. (13 October 2007 C. E.), *A Common Word Between Us and You: An Open Letter and Call from Muslim Religious Leaders,* to "Leaders of Christian Churches, everywhere," was promulgated. The Archbishop of Canterbury was one of twenty-eight international Christian leaders to be greeted by name. His copy of the letter was hand-carried to him by one of the 138 signatories, each significant in stature and influence, and together embodying the breadth of Islam, geographically and otherwise. *A Common Word* makes five key points: that the ground shared by Muslims and Christians is located in our respective scriptural mandates to love God and neighbor; that, for Muslims, dialogue is a divine imperative; that Islam is not inherently anti-Christian; that exploration of our shared ground requires that we move beyond mere polite conversation to action in concert with each other; that striving together for fairness, justice, and mutual goodwill is absolutely necessary for the welfare of the world. Such a substantial document deserves a substantial response. The following is offered as a contribution from the national Episcopal Church to such a response from the Office of the Archbishop of Canterbury.

The equivalence of the "Best Remembrance" and the "Great Commandment"

2. Much of the body of *A Common Word* is devoted to careful and detailed textual analysis of the Bible and the Qur'ān in support of the contention that what Christians know as the Great Commandment—*You shall love the Lord your God with all your heart, and with all your soul, and with all your mind, and with all your strength* (Mark 12:30)—is equivalent in meaning and import to what Muslims know as the Best Remembrance—*There is no god but God* (al-Fath 48:29). This argument is perhaps the most interesting and enlightening aspect of this document, in that it provides us Christians with a helpful opportunity to experience the Islamic exegetical process.

Further, such a close reading of the Bible implicitly encourages Christians to take up close reading of the Qur'ān.

3. We concur that complete devotion to God is the duty, privilege, and hallmark of observant Muslims and Christians alike. For Christians, love of God with heart, soul, mind, and strength is indeed paramount. We Episcopalians therefore sing: "Splendor and honor and kingly power are yours by right, O Lord our God, For you created everything that is, and by your will they were created and have their being...."

4. We Episcopalians applaud A Common Word's careful analysis of the Great Commandment. Even more so, we are grateful to learn that "the Best Remembrance" is an honorific bestowed by the Prophet Muhammad on the first of the two parts of the Shahadah. Drawing upon various Qur'ānic phrases, Muhammad expanded it thus: "There is no god but God, He alone, He has no associate [sharīk, sometimes translated "partner"], His is the sovereignty and His is the praise and He has power over all things." A Common Word's exegesis of this expansion is a fine educational resource for us Episcopalians as we strive to help our fellow Christians understand Muslim thought more fully. For example, whereas a Christian reader might have anticipated the phrase Lā sharīka lah (He has no associate) to be interpreted as a refutation or rejection of the Christian doctrines of Trinity and Incarnation, A Common Word takes a different tack: "The words: He hath no associate, remind Muslims that they must love God uniquely, without rivals within their souls, since God says in the Holy Qur'ān [al-Baqarah 2:165a]: Yet there are men who take rivals unto God: they love them as they should love God...." We read this and recall the Lord said to Moses, You shall have no other gods before me (Exodus 20:3); and, that Jesus said, No one can serve two masters;...You cannot serve God and wealth (Matthew 6:24).

Dialogue as required by God

5. David Lochhead identifies four common ideological responses to the fact of an increasingly interreligious world: Isolation, Hostility, Competition, and Partnership. In each case, Christian theologians have demonstrated its authentic Christian-ness. Muslim examples of all four positions vis-à-vis the non-Muslim certainly can be found as well. While these ideologies continue to be popular in each of our religion-communities, a vastly preferable alternative is the dialogical relationship (as Lochhead names it): a relationship of openness and trust which is clear, unambiguous, and has no other purpose than itself. Just as the other four ideologies have been advocated traditionally with scriptural support, so, too, is the relationship of dialogue. In fact, Lochhead asserts, Christians have a biblically-based mandate to unconditional openness to the neighbor: a biblical "imperative to seek dialogue and to be open to dialogue whenever and from whomever it is offered."

6. A Common Word lays out Islam's own dialogical imperative, and declares: "As Muslims, and in obedience to the Holy Qur'ān, we ask Christians to come together with us on the common essentials of our two religions...that we shall worship none but God...Let this common ground be the basis of all future interfaith dialogue between us, for our common ground is that on which stands all the Law and the Prophets (Matthew 22:40)." A Common Word's invitation to dialogue is taken directly from the Qur'ān itself: Come to a common word between us and you: that we shall worship none but God, and that we shall ascribe no partner unto Him, and that none of us shall take others for lords beside God. (al-'Imran 3:64a) The document's interpretation of associate (as noted above) enables us Christians to accept the invitation with integrity.

Islam is not inherently anti-Christian

7. A Christians, we take delight in the Qur'ān's assertion, *O humanity! We created you from a single male and female, and made you into nations and tribes, that you might know each other. Certainly the most honored of you in the sight of God is the most righteous of you.* (al-Hujurāt 49:13) Inherent here is a reminder of the necessity of humility. We recall St. Paul's admonition: *By the grace given to me I say to everyone among you not to think of yourself more highly than you ought to think, but to think with sober judgment, each according to the measure of faith that God has assigned.* (Romans 12:3) We are grateful that *A Common Word* (in Section III) acknowledges the very real differences between Muslims and Christians in terms of doctrine and practice: such difference will (and must) persist. Be such differences as they may, A Common Word moves toward its conclusion by asserting: "As Muslims, we say to Christians that we are not against them and that Islam is not against them—so long as they do not wage war against Muslims on account of their religion, oppress the, and drive them out of their homes." This apology leads in the document to the obverse query: "Is Christianity necessarily against Muslims?"

8. A Common Word answers its own question by arguing that Mark 9:40 and Luke 9:50 (*Whoever is not against us is for us*) need not be read as a contradiction of Matthew 12:30 (*Whoever is not with me is against me.*) We would suggest that a more robust answer be found in the biblical imperative toward hospitality and neighbor-love. Thus we take delight in the fact that much of *A Common Word* is given over to demonstration that love of neighbor as oneself is mandated of Muslims and Christians alike.

9. For Episcopalians, it can be argued, the mandate to be "for" Muslims is latent in our Baptismal Covenant. This formula, which begins with the Apostles' Creed, is of course an affirmation of our identity and allegiance; but in it we may also discern the imperative to promote positive inter-religious relations. Notably, in every reaffirmation of this covenant, we promise to seek and serve Christ in *all* persons. We recall that the interfaith documents of the 1988 Lambeth Conference of Bishops of the Anglican Communion articulate in depth an Anglican theology of religious difference, which they do in profoundly incarnational terms.

10. As Christians, we insist that the One and Only God is Triune. That is, we understand the One and Only God to be *Relationship Itself.* That is, "the very life of God [as] a 'being with," as the Lambeth documents assert. We celebrate that in Jesus we have come to know Immanu-el: *God With Us.* We recall that the Christ whom we promise to seek and serve in all persons is he who told us that the Greatest Commandment is to love both God *and* Neighbor; and, through the story of the Good Samaritan, defined "neighbor" in terms of the *other* who makes a claim on us by virtue of his or her *nearness.* When we are commanded to love God and to love our neighbors as ourselves—we are, in effect, commanded to "be with" our neighbors. When it comes to neighbors whose religions are different from ours, our Anglican Communion interfaith documents teach that we can begin by taking advantage of each opportunity of encounter to eavesdrop: "to overhear what dialogue there may be between God and these people, between the God who calls all into being by a process of sharing and communication, and other peoples in their religious cultures."

11. Turning again to the *A Common Word's* question, *Is Christianity necessarily against Muslims?*, we note well that the Ninth of the Ten Commandments received by Moses orders us not

to bear false witness against our neighbor (Exodus 20:16). In fact, we are hard pressed to bear accurate witness to the religion of our neighbors if we have little sense of what their religion is about. Bearing truthful witness regarding our neighbor includes what we say about their religions' beliefs and practices. Certainly, we can be of better service, more loving, more respectful of dignity, more likely to establish justice and peace (all of which we promise to do by means of our reaffirmation of our Baptismal Covenant) if we bring to that effort an understanding of how our neighbor "establishes, maintains, and celebrates a meaningful world"—which is a helpful working definition of religion itself.

12. As a consequence of the engagement for which *A Common Word* calls, we will have the opportunity to become "theologically and religiously multilingual" (as Martin Forward puts it) so that we can bear truthful witness about our neighbors. All the while we are striving to become theologically multilingual, we Christians must take seriously the necessity to "continue in the apostles' teaching and fellowship, in the breaking of bread, and in the prayers" (Acts 2:42), just as Muslims must continue to follow the Qur'ān and the Prophet's *Sunnah*. Thus love of neighbor as oneself also entails delighting in our differences—even the deepest ones. In effect, we are for what Diana Eck calls the encounter of commitments, thus allowing neighbors to remain "other"—indeed, to *thrive* as other.

13. This provokes yet another issue: that of intra-religious education. Worldwide, Christians and Muslims have much work to do to teach our co-religionists that we have no inherent necessity to be "anti-" the other in order to be true to our own religion-community.

More is demanded than mere "polite ecumenical dialogue"

14. "Finding common ground between Muslims and Christians is not simply a matter for polite ecumenical dialogue between selected religious leaders," *A Common Word* declares. Certainly, we concur. However, properly understood, dialogue (while it is indeed characterized by courtesy and forbearance) is never mere polite conversation. Rather, dialogue is dialectical and reciprocal; unlike debate, its purpose is the gaining of clarity on a matter rather than winning an argument. For Daniel Yankelovich, *dialogue* is a technical term which names *transformative activity*—a constellation of strategies employed for the purpose of strengthening relationships or solving problems. The transformative nature of dialogue is acknowledged in the agreement (signed January 2002) to sustain a relationship between the offices of the Archbishop of Canterbury and the Grand Imam of al-Azhar: "We believe that friendship which overcomes religious, ethnic and national differences is a gift of the Creator in whom we all believe.…We believe that direct dialogue results in restoration of the image of each in the eyes of the other."

15. As a way forward, a useful model can be elicited from the *Building Bridges Seminar*, a project of scholarly engagement which the Anglican Communion facilitates between Muslims and Christians, and which has met annually since 2002. The project's aim has been "to create an environment for bridge-building in the sense of "creating new routes for information, appreciation and respect to travel freely and safely in both directions between Christians and Muslims, Muslims and Christians." Of the various methods used in these gatherings, studying the Bible and the Qur'ān together has been particularly fruitful. As Michael Ipgrave stresses in his reflections on the project, "for Muslims and Christians, our mutual recognition of one another as people who bear within ourselves the transforming burden of the divine Word is the surest ground on which to build friendship, trust and cooperation."

16. The *Building Bridges* model is replicable on the local and national level. The topics explored and the texts studied are reported in the seminar's digests. It offers resources which laypersons as well as scholars and religious leaders, or congregants of a neighboring mosque and church, might adapt to weekly or monthly sessions. This is one method; there are others.

17. Regardless of the choice of method, we acknowledge the need to develop deep knowledge of the contents of each other's sacred texts, and also of the ways in which each community reads and understands them. There is need to deepen our knowledge of each other, not only through mutual theological engagement and reflection, but through conversation at every level on such matters as human rights, the rule of law, and care for our fragile planet. There is need to consider together the relationship between faith and national identity; between governance, divine justice, political authority, and religious freedom—taking into account both majority and minority situations for Christians and Muslims, and the implications of secularism as well. However, to undertake this in any location and at any level (even the grassroots) will require considerable institutional support, advocacy, and commitment from Muslims and Christians alike.

18. What truly is at stake here is this question: How are we to broaden the conversation between "us" and "you"? That is, How exactly do we enter into "a common word between us and you"? In recent years, we have become increasingly aware of the complexity of Islam, a point made by a number of scholars—from Bruce Lawrence (himself an Episcopalian) to the Pakistani-American Muslim Jamal Elias. As Elias reminds us:

> [Islam is] the majority religion in countries as diverse as Morocco in the west and Indonesia in the east, and from Senegal in the south to Kazakhstan in the north. In each of these countries Islam is practiced in a distinct way…It is therefore possible to speak of numerous "fault-lines" of identity along which one can differentiate Muslims, these being lines of language, ethnicity, race, nationhood, gender, attitudes toward the modern world, experience with colonialism, age, economic status, social status, sectarian identity, and so on. Any statement about Muslim beliefs that claims to be universal ends up being disproved by exceptions somewhere in the Muslim world.

19. With just a few adjustments, Elias's description of the complexity of Islam can become a description of the reality of the Anglican Communion's own diversity (thus complexity). Anglicanism has its own range of temporal and geographical particularities, its own multiplicity of expression and experience. Furthermore, a description in the style of Elias aptly lays out the multiplicity of temporal, geographical, and contextual particularities in Anglicanism's relationship to Islam, thus of Anglicans to Muslims. This cross-faith relationship has had its positive and negative dimensions over the centuries, and it has been played out on most of the earth's continents and in a great many countries.

20. If Anglicanism brings a unique charism to the invitation to improve Christian-Muslim relations worldwide, it is our very nature as *communio oppositorum*. Anglicanism at its core is an ongoing attempt to hold "difference" together. We say of ourselves that—by virtue of the Elizabethan Settlement—our communion is a *via media*, at once Catholic and Reformed. The worldwide Anglican Communion comprises more than 80 million Christians in 44 regional and national member churches in more than 160 countries. We hold together difference across fault-lines of culture, economics, politics, experience of colonialism, and experience of (and attitude toward) the Other-Than-Christian. All of this is prefatory to saying that there is not—indeed,

there cannot be—a single Anglican way of proceeding. There will be a range of responses to *A Common Word*. What will be decidedly Anglican will be the effort to hold together diverse answers.

21. We wish to respond to the Muslim invitation to share a common word by living these realities out at the local level at least as much as at the national and international levels. As important as be official statements and documents, we want *A Common Word's* initiative to take flesh. We must move toward action, and we are ready to do so. Indeed, in 2003 the General Convention of the Episcopal Church determined to "embody and strengthen" its commitment to Christian-Muslim dialogue. *A Common Word* serves to remind us of our pledge.

The necessity for global welfare of mutual striving toward fairness, justice, and goodwill

22. Having laid out the consequences for behaving otherwise, *A Common Word* concludes: "Let our difference not cause hatred and strife between us. Let us vie with each other only in righteousness and good works. Let us respect each other, be fair, just and kind to [one] another and live in sincere peace, harmony and mutual goodwill." We hear in this invitation its Qur'ānic basis: *If God had so willed, He could have made you one people. But He wanted to test you by that which He has given you. So vie, then, with one another in doing good deeds. To Him will you all return in the end, that He may instruct you regarding that on which you differed.* (al-Ma'idah 5:48b) *And again, Each has a goal toward which he turns. Vie, therefore, with one another in doing good deeds. Wherever you are, God will bring you all together. Certainly God has power over all things.* (al-Baqarah 2:148)

23. We listen to this challenge, and recall that Jesus has taught us: *Blessed are the peacemakers, for they will be call children of God.* (Matthew 5:9) We hear Micah ask: *What does the Lord require of you but to do justice, and to love kindness, and to walk humbly with your God?* (Micah 6:8) The Psalmist enjoins us to *seek peace and pursue it.* (Psalm 34:14) The result, says Isaiah: *justice will dwell in the wilderness, and righteousness abide in the fruitful field. And the effect of righteousness will be peace.... Righteousness and peace will kiss each other.* (Isaiah 32:16-17; 85:10) We take seriously the admonition of St. Paul: *Whatever is true, whatever is honorable, whatever is just, whatever is pure, whatever is pleasing, whatever is commendable, if there is any excellence and if there is anything worthy of praise, think about these things. ...and the God of peace be with you.* (Philippians 4:8-9). Therefore, by our Baptismal Covenant, we Episcopalians promise to "strive for justice and peace among all people, and respect the dignity of every human being," each of whom, according to Genesis 1:26, is made *in God's image and after God's likeness.*

24. For reasons such as these, the Episcopal Church's House of Bishops, at its first meeting following the events of 9/11/01, called upon the Episcopal Church to "wage reconciliation," asserting, in part:

> As members of a global community and the worldwide Anglican Communion, we are called to bear one another's burdens across the divides of culture, religion, and differing views of the world.... We are called to self-examination and repentance: the willingness to change direction, to open our hearts and give room to God's compassion as it seeks to bind up, to heal, and to make all things new and whole. God's project, in which we participate by virtue of our baptism, is the ongoing work of reordering and

transforming the patterns of our common life so they may reveal God's justness—not as an abstraction but in bread for the hungry and clothing for the naked. The mission of the Church is to participate in God's work in the world. We claim that mission. Let us therefore wage reconciliation. Let us offer our gifts for the carrying out of God's ongoing work of reconciliation, healing and making all things new. To this we pledge ourselves and call our church.

Thus we Episcopalians cannot but concur with the claim of *A Common Word* that "the basis for peace and understanding already exists [and that] it is part of the very foundational principles of both faiths." However, these principles must be seen and experienced together in the crucible of lived encounter. Vying with one another in good works is crucial in our day; and while it can be framed in (or lead to) theological reflection, our mutual effort in good works can be wonderfully successful even if we grow but little in understanding each other's doctrines and practices.

25. Yet it bears repeating: we have as much vying with one another to do within our respective religion-communities as between them. Adherents of each religion—as individuals and as various local communities—have fallen short of our ideals and we need to be honest about that, together and in dialogue. Only then can the prophet Isaiah's vision of peace begin to be fulfilled: The wilderness and the dry land shall be glad, the desert shall rejoice and blossom; like the crocus it shall blossom abundantly, and rejoice with joy and singing. (Isaiah 35:1-2a). Borrowing the words of St. Francis of Assisi, who by his own example modeled positive Christian-Muslim relations, we therefore pray: "Lord, make us instruments of your peace. Where there is hatred, let us sow love;…where there is sadness, joy. Grant that we may not so much seek…to be understood as to understand."

Wa alaykum as-salām.

Theological Statement on Interreligious Relations
adopted by
The 76th General Convention
of
The Episcopal Church
2009‡

I. Introduction

We affirm the foundational Gospel proclamation that "Jesus is Lord" (I Corinthians 12:3 NRSV here and hereafter), and therefore [we affirm] Summary of God's Law: "love the Lord your God with all your hearts, with all your souls, and with all your minds, and to love your neighbor as yourself" (Mark 12:29-31; BCP, Catechism, page 851). For this reason we reach out in love and genuine openness to know and to understand those of other religions.

‡   Used with permission from The Archives of The Episcopal Church.

Therefore, we commend to all our members: dialogue for building relationships, the sharing of information, religious education, and celebration with people of other religions as part of Christian life, [with a reminder that]

1. dialogue begins when people meet each other;

2. dialogue depends upon mutual understanding, mutual respect and mutual trust;

3. dialogue makes it possible to share in service to the community;

4. dialogue is a medium of authentic witness by all parties and not an opportunity for proselytizing.

We believe that such dialogue may be a contribution toward helping people of different religions grow in mutual understanding and making common cause in peacemaking, social justice, and religious liberty.

We further encourage dioceses, congregations, and other organizations of The Episcopal Church to initiate such dialogue in partnership with other Christian Churches and in consultation with other provinces of the Communion, where appropriate.

2. As we engage other religious traditions, our work must be grounded in thoughtful exploration of and reflection on the appropriate ways to profess Christianity in the context of other religious traditions. This document is an initial reflection on why we are participating in multireligious relationships. It explores the contexts for doing so and seeks to discern the unique contribution of The Episcopal Church to such relationships. As Christians we celebrate and affirm our witness to the gospel of Jesus Christ. "He is the image of the invisible God, the firstborn of all creation" (Colossians 1:15). We rejoice in our call to spread the good news of God's love and reconciliation through engaging in life-enhancing relationships with all of God's people.

II. Historical Context

3. The Episcopal Church and the Anglican Communion have had a long interest and involvement in interreligious matters, which have historically been addressed in the context of mission. Prominent Episcopalians were involved in the first World Parliament of Religions in 1893. The Episcopal Church and Anglican Communion were well represented at the 1910 Edinburgh Missionary Conference, which was called to discuss cooperation in the global mission field and gave birth to the modern ecumenical movement. In the decades that followed, the Anglican Communion and The Episcopal Church were influenced by the important theologies of mission developed by John V. Taylor (Bishop of Winchester and General Secretary of the Church Mission Society) and Lesslie Newbigin (a minister of the Church of Scotland and later a Bishop in the Church of South India). In The Episcopal Church, engagement with Native American culture has resulted in the establishment of significant missionary presence in certain areas.

4. The groundbreaking 1965 document from Vatican Council II, *Nostra Aetate* (In Our Time), helped to inaugurate a new era of dialogue between Christians and those of other religions. In the Anglican Communion, the 1988 Lambeth Conference issued a major report commending dialogue with people of other faiths as part of Christian discipleship and mission. It also produced the first Anglican Communion document on dialogue with Abrahamic traditions, *Jews,*

Christians and Muslims: The Way of Dialogue. This document was recommended for study; and the Provinces were asked to initiate talks wherever possible on a tripartite basis with both Jews and Muslims. Other important resources we have used here include *Generous Love: the Truth of the Gospel and the Call to Dialogue,* issued in 2008 by the Network for Interfaith Concerns (NIFCON) of the Anglican Communion; the Archbishop of Canterbury's 2007 reply to *A Common Word,* an overture from Muslim scholars for dialogue with Christians; and *Relations with Other World Religions,* Section F of the 2008 Lambeth Conference Indaba Reflections.

5. The Episcopal Church's primary participation in interreligious dialogue has taken several forms:

- Ecumenical efforts with other Christians, through the Interfaith Relations Commission of the National Council of Churches of Christ. The 1999 Assembly of the National Council of Churches unanimously approved a policy statement giving a theological rationale for participating in interreligious dialogue.

- International efforts through the Anglican Communion Office, including the Network for Interfaith Concerns.

- Particular initiatives taken by the Presiding Bishop as primate and chief pastor of the church.

- Task force initiatives, first the Presiding Bishop's Advisory Committee on Interfaith Relations (through 1997) and then the Standing Commission on Ecumenical Relations (from 1997-2003).

- Diocesan, congregational and individual efforts in peace making and interreligious dialogue.

6. In addition, in response to the terrorist attacks of September 11, 2001, Episcopal Relief and Development funded the Interfaith Education Initiative, a three-year program in conjunction with the Office of Ecumenical and Interfaith Relations that surveyed the interfaith work of The Episcopal Church and developed educational resources for interreligious dialogue. This project culminated in a conference held at Washington National Cathedral in 2004, and in the publication of the *IEI Manual on Interfaith Dialogue.*

7. In 2003, the General Convention officially located oversight of the church's interreligious work with the Standing Commission on Ecumenical Relations, which was renamed the Standing Commission on Ecumenical and Interreligious Relations (SCEIR).

III. Current Context

8. As the Indaba Reflections from Lambeth note, "The contexts within which the Church ministers around the world vary widely and the potential for interfaith dialogue will vary accordingly" (¦ 93). The following paragraphs are an attempt to note some of the ways in which our context informs our approach to interreligious relations.

9. Today the picture of the world we have to carry is of the earth seen from space. Borders and boundaries are fluid, easily fractured, and unstable. The peoples of the earth will either survive together or perish together. Paradoxically our entire world is, at the same time, housed inside

the flat screens of computers that provide immediate access to almost anyone or anything at any-time, anywhere on the planet. Crises and conflicts that were once local matters and seemed to be none of our concern are now global. Social strife, political upheaval and violence-predominantly fueled by greed and/or religious fanaticism-are not distant from us.

10. In the United States, the naive image of the world as a safe and stable place was shattered on September 11, 2001. Those killed in the attacks on the World Trade Center in New York came from many lands, prayed in many languages, called God by many names. They are a true micro-cosm of the shifting reality of who lives in the United States today, citizens and foreign nationals alike. For the first time in decades, people in the United States experienced what other people in other lands have experienced for generations: fear, grief and loss following from an assault on their homeland, the devastation of their people, and the shattering of a sense of well being. While grief and loss are certainly appropriate, fear is the opposite of truth, and fear has led some people of all religions to collude with, participate in, and justify political acts of violence and oppression which dishonor all concepts of the Sacred.

11. As Episcopalians, we recognize that our neighbors come from a variety of different beliefs and backgrounds, and we are unfamiliar with many of if not most of them. Christians continue to struggle to find common ground and mutual respect with Jews and Muslims who are fellow children of Abraham. Whether we intend to or not, we impact and are impacted in return—pow-erfully and profoundly—by each other's lives, cultures and beliefs. For each of us, the neighbor often seems to be the Other rather than the one whom Christ calls us to receive as a gift and to love as we would be loved ourselves.

12. In contemporary local and global contexts, The Episcopal Church faces crucial opportu-nities and challenges for developing new creative relationships with people of other religious heritages. Throughout the world, people of different religions can be seen searching for compat-ible if not common ways toward justice, peace and sustainable life. Our theological and ecclesial heritage offers significant resources for participating in this global quest.

IV. Scripture, Reason and Tradition as Resources in Interreligious Dialogue

13. As part of the Anglican Communion, The Episcopal Church seeks to be a community living in obedience to the Word of God revealed through Scripture, and to identify the contemporary message of that Word through bringing the insights of tradition and reason, to theological reflec-tion on interreligious relations.

Scripture and Reason

14. We understand the Holy Scriptures to be inspired by the Holy Spirit of God and at the same time the work of human authors, editors, and compilers. "All scripture is inspired by God and is useful for teaching, for reproof, for correction, and for training in righteousness" (2 Timothy 3:16). The Scriptures "contain all things necessary for salvation" (BCP, 513). In the Scriptures we discover the nature of God, by their witness to Jesus Christ, in their record of his teaching, and through their proclamation of the Good News of God's Reign for all people. We believe the Holy Spirit continues to guide us in our growing understanding of the Scriptures, which are always to be interpreted in the widest possible context of God's redeeming love for all people. Throughout our history, Episcopalians have wrestled with varying interpretations of the Scriptures. Such dif-

ferences are to be expected and appreciated as a direct consequence of our dynamic relationship with the Word of God and our experience of faith over time.

15. Christianity's Holy Scriptures reveal to us both the invitation and the direction to engage with people of other religions. In Genesis 1:26 we meet the loving God who created all people and all nations, and the awesome majesty of creation bids us humbly acknowledge that the fullness of God's intention is beyond the scope of our limited understanding; God's gracious love is not confined to the Christian community alone. Because of our faith in the incarnation of God in Jesus Christ, we expect to meet God in our neighbor, whom God commands us to love as we love ourselves (Mark 12:29-31).

16. The sixteenth-century Anglican theologian Richard Hooker helped form our tradition of Scriptural interpretation. In his major work, Of the Laws of Ecclesiastical Polity, Hooker argued that the Holy Spirit requires the church to use Reason to interpret scripture. For Hooker, the Scriptures reveal to us essential truths about God and ourselves that we cannot learn by any other means. In other matters of human life, God expects us to use our minds in order to reason together and thus discover, through conversation, debate, and argument, the right way forward. This requires respect for the opinions of other people of good will.

17. This Biblically-based respect for the diversity of understandings that authentic, truth-seeking human beings have is essential for communal reasoning and faithful living. The revelation of God in Christ calls us therefore to participate in our relationship with God and one another in a manner that is at once faithful, loving, lively, and reasonable. This understanding continues to call Episcopalians to find our way as one body through various conflicts. It is not a unity of opinion or a sameness of vision that holds us together. Rather, it is the belief that we are called to walk together in Jesus' path of reconciliation not only through our love for the other, but also through our respect for the legitimacy of the reasoning of the other. Respect for reason empowers us to meet God's unfolding world as active participants in the building of the Kingdom and to greet God's diverse people with appropriate welcome and gracious hospitality.

Tradition

18. Tradition is also an important aspect of Anglican theological understanding. As Anglicans we have always understood ourselves to be in continuity with the Catholic faith reaching back to the ancient, patristic church; we therefore hold the church's tradition in high regard. Anglicans have used tradition to inform our common reasoning as the church responds to new challenges and developments, using accumulated wisdom to show how similar challenges have been met in the past. For example, the English Reformers allowed tradition to shape the reformation of the Christianity they had received. Similarly, the founders of The Episcopal Church also placed great emphasis in tradition by continuing important beliefs and practices of the Church of England, such as its liturgy and ministry, and adapting them to the new context of the American republic, as in the American revival of the ancient practice of electing bishops. Tradition informed and shaped how Anglicans in these contexts responded to new situations.

19. Historically The Episcopal Church encountered religious pluralism and engaged in inter-religious relations in the context of the foreign mission field. In many cases this work was the product of dedicated missionaries called to spread the Gospel in faithfulness to the Great Commission. We are also aware that in many cases this work went hand in hand with American

expansionism in a combination of mission and empire. We need no better example than the ship sent to the newly-conquered Philippines that carried William Howard Taft as appointed governor and Charles Henry Brent as missionary bishop. We are shaped by these traditions: we are inspired by the energy, engagement, and faithfulness to the Gospel exhibited in the Anglican missionary engagement. Yet we recognize the need to be aware of the socio-religious implications of mission.

20. In turn, we hope that these examples from our history will help to shape future interreligious relationships. We pray for the same energy, engagement, and faithfulness to the Gospel that the Anglican missionary traditions display. We hope that these traditions will in turn shape our future relationships as missional ones of dialogue and companionship. *Companions in Transformation*, the official Global Mission vision statement adopted at the 2003 General Convention, emphasizes the importance of dialogue and companionship in engagement with other religious traditions. We believe the theological principles articulated there are also part of creating new traditions in interreligious relations, informed in classic Anglican fashion by our past.

21. We believe that interreligious work will carry forth God's intention for God's creation. It will provide us the opportunity to reflect the love of God we know through our redemption through the Incarnation of Christ; and it will provide us with the opportunity to build faithful communities that live out the majesty of God's will for the earth with more depth and in more forms than we currently experience within the limitations of our own rich religious community. And we believe that Episcopalians find our best resources in our historic understandings of Scripture, reason, and tradition to engage in this work of transformation.

V. Salvation in Christ and Interreligious Relations

22. The most sensitive aspects of interreligious relations concerns any religion's claims to unique or exclusive authority or revelation, including Christian traditions and teachings such as the incarnation, cross, and the resurrection of Jesus Christ. Christians affirm that God "has created all men and women in his image, and he wishes all to enjoy that fullness of life in his presence which we know as salvation" (*Generous Love*, Section 1). We also recognize that our efforts toward this goal are futile without the assistance of God in Christ through the power of the Holy Spirit. We are dependent on the grace of God—God's unconditional, undeserved love for those God has made. The source of salvation is God alone. Christians believe salvation comes through Jesus Christ, the Son of God.

23. As Christians "we are saved by grace through faith, and this is not our own doing, but the gift of God, not the result of works so that no one may boast. For we are what God has made us, created in Christ Jesus for good works, which God has prepared beforehand to be our way of life" (Ephesians 2: 8-10). In various ways, language of salvation refers to a form of deliverance from sin and the finiteness of this life as we experience it, with all its hardships and joys. Our hope of salvation expresses our expectation that we shall share in the life of God, and do so not only after death, but now.

24. The Christian scriptures proclaim that Jesus is "the Word made flesh" (John 1:14) and as such he is "the Way and the Truth and the Life" (John 14:6). As stated in our creeds (Apostles', and Nicene) and liturgy, Jesus Christ is the full revelation of God. Since God has chosen to share our life, we affirm that God is intensely concerned about every human life. Among Christians,

Episcopalians have a particular appreciation of this teaching, in that we believe that the coming of God in Christ has already begun to transform all of creation.

25. The human response to God's incarnate love was "to crucify the Lord of Glory" (1 Corinthians 2:8). The cross is the Christian symbol and act of self-emptying, humility, redemptive suffering, sacrificial self-giving, and unvanquished love. We believe that we have been reconciled to God through the cross.

26. In the resurrection we believe "Christ is risen from the dead, trampling down death by death, and giving life to those in the tomb" (BCP, p. 483). By our baptism into Christ's death and resurrection we enjoy new life as members of the Body of Christ, called therefore to become ourselves ambassadors of reconciliation (Romans 6:4; 2 Corinthians 5:14-20).

27. Professing salvation in Christ is not a matter of competing with other religious traditions with the imperative of converting one another. Each tradition brings its own understanding of the goal of human life to the interreligious conversation. Christians bring their particular profession of confidence in God's intentions as they are seen in and through the incarnation, death and resurrection of Jesus Christ. As the bishops at Lambeth 2008 noted, "The purpose of dialogue is not compromise, but growth in trust and understanding of each other's faith and traditions. Effective and meaningful dialogue will only take place where there is gentleness, honesty and integrity. In all of this, we affirm that Christianity needs to be lived and presented as 'a way of life', rather than a static set of beliefs (89)."

28. Claiming Jesus as the Way, therefore, requires us to "respect the dignity of every human being" (BCP, p. 305). This grounds our expectation that we shall discover new insights and develop new relationships through interreligious dialogue. In mutual encounters and shared ascetic, devotional, ethical, and prophetic witness, we dare to hope that God will reveal new and enriching glimpses of a reconciled humanity.

VI. Mission and Evangelism

29. Another sensitive and important aspect of interreligious relations concerns how we as Christians are called to offer life abundant (John 10:10) and to "make disciples of all nations" (Matthew 28:16-20). Christianity (including Anglicanism) is an actively evangelical religion. As we consider mission and evangelism in a pluralistic, globalized world, we are mindful of our particular cultural contexts. We are aware that The Episcopal Church is an international church, with congregations in over sixteen different nations. We are also part of the larger Anglican Communion. We should always be mindful of how encounters with people of other religions in the United States may have differences as well as similarities with encounters in different contexts outside the US. We seek to be informed by the experience and reflection of our sisters and brothers living among men and women of many religious traditions in many nations. We stand in solidarity with each other, each seeking in our own circumstances to be faithful to the gospel.

30. We have spoken in this statement of the need to love one's neighbor. We see that love taking a variety of forms. Commitment to justice and mutual respect is the paramount consideration for some, for whom the practice of Christian love is the most powerful witness to the truth of the Gospel. Others, while not denying the witness of faithful lives, believe that love demands the verbal proclamation of the Gospel and an open invitation to all people to be reconciled to God

in Christ. Still others understand evangelization as our participation in God's transformation of human society. The love of God that Jesus expressed in presence, compassion, healing, and justice: this we are called to live in mission. The reconciliation that God offers a sinful and broken world in Jesus' death and resurrection: this is the hope we offer the world in mission. As we seek to respond to God's call to love our neighbor, we all must seek to avoid ways of interaction which do violence to the integrity of human persons and communities.

31. We look for a way forward in the theology of companionship, as articulated in *Companions in Transformation*. This statement, produced by the Standing Commission on World Mission, reflects important developments in The Episcopal Church's understanding of how we participate in global mission; it is currently in a process of reception and review by the Church. *Companions in Transformation* outlines different ways in which Episcopalians are called to engage in mission and witness, and we believe these ways are also important in the service of interreligious dialogue. Companions states that a church participating in God's mission may not be able to solve the anguish, violence, and injustice suffered by companion churches. Even so, simply being present in the place of fear, loss and isolation expresses the love of Christ. We seek to be in companionship with our interreligious partners as we present ourselves in a variety of ways:

- *Witness:* "You are witnesses of these things," said Jesus to his disciples (Luke 24:48). Witness in word means sharing the story of what God has done with us in light of the story of what God has done in Christ Jesus. Such witness is a natural and inevitable fruit of life in Christ, and it is the heart of evangelism as a mission imperative. Sharing the story with those who have never heard it is a crucial gift. Sharing our story with others must be part of a dialogue in which we listen to the stories others share with us, whether from places of little faith or from other religious paths. The religious diversity of the 21st century, like that of the early centuries of Christianity, calls us to hold together the multiple tasks of listening, learning, and bearing witness to Christ.

- *Pilgrim:* Pilgrims grow in their knowledge of God, learning as much as they share, receiving as much as they give. The humility of this orientation and the eagerness to learn from companions nurtures deep and lasting relationships. The pilgrim motif opens the door to true mutuality, where, as the 1966 Anglican Congress said about partnership, "all are givers and all are receivers."

- *Servant:* Servanthood means that we listen to the stated needs of our companions and look for signs of God's work in them. It means that we seek to meet Christ in all situations. For Episcopalians, authentic servanthood is a crucial counter to the assumptions we develop on the basis of our extraordinary access to the power of information, technology, and money. Servanthood is a key mark for our church as a whole, though it is sometimes perceived as a domineering church in a superpower nation.

- *Prophet:* In companionship we often find our views of political, racial and economic relationships in the world challenged and transformed. Episcopalians in the 21st century are called to prophesy both to our own church and to the world church that the Body of Christ may be a mustard seed of God's Jubilee in the world, working justice for the whole human family from all faiths.

- *Ambassador:* In addition to witnessing in word and deed as ambassadors of Christ, in companionship with interfaith partners we are ambassadors of our own church. As

Episcopalians in dialogue, we must be aware always that companions are experiencing the vision, faithfulness, and integrity of The Episcopal Church through our conversation, conduct, and life. The role of ambassador also entails a commitment to represent fairly the life of The Episcopal Church. We should not be hesitant in being Episcopalian Christians, just as our interreligious partners are not hesitant in being faithful Muslims, Jews, Buddhists, Hindus, Jains, Sikhs, Bahai, or other faiths, as we are in dialogue with each other.

- **Host:** "Let a little water be brought, and wash your feet," said Abraham to the three strangers who appeared at Mamre (Genesis 18:4). "Let it be to me according to your word," said Mary to the angel Gabriel (Luke 1:38). God is not forcible but invites a response of hospitality. As we engage in interreligious dialogue, hospitality must be central in our response. Hospitality means that we listen to what our companions say, offer them opportunities to experience the breadth of our church, and care for one another. We are likewise called to be generous and hospitable with those whom God brings to us, always respecting the practices and customs of our partners.

- **Sacrament:** As the body of Christ, the church is a sacrament of Christ, an outward and visible sign of Christ's inward and spiritual grace. We are called to be signs of God's mission to reconcile all people with one another and with God in Christ. The people and communities we meet are likewise sacramental signs of God's global presence. This sacramental emphasis helps us to retain an incarnational focus on people, relationships, and community, where God truly lives and where the most lasting impacts are made.

32. We are called and committed to be in companionship and partnership in interreligious dialogue in these different ways. We believe that religions must stand together in solidarity with all who are suffering and witness to the dignity of every human being. In these ways, presence in mission becomes a courageous mode of peace-making in a violent world. With ecumenical and interreligious groups, initiatives to encourage contact and dialogue and to advocate for religious freedom are imperative for reconciliation amid today's heightened tensions among religions. God is calling us to join hands with all, and to speak out when religious freedom is curtailed and when the social, environmental, economic, or political welfare of communities is damaged. We believe that authentic Christian witness and evangelism that serve God's mission are compatible with authentic interreligious dialogue.

33. At the outset of this statement, we recalled that one hundred and twenty years ago in the Chicago Quadrilateral, The Episcopal Church formulated a definition of what it considered essential to engage in ecumenical relations. Today Christianity lives and serves in a global setting in which all of God's human creation is challenged to find common ground for our mutual flourishing. Interreligious relations are vital to this. In seeking to articulate for this century the principles to be considered for authentic interreligious relations and dialogue, we offer three gifts from The Episcopal Church and the Anglican way:

- Our comprehensive way of thinking by which we balance Scripture, reason, and tradition in relationship building;

- Our belief system that centers on the incarnation of God in Christ, and on the Crucified One who leads us to self-emptying, forgiveness, and reconciliation; and

- Our practice of focusing mission in terms of service, companionship, and partnership between people as demonstrative of God's embrace of human life.

34. These gifts are especially suited for our time. The late Martin Luther King, Jr.., celebrated in Lesser Feasts and Fasts, foresaw a time when as one all human beings of every religion would have to learn to choose "a non-violent coexistence" over a "violent co-annihilation", and to seek community over chaos. Interreligious relations are no longer about competing religions but about mutual demonstrations of Love Incarnate. We close this statement encouraged by Dr. King's word: "Love is the key that unlocks the door which leads to ultimate reality. This Hindu-Muslim-Christian-Jewish-Buddhist belief about human reality is beautifully summed up in the first Epistle of St. John: 'Let us love one another; for love is of God; and everyone that loves is born of God and knows God. The one who loves not does not know God, for God is love. If we love one another God dwells in us, and God's love is perfected in us.'"

BIBLIOGRAPHY

Books

Albanese, Catherine. *America: Religions & Religion*, 4th ed. Belmont, CA: Thomson Wadsworth, 2007.

Allen, Ronald J., and Williamson, Clark M. *Preaching the Gospels Without Blaming the Jews: A Lectionary Commentary*, Westminster John Knox: 2004.

———. *Preaching the Letters without Dismissing the Law*. Westminster John Knox, 2006.

Anglican Communion Network for Inter Faith Concerns. *Generous Love: The Truth of the Gospel and the Call to Dialogue, an Anglican Theology of Inter Faith Relations*. London: The Anglican Consultative Council, 2008.

———. *Preaching the Old Testament: A Lectionary Commentary*. Westminster: John Knox, 2007.

Banchoff, Thomas. *Democracy and the New Religious Pluralism*. New York: Oxford University Press, 2007.

Book of Common Prayer and Administration of the Sacraments and Other Rites and Ceremonies of the Church…According to the use of The Episcopal Church (1979), The. New York: The Church Hymnal Corporation, 2001.

Borowitz, Eugene B., with Naomi Patz. *Explaining Reform Judaism*. Behrman House, 1985.

Boys, Mary C. *Has God Only One Blessing? Judaism as a Source of Christian Self-Understanding*. Mahwah, New Jersey: Paulist Press, 2000.

Boys, Mary C., ed., *Seeing Judaism Anew: Christianity's Sacred Obligation*. Sheed and Ward, 2005.

Braybrooke, Marcus. *Faith and Interfaith in a Global Age*. Grand Rapids: CoNexus, 1998.

Brill, Earl H. et al. *The Christian Moral Vision*. New York: Seabury Press, 1979.

Carroll, James. *Constantine's Sword: The Church and the Jews: A History*. Boston: Houghton Mifflin, 2001.

Charlesworth, James H., ed. *Jews and Christians: Exploring the Past, Present, and Future*. New York: Crossroad, 1993.

Charlesworth, James H., ed., with Frank X. Blisard and Jerry L. Gorham. *Overcoming Fear Between Jews and Christians*. New York: Crossroad, 1992.

Clooney, Francis X., S. J. *Theology After Advaita Vedanta: An Experiment in Comparative Theology*. Albany, New York: SUNY Press, 1993.

Cross, F. L., and E. A. Livingstone. *The Oxford Dictionary of the Christian Church*, third edition. New York: Oxford University Press, 1997.

Davies, J. G. *Holy Week: A Short History, Ecumenical Studies in Worship 11*. Richmond, Virginia: John Knox Press, 1963.

D'Costa, Gavin. *The Meeting of the Religions and the Trinity*. Maryknoll, New York: Orbis, 2000.

DiNoia, J. A. *The Diversity of Religions: A Christian Perspective*. Washington, DC: Catholic University of America Press, 1992.

Douglas, Ian. *Fling Out the Banner! The National Church Ideal and the Foreign Mission of the Episcopal Church*. New York: Church Hymnal Corporation, 1996.

Douglas, Ian, ed. *Waging Reconciliation: God's Mission in a Time of Globalization and Crisis*. New York: Church Publishing, 2003.

Dupuis, Jacques. *Toward a Christian Theology of Religious Pluralism*. Maryknoll, New York: Orbis, 1997.

Earhart, H. Byron. *Religious Traditions of the World: A Journey Through Africa, North America, Mesoamerica, Judaism, Christianity, Islam, Hinduism, Buddhism, China, and Japan*. New York: HarperCollins, 1992.

Eck, Diana L. *A New Religious America: How a "Christian Country" Has Become the World's Most Religiously Diverse Nation*. San Francisco: HarperSanFrancisco, 2002.

Eckel, M. David. *Buddhism: Origins, Beliefs, Practices, Holy Texts, Sacred Places*. New York: Oxford University Press, 2002.

Elwell, Walter A., ed. *Evangelical Dictionary of Theology*. Grand Rapids, Michigan: Baker Book House, 1984.

Farquhar, John N. *The Crown of Hinduism*. London: Oxford University Press, 1913.

Fredericks, James. *Faith Among Faiths: Christianity & the Other Religions*. Mahwah, New Jersey: Paulist Press, 1999.

Fredriksen, Paula, and Reinhartz, Adele, eds. *Jesus, Judaism and Christian Anti-Judaism: Reading the New Testament after the Holocaust*. Louisville, Kentucky: Westminster John Knox Press, 2002.

Frymer-Kensky, Tikva, et al. *Christianity in Jewish Terms*. New York: Basic Books, 2000.

General Convention of The Episcopal Church. *The Journal of General Convention...of The Episcopal Church*. New York: General Convention, 1880–2009.

———. *Reports to the...General Convention otherwise known as The Blue Book*. New York: General Convention, 1976–2012.

Harrington, S. J., and Yehezkel Landau. *The Synoptic Gospels Set Free: Preaching Without Anti-Judaism*. Mahwah, New Jersey: Paulist Press, 2009.

Heim, S. Mark. *Salvations: Truth and Difference in Religion*. Maryknoll, New York: Orbis, 1995.

Hick, John, and Paul F. Knitter, eds. *The Myth of Christian Uniqueness: Toward a Pluralistic Theology of Religions*. Maryknoll, New York: Orbis Books, 1995.

Hickman, H. L., Don E. Saliers, L.H. Stookey, J.F. White, *The New Handbook of the Christian Year: Based on the Revised Common Lectionary*. Nashville, Tennessee: Abingdon Press, 1986, 1992.

Hocking, William Ernest, ed. *Re-Thinking Missions—A Layman's Report After One Hundred Years*. New York: Harper & Brothers, 1972.

Holmes III, Urban T. *What is Anglicanism?* Wilton, Connecticut: Morehouse-Barlow, 1982.

Hood, Robert E. *Social Teachings in the Episcopal Church: A Source Book.* Harrisburg, Pennsylvania: Morehouse Publishing, 1990.

Jefferts Schori, Katharine. *The Gospel in the Global Village: Seeking God's Dream of Shalom.* New York: Morehouse Publishing, 2009.

Joddock, Darrell, ed. *Covenantal Conversations: Christians in Dialogue with Jews and Judaism.* Minneapolis, Minnesota: Fortress Press , 2008.

Kärkkäinen, Veli-Matti. *An Introduction to the Theology of Religions: Biblical, Historical & Contemporary Perspective.* Downers Grove, Illinois: InterVarsity Press Academic, 2003.

Knitter, Paul F. *Introducing Theologies of Religions.* Maryknoll, New York: Orbis, 2002.

Knitter, Paul F. ed. *The Myth of Religious Superiority: Multifaith Explorations of Religious Pluralism.* Maryknoll, New York: Orbis, 2005.

Kushner, Rabbi Harold. *To Life! A Celebration of Jewish Being and Thinking.* New York: Warner Books, 1993.

Levine, Amy-Jill, and Marc Z. Brettler. *The Annotated Jewish New Testament.* New York: Oxford University Press, 2011.

Levine, Amy-Jill. *The Misunderstood Jew: The Church and the Scandal of the Jewish Jesus.* New York: HarperCollins, 2007.

Lochhead, David. *The Dialogical Imperative: A Christian Reflection on Interfaith Encounter.* Maryknoll, New York: Orbis, 1988.

Lott, David, ed. *New Proclamation Year C, 2006-07, Advent through Holy Week.* Minneapolis, Minnesota: Fortress Press, 2006.

Maurice, Frederick Denison. *The Religions of the World and Their Relation to Christianity Considered in Eight Lectures.* London: John W. Parker, 1847.

McCarthy, Kate. *Interfaith Encounters in America.* Piscataway, New Jersey: Rutgers University Press, 2007.

McClendon, James Wm., Jr., and James M. Smith. *Convictions: Diffusing Religious Relativism.* Harrisburg, Pennsylvania: Trinity Press International, 1994.

Mosher, Lucinda. *Belonging.* New York: Seabury Books, 2005.

Mosher, Lucinda A., and Claude Jacobs. "The University of Michigan-Dearborn Worldviews Seminar." In *Teaching Religion and Healing,* edited by Linda Barnes, 261–70. New York: Oxford University Press, 2006.

Nazir-Ali, Michael, and Pattinson, Derek.,Editors. *The Truth Sall Make You Free: The Lambeth Conference 1988.* London: Anglican Consultative Council, 1988, and Church House Publishing, 1994.

Newbigin, Lesslie. *The Gospel in a Pluralist Society.* London: SPCK, 1989.

Nhat Hanh, Thich. *Being Peace.* Berkeley, California: Parallax Press, 1987.

Ogden, Schubert. *Is There Only One True Religion or Are There Many?* University Park, Texas,: Southern Methodist University Press, 1992.

Pearson, Sharon Ely, ed. *Remembering a Time that Changed US: Worship & Education Resources for the 10th Anniversary of 9/11.* New York: Church Publishing, Inc., 2011.

Pedersen, Kusumita P. "The Interfaith Movement: An Incomplete Assessment." *Journal of Ecumenical Studies* 41, no. 1 (Winter 2004).

Pratt, Douglas. "Pluralism and Interreligious Engagement: The Contexts of Dialogue." In *A Faithful Presence: Essays for Kenneth Cragg*, edited by David Thomas and Clare Amos. London: Melisende, 2003.

Presler, Titus, ed. *Companions in Transformation: The Episcopal Church's World Mission in a New Century.* Harrisburg, Pennsylvania: Morehouse Publishing, 2003.

Presler, Titus. *Going Global With God: Reconciling Mission in a World of Difference.* Harrisburg, Pennsylvania: Morehouse Publishing, 2010.

———. *Horizons of Mission.* Cambridge, Massachusetts: Cowley Publications, 2001.

Putnam, Robert D., and David E. Campbell. *American Grace: How Religion Divides and Unties Us.* New York: Simon & Schuster, 2010.

Race, Alan, and Paul M. Hedges. *Christian Approaches to Other Faiths.* Norwich, UK: SCM Press, 2008.

Race, Alan. *Christians in Religious Pluralism: Patterns in the Christian Theology of Religions.* London: SCM Press, 1983.

Reuther, Rosemary Radford. *Faith and Fratricide: The Theological Roots of Anti-Semitism.* Eugene, Oregon: Wipf & Stock, 1996.

Salmon, Marilyn J. *Preaching Without Contempt: Overcoming Unintended Anti-Judaism.* Minneapolis, Minnesota: Augsburg Fortress Press, 2006.

Samartha, Stanley J., ed. *Living Faiths and Ultimate Goals.* Geneva: World Council of Churches, 1974.

———. *Towards World Community: Resources and Responsibilities for Living Together.* Geneva: World Council of Churches, 1975.

Sandmel, David F. et al. *Irreconcilable Differences? A Learning Resource for Jews and Christians.* Boulder, Colorado: Westview Press, 2001.

Selmanovic, Samir. *It's Really All About God: Reflections of a Muslim Atheist Jewish Christian.* Hoboken, New Jersey: Jossey-Bass, 2009.

Shermis, Michael and Arthur E. Zannoni, eds. *Introduction to Jewish–Christian Relations.* Mahwah, New Jersey: Paulist Press, 1991.

Smart, Ninian. *Worldviews: Crosscultural Explorations of Human Beliefs.* Upper Saddle River, New Jersey: Prentice Hall, 1999.

Smiga, George M. *The Gospel of John Set Free: Preaching Without Anti-Judaism.* Mahwah, New Jersey: Paulist Press, 2008.

Stassen, Glen H. ed. *Just Peacemaking: The New Paradigm for the Ethics of War and Peace.* Cleveland, Ohio: Pilgrim Press, 2008.

Suchocki, Marjorie. *Divinity and Diversity: A Christian Affirmation of Religious Pluralism*. Nashville, Tennessee: Abingdon Press, 2003.

Swanson, Richard W. *Provoking the Gospel of Luke: A Storyteller's Commentary, Year C*. Cleveland, Ohio: Pilgrim Press, 2005.

———. *Provoking the Gospel of Mark: A Storyteller's Commentary, Year B*. Cleveland, Ohio: Pilgrim Press, 2005.

———. *Provoking the Gospel of Matthew: A Storyteller's Commentary, Year A*. Cleveland, Ohio: Pilgrim Press, 2007.

Telushkin, Rabbi Joseph. *Jewish Literacy: The Most Important Things to Know About the Jewish Religion*. New York: HarperCollins, 2008; originally published 1991.

Thistlethwaite, Susan Brooks. *Interfaith Just Peacemaking: Jewish, Christian, and Muslim Perspectives on the New Paradigm of Peace and War*. New York: Palgrave Macmillan, 2011.

Thomas, Owen C. *Attitudes Toward Other Religions*. London: SCM Press, 1969.

Tilley, Terrence W. et al. *Religious Diversity and the American Experience: A Theological Approach*. New York: Continuum, 2007.

Trachtenberg, Joshua. *The Devil and the Jews: The Medieval Conception of the Jew and Its Relation to Modern Anti-Semitism*, 2nd. Ed. Philadelphia, Pennsylvania: The Jewish Publication Society, 2002.

Wuthnow, Robert. *America and the Challenges of Religious Diversity*. Princeton, New Jersey: Princeton University Press, 2005, 2007.

Yankelovich, Daniel. *The Magic of Dialogue:T transforming Conflict into Cooperation*. New York: Simon & Schuster, 1999.

Zizioulas, John. *Communion and Otherness*. London: T&T Clark, 2006.

Articles

A Sermon Preached by the Most Rev. Frank T. Griswold, Presiding Bishop and Primate of The Episcopal Church, at St. Paul's Cathedral, Burlington, Vermont. Episcopal News Service 2001-271 (24 September 2001).

Adams, William Seth. "Christian Liturgy, Scripture, and the Jews: A Problematic in Jewish-Christian Relations." *Journal of Ecumenical Studies*. 25, no. 1 (Winter 1988).

Breidenthal, Thomas E. "Neighbor-Christology: Reconstructing Christianity Before Supersessionism." *Cross Currents* (Fall 1999): 320–48.

Bishops Call 'Waging Reconciliation' the Answer to Globalization, Terrorism. Episcopal News Service 2001-277 (28 September 2001).

Coddaire, Louis, and Louis Weil. "The Use of the Psalter in Worship." In *Worship* 52, no. 4 (July 1978): 342–348.

Daw, Jr., Carl P. "The Spirituality of Anglican Hymnody: A Twentieth-Century American Perspective." In *The Hymnal 1982 Companion*. Volume One, edited by Raymond F. Glover. New York: The Church Hymnal Corporation, 1994.

D'Costa, Gavin. "The Impossibility of a Pluralist View of Religion," *Religious Studies* 32 (1996): 223–32.

Episcopal Interfaith Officer Addresses Muslim Convention. Episcopal News Service 070904-1 (7 September 2004).

Episcopalians in Ecumenical Delegation Seek Understanding of Mideast Conflict. Episcopal News Service 2000-240 (20 December 2000).

General Convention. *Journal of the General Convention of...The Episcopal Church*. (New York: General Convention, 1892–2009).

Hockin, Katharine B. "My Pilgrimage in Mission." *International Bulletin of Missionary Research* (January 1988).

Ipgrave. M. "Understanding, Affirmation, Sharing: *Nostra Aetate* and an Anglican Approach to Inter-Faith Relations," *Journal of Ecumenical Studies*, Volume 43, No. 1 (Winter 2008): 1–16.

Joslyn-Siemiatkoski, Daniel. *Anti-Judaism and the Liturgy: Theological Reflections on Covenant and Language*. Unpublished paper, 2012.

———. "'Moses Received the Torah at Sinai and Handed It On' [Mishnah Avot 1:10]: The Relevance of the Written and Oral Torah for Christians," *Anglican Theological Review* 91, no. 3 (2009): 443–66.

Markham, Ian. "Creating Options: Shattering the Exclusivist, Inclusivist, Pluralist Paradigm." *New Blackfriars* 74, no. 867 (1993): 33–41.

Muck, Terry. "Instrumentality, Complexity, and Reason: A Christian Approach to Religions," *Buddhist-Christian Studies* 22 (2002): 115–21.

Nunley, Jan. *Episcopalians Begin to Battle "Backlash Violence" Against Muslim Neighbors*. Episcopal News Service 2001-264 (20 September 2001).

Race, Alan. "Religious Plurality and Contemporary Philosophy: A Critical Survey." In *Harvard Theological Review* 87, no. 2 (1994): 197–213.

Salmon, Marilyn J. "In Our Times: What Has Changed Between Jews and Christians?" *Proceedings of the Center for Jewish-Christian Learning*. 1992 Lecture Series, Vol. 7 (Spring 1992).

Tilley, Terrence W. "'Christianity and the World Religions': A Recent Vatican Document," *Theological Studies* 60 (June): 318–37.

Thomas, Owen C. "Religious Plurality and Contemporary Philosophy: A Critical Survey," *Harvard Theological Review* 87, no. 2 (1994): 197–213.

'We Are Called to Another Way': Presiding Bishop Griswold on the September 11 Attacks, Episcopal News Service 2001-239 (11 September 2001).

Zscheile, Dwight J. "Beyond Benevolence: Toward a Reframing of Mission in the Episcopal Church," *Journal of Anglican Studies* 8, no. 1 (2009): 83.

Online Resources

A Common Word Between Us and You. www.acommonword.com.

Archives of the Episcopal Church, The. *Episcopal Press and News 1962–2006.* http://www.episco-palarchives.org/e-archives/ENS/.

———. *Reports to the...General Convention otherwise known as The Blue Book 1976–2009.* http://www.episcopalarchives.org/e-archives/blue_book/.

———. *The Acts of Convention 1976–2009.* http://www.episcopalarchives.org/e-archives/acts/.

———. *The Resolves of Executive Council 1976–2011.* http://www.episcopalarchives.org/e-archives/executive_council/.

Attridge, Harold W., et al. *Loving God and Neighbor Together.* http://www.acommonword.com/lib/downloads/fullpageadbold18.pdf. Last accessed: 6 July 2012.

Becker, Scott. "Responding to Violence with Wisdom and Morality." *The Seattle Times* (26 October 2001). http://community.seattletimes.nwsource.com/archive/?date=20011026&slug=becker26. Last accessed: 5 July 2012.

Breiner, Bert. *Interfaith Relations and the Churches: A Brief Theological Introduction to the Policy Statement.* htttp://www.ncccusa.org/interfaith/brieftheocom.html.

Breuer, Sarah Dylan. *dylan's lectionary blog.* www.sarahlaughed.net.

Harris, Mark. "What's in a Name?" *Preludium.* anglicanfuture.blogspot.com.

Henderson, Frank. *Critical Reflections on the Reproaches of the Good Friday Liturgy,* http://www.jfrankhenderson.com/pdf/goodfriday2.pdf. Last accessed: 4 April 2012.

General Convention. *Report to the 77th General Convention Otherwise Known as The Blue Book. Indianapolis, 2012.* http://www.generalconvention.org/gc/prepare.

Getting to Know Neighbors of Other Faiths: A Theological Rationale for Interfaith Relationships. National Council of Churches. http://www.ncccusa.org/pdfs/neighbors3.pdf. Last accessed: 9 July 2012.

"Ideas & Trends: 'Supersessionism' Reconsidered; A Leap Toward Closing the Basic Gap Between Christians and Jews." *The New York Times,* 24 July 1988. http://www.nytimes.com/1988/07/24/weekinreview/ideas-trends-supersessionism-reconsidered-leap-toward-closing-basic-gap-between.html?scp=6&sq=episcopal+church&st=nyt. Last accessed: 2 August 2012.

Interfaith Relations and the Church: The Ecumenical Challenge. National Council of Churches U.S.A. http://www.ncccusa.org/interfaith/IFRecumenical.pdf. Last accessed: 9 July 2012.

Interfaith Relations and the Church: The Identity Challenge. National Council of Churches U.S.A. http://www.ncccusa.org/interfaith/IFRidentity.pdf. Last accessed: 3 August 2012.

Interfaith Relations and the Church: The Missional Challenge. National Council of Churches U.S.A. http://www.ncccusa.org/interfaith/IFRmission.pdf. Last accessed: 3 August 2012.

Interfaith Relations and the Church: The Moral Challenge. National Council of Churches U.S.A. http://www.ncccusa.org/interfaith/IFRmoral-1.pdf. Last accessed: 3 August 2012.

Interfaith Relations and the Church: The Theological Challenge. National Council of Churches U.S.A. http://www.ncccusa.org/interfaith/IFRtheology.pdf. Last accessed: 3 August 2012.

Lambeth Conference 1978. *Resolution 37: Other faiths: Gospel and dialogue.* http://www.lambethconference.org/resolutions/1978/1978-37.cfm. Last accessed: 3 August 2012.

Mosher, Lucinda. *Appreciative Conversation: The Archbishop of Canterbury's 'Building Bridges Seminars.'* May, 2010. http://repository.berkleycenter.georgetown.edu/Mosher-Building-Bridges-Article.pdf. Last accessed: 3 August 2012.

Nostra Aetate (Declaration Concerning the Relationship of the Church to Non-Christian Religions). Second Vatican Council, promulgated 28 October 1965. http://www.vatican.va/archive/hist_councils/ii_vatican_council/index.htm.

Thomas, Margaret Orr. *A Liturgy Based on Interfaith Relations and the Churches.* http://www.ncccusa.org/interfaith/ifrliturgy.html. Last accessed: 13 July 2012.

Tutt, Daniel. "Malleable Stereotypes: How Media is Improving the Image of American Muslims." *Institute for Social Policy and Understanding Policy Brief.* #48 (September 2011). http://ispu.org/pdfs/ISPU_Policy%20BriefTutt_WEB.pdf. Last accessed: 21 July 2012.

Weil, Louis. "Some Words About the Anti-Judaism Resolution." *SCLM Blog* (March 29, 2012). http://liturgyandmusic.wordpress.com.

Weller, Paul. *Four Principles of Dialogue: Christian Origins.* http://www.dialoguesociety.org/download/Transcripts/Transcript-DS-Seminar-Four-Principles-of-Dialogue-Christian-Origins-by-Prof-Paul-Weller-090127.pdf.

Williams, Rowan. A Common Word for the Common Good. http://www.archbishopofcanterbury.org.

INDEX

STUDIES IN EPISCOPAL AND ANGLICAN THEOLOGY

C. K. Robertson
General Editor

"The links which bind us to that historic past are not fetters upon the free and enterprising spirit which is essential to progress." (Encyclical Letter of the Fifth Lambeth Conference of Bishops, 1908)

In these early years of the twenty-first century, we who claim an Anglican identity are reminded again of the importance of both our historic past and an enterprising spirit as we engage numerous theological issues and controversies which occupy our time, energy, and imagination. Through the work of both established and emerging scholars within the Episcopal Church and the worldwide Anglican Communion, this series explores a broad range of topics, including ecumenical and interfaith relations, human sexuality and gender equality, biblical authority and ecclesial structures, ministry theory and praxis, sacramental theology, and religious foundations for advocacy. Volumes in the series are in the form of monographs, revised dissertations, and compilations of essays.

For further information about the series, as well as the submission of proposals or manuscripts, please contact:

The Rev. Canon C. K. Robertson, Ph.D.
Canon to the Presiding Bishop, The Episcopal Church
Distinguished Visiting Professor, General Theological Seminary
815 2nd Ave., New York, NY 10017
e-mail:crobertson@episcopalchurch.org

To order other books in this series, please contact our Customer Service Department:

(800) 770-LANG (within the U.S.)
(212) 647-7706 (outside the U.S.)
(212) 647-7707 FAX

Or browse online by series:

www.peterlang.com